The Architecture of Full-Scale Mock-Ups

The Architecture of Full-Scale Mock-Ups looks at the theory and contemporary practice of creating full-scale architectural mock-ups.

This book serves as an introduction to the various forms of full-scale mock-ups which occur today. To broaden the definition of mock-ups, Nick Gelpi dives deep into the use of mock-ups in seven high-profile and global contemporary case studies. Instead of the presentation drawings and final building photos, the documentation of case studies relies on process photos, interviews, and moments of tension in the execution of each building. With never before published content, case studies include buildings from all over the world, including the Quincho Tia Coral and Teleton Building, Copper House II, the Pérez Art Museum Miami, the Cité de L'Océan et du Surf Museum, and more.

Investigating unique case studies to answer how and when full-scale mock-ups occur today, this book is ideal for professionals and students of architecture studying materials and representation, design-build, and professional practice.

Nick Gelpi is a licensed architect in the state of Florida, and a Professor of Architecture who has lectured and published widely on the tensions between materials, construction, and representation in architecture. Currently Gelpi is an Associate Professor of Architecture at Florida International University in Miami, Florida.

The Architecture of Full-Scale Mock-Ups

From Representation to Reality

Nick Gelpi

Taylor & Francis Group
NEW YORK AND LONDON

First published 2020
by Routledge
52 Vanderbilt Avenue, New York, NY 10017

and by Routledge
2 Park Square, Milton Park, Abingdon, Oxon, OX14 4RN

Routledge is an imprint of the Taylor & Francis Group, an informa business

© 2020 Taylor & Francis

The right of Nick Gelpi to be identified as author of this work has been asserted by him in accordance with sections 77 and 78 of the Copyright, Designs and Patents Act 1988.

All rights reserved. No part of this book may be reprinted or reproduced or utilised in any form or by any electronic, mechanical, or other means, now known or hereafter invented, including photocopying and recording, or in any information storage or retrieval system, without permission in writing from the publishers.

Trademark notice: Product or corporate names may be trademarks or registered trademarks, and are used only for identification and explanation without intent to infringe.

Library of Congress Cataloging-in-Publication Data
Names: Gelpi, Nick, 1979- author.
Title: The architecture of full-scale mock-ups : from representation to reality / Nick Gelpi.
Description: New York : Routledge, 2020. | Includes bibliographical references and index.
Identifiers: LCCN 2019050129 (print) | LCCN 2019050130 (ebook) | ISBN 9781138891043 (hardback) | ISBN 9781138891050 (paperback) | ISBN 9781315709888 (ebook)
Subjects: LCSH: Architectural models. | Ratio and proportion.
Classification: LCC NA2790 .G45 2020 (print) | LCC NA2790 (ebook) | DDC 720.22/2—dc23
LC record available at https://lccn.loc.gov/2019050129
LC ebook record available at https://lccn.loc.gov/2019050130

ISBN: 978-1-138-89104-3 (hbk)
ISBN: 978-1-138-89105-0 (pbk)
ISBN: 978-1-315-70988-8 (ebk)

Typeset in Franklin Gothic and Garamond
by Swales & Willis, Exeter, Devon, UK

For my family, particularly my parents Doug and Candi, for giving me the freedom to fail; to my four children Olive, Miles, Mimi, and Sally, and most of all to Estee for her patience while I was absent from family vacations, giving me the space to write this book. I love you all, and dedicate my best efforts at writing with thoughtfulness, to each of you.

Contents

Acknowledgments   ix
Foreword   xiii

Introduction   1

1. **An Alchemy of Bricks**   29
   The Teletón Children's Rehabilitation Center and Quincho Tía Coral, Asunción, Paraguay
   Solano Benitez and Gabinete de Arquitectura

2. **Drawing without Paper and Building without Buildings: Large Representations in the Field**   61
   Copper House II, the House with White Net and Saat Rasta, Mumbai, India
   Bijoy Jain/Studio Mumbai

3. **The Impossibly Real: In Pursuit of New Translations**   89
   The Physical Motivations of Round Room and La Voûte de LeFevre
   Matter Design/Brandon Clifford and Wes McGee

4. **Unpredictable Petrifications: The Unnatural Forms and Transformations of a Concrete Museum**   115
   The Pérez Art Museum Miami, Miami, FL, USA
   Herzog & de Meuron, Basel, Switzerland

5. **Massive Impressions: The Materials of Representation**   141
   The Cité de L'Océan et du Surf Museum, Biarritz, France
   Steven Holl Architects

6. **Acclimated Transformations: The Surprising Materialities of the Harvard Art Museums and its Surroundings**   171
   Renzo Piano Building Workshop, Genoa, Italy
   Harvard Art Museums Renovation and Expansion, Cambridge, MA, USA

7. **Mocked-Illuminations: The Transformed Environments Refracted in the Complex Surfaces of 7 World Trade Center**   197
   7 World Trade Center, New York City, USA
   Skidmore, Owings & Merrill and James Carpenter Design Associates

Index   227

Acknowledgments

Like all productive mock-ups, there were times when this book seemed likely to fail. The current form of this book owes its outcome to many individuals, without whom it would not have been possible.

To my colleague and oldest friend Joe Chase, for first helping me to put thoughts into words and arguments, and spending countless hours discussing and debating many of the ideas found here.

To my former colleagues Mike Cadwell and Steve Turk for nurturing these ideas in their formative years during my time at Ohio State as the Howard E. LeFevre Fellow. Separately I must thank John McMorrough and Jeffrey Kipnis, for critically challenging these ideas, and helping me to clarify them during this time.

I am so grateful to Terrence Riley, for his willingness to vouch for the merits of this project very early on, and throughout the process. In particular the chapter on Herzog & de Meuron's Pérez Art Museum Miami would not have been included without his generous diplomacy.

I would be remiss if I didn't recognize the key contributions of my colleagues from the School of Architecture, at Florida International University. I particularly must thank Henry Rueda, for his attentive proofreading of the many early drafts of the chapters found in the book, and for the constructive direction he provided. Additionally I must thank Jason Chandler, who first suggested I expand a lecture I had given at FIU into the format of this book. On occasion I experienced the effects of tunnel vision and uncertainty while trying to complete the manuscript and must acknowledge Gray Read and David Rifkind, both for their patience to discuss these topics and for the many helpful suggestions and references I had not previously considered, and for their cheerleading of this process. Lastly, I must thank John Stuart, for his calming advice in regards to many of the complex publishing conundrums I encountered, and for making such a sustained enterprise seem manageable and enjoyable. In addition, I want to generally thank my colleagues from Florida International University who encouraged me including Eric Goldenberg, Camilo Rosales, Shahin Vassigh, Marilys Nepomechie, Jaime Canaves, Thomas Spiegelhalter, Alfredo Andia, Felice Grodin, Nik Nedev, and Eric Peterson.

Acknowledgments

The early forms of this book were quite rough around the edges, and to the degree that this book is more refined, I must acknowledge the tireless efforts of Adam Bierman, for serving as my writing coach, punching holes in the arguments, and teaching me to take more time to write shorter paragraphs, and to Maria Flores, for helping me to selectively trim down and edit the very long final text in its entirety. I share this text with both of you.

I must acknowledge two more individuals, who provided both direct and indirect support. First, I have to thank Nader Tehrani, for the encouragement and enthusiasm he showed for the book, and for the significant generosity and thoughtfulness of the foreword he contributed to this text.

Second, I must acknowledge the significant influence of Steven Holl, who indirectly guided the construction of these thoughts during my time working in his office, teaching with him, and our many subsequent discussions. I am grateful for the conversations we have had over the years, many of which were instrumental in forming a basis for the observations found here, and for his support of me as a young architect.

Last, I must acknowledge the architects who allowed me the pleasure of reflecting on their work in such depth. Without the care of many individuals including staff in the offices of each architect this book would certainly not be possible.

For the chapter on the work of Solano Benitez and Gabinete De Arquitectura I must thank Solano Benitez and Gloria Cabral, for generously hosting my visit to Paraguay, and to Alejandro Aravena for first suggesting that I focus one of the chapters on Solano's work, with which I had not been previously familiar with.

For the chapter about the work of Matter Design, I must thank Brandon Clifford, for his interview and providing open access to his work, and process.

For the chapter on Studio Mumbai, I must thank Bijoy Jain, first for his reply to the email I sent to his general office delivery, and then also for providing such compelling documentation and feedback. In support of this chapter I must than Mitul Desai, for our numerous phone interviews and his patience in explaining the unique processes of each projects.

For the chapter on Herzog & de Meuron's Pérez Art Museum Miami, I must thank Stefan Horner for his deliberate interview, Jack Brough for answering my follow up questions, and Alienor de Chambrier, Edward Haynes, and Patrick Ilg for organizing and sharing the content for the chapter, and lastly to Christine Binswanger for her generous participation.

For the chapter on Steven Holl Architects' the Cité de l'Océan et du Surf, I must thank Steven Holl for his inspiring interview and Rodolfo Dias for his methodical organization and summaries of the mock-up process. Additional acknowledgment must be given to Chris McVoy for his insights generally, and to the brief conversations I had with Garrick Ambrose, Olaf Schmidt, Marcus Carter, Noah Yaffe, and lastly to Julia van den Hout.

For the chapter on the Harvard Art Museums I thank Stefania Canta, for her tireless effort in providing the necessary content and explanations, and to Elissibetta Trezzani for her generous phone interview. Lastly I want to acknowledge the many phone interviews I had with Ron Anthony, whose insight into the particularities of wood science provided surprising depth to the chapter.

For the chapter on 7 World Trade Center, I would like to thank James Carpenter and Richard Kress for clarifying the particularities of the design details, and to Ben Colebrook for fostering the lengthy process of organization and insightful feedback and editing of the text.

Lastly, I wish to mention my gratitude to the various editors from the publisher who showed patience in the process of completing the project, Wendy Fuller, Grace Harrison, and Julia Pollacco.

Foreword

The Indispensable Failure

Nader Tehrani

While the advent of the mock-up is nothing new, there is something that each historical era brings to its purpose that redefines its conceptual potential. In effect, it has had a transformational role as a medium of persuasion, giving rhetorical strength for great patronage, while also serving as a testing ground key technological innovations. This book brings urgency to the idea of the mock-up as artifact, and a view into the architectural discipline's recent history might explain a few things about its renewed relevance.

Building the Historical Moment

Revisiting the early-1990s, when after an era of repressed presence, the return of construction as a theme within architectural discourse engendered an important turn-around for the discipline. The preamble, of course, was not insignificant, and nor was it historically monolithic. The intellectual contributions of post-modernism and deconstruction did much to advance architectural thinking from the 1960s through the 1980s, and yet fell short of addressing building construction as the locus of academic speculation.

If post-modernism brought a renewed self-consciousness to the architectural act, it also expanded the historical framework from which we looked at history, culture, and architectural morphologies, overturning an era that had appealed to positivism as architecture's main narrative. In tandem, the advent of deconstruction, drawing from philosophy, literary criticism, and other fields did much to challenge architecture as an institution, but the forms it produced in the context of architecture did little to dismantle the very politics that drove patronage, construction, and tectonic thinking. In fact, arguably, while on the surface the forms produced by both movements may have seemed different at that time, in retrospect they shared much in common, relying on the integrity of architectural types (or fragments) on the one hand, and the techniques of collage and montage as the basis of their assembly, on the other. More importantly, neither were invested in the materiality of building or a theory of construction as a site of intellectual inquiry.

Of course, while these movements were predominantly shared between the United States and Europe, its results were also neither singular nor monolithic. In the Iberic peninsula both Spain and Portugal enjoyed relative autonomy from these tendencies as they overcame an era of centralized governance. Spanish culture, having only recently come out from under the reign of Franco, maintained a relatively isolated relationship to architectural thinking from the rest of Europe; under Franco, the continued presence of the modernist project with the radical experiments of Miguel Fisac, Francisco Javier Saenz de Oiza, and Fernando Higueras produced a robust engagement with building experiments, while the post-Franco period of the 1980s extended the modernist project in a much more orthodox manner, save the work of very few like Enric Miralles and Carme Pinos, whose experiments held to the extremities posed by their predecessors. Still, both the Barcelona and Madrid School held tight relationships with practice and their engagement with "building" projects maintained a strong experimental thrust, always deeply invested in architecture as an act of fabrication.

Meanwhile in the 1980s, even while Switzerland was marked by characters like Mario Botta, Bruno Reichlin, and Fabio Reinhardt, all protagonists of the post-modern era, their work maintained a committed relationship to the ethics of construction as basis for speculation; this is also later evidenced in the work of the then-emerging names of Herzog & de Meuron, who double-handedly transported the theme of materiality – aligned with a reformed definition of craft – toward a new era, much of which today's generations have inherited as a foundation. Much of this work, in both Spain and Switzerland, while alien to practice in the United States was becoming common to its academic institutions, especially after the arrival of Rafael Moneo, who played a pivotal role in bringing some of those voices to the Harvard Graduate School of Design.

The Mock-Up Installed

By the 1990s, the academy in the United States was split between a yearning for the type of construction experimentation seen in both Spain and Switzerland, on the one hand, and the emergence of the digital platform that, on the other hand, had seen its outlet in computer visualization and formal research as witnessed through the paperless studios of Columbia.[1]

In contradistinction, a few practices were engaged in the difficult synthesis that would emerge out of these two tendencies, among them Foreign Office Architects (FOA), SHOP architects, and my own collaboration with Rodolphe El Khoury and Monica Ponce de Leon under the banner of Office dA. Our installation for MOMA's exhibition "Fabrications: The Tectonic Garden," curated by Terry Riley, was a precise response to this false dichotomy. The folded steel plate construction, anamorphically conceived, meticulously calculated and drawn in the computer, and then fabricated by Milgo Bufkin, was a stitching together of a pictorial idea that could only be delivered through computer-aided manufacturing. That is, in order to create a series of mass-customized panels that would appear to be completely plumb, level, and flat from one perspectival station point, it would require a fabrication technique that could eliminate conventional tolerances as defined by the construction industry.

For Riley, this exhibition was an important dress-rehearsal for many things that were to come in the next two decades; in fact, the PS1 summer installations are an extension of the very premise he laid out: the idea that an architectural exhibition revolves not around representations such as drawings and models, per se, but the actual architectural fragment at full-scale. Maybe most importantly, one of the underlying aspects of this exhibition was a critique of both practice and the academy as they had evolved, with the academy becoming ever more submerged under meta-discursive aspects of theory and criticism, and with practice becoming increasingly acquiescent as a service industry with a total abdication of its agency to transform the built reality of the world around us. This was also an indication of the increasing calcification of patronage in the United States; few if any clients would place importance – or funding – in building innovation, while also handing over a great part of the architect's instrumentality to the platform of contractors, project managers, and the building industry at large. From our perspective as thinkers and practitioners, the re-claiming of the means and methods of production was the most important challenge to architectural practice, and in great part what has led to a transformation of practice today.

It is, then, maybe a fortuitous coincidence that FOA's Yokohama project was also premised on the idea of the fold, and the subsequent construction of the terminal while remaining faithful to its original idea transformed considerably, creating a composite structure with a vector active truss vault in combination with plate steel veneers that gave surface to its many folded facets. In contrast to the pure folded "stitched" details of the Office dA Fabrications installation, the FOA project required a mediated process of translation due to its shift in scale. If the Office dA mock-up adopted an invented detail as a catalyst for part-to-whole relationships, the FOA project needed to rely on three different Japanese ship manufacturers, who served as builders for the terminal, to mock-up slightly different variations of a design intent. This also helps to underscore the difference between the building of infrastructure on the one hand, and the bespoke development of an installation, on the other: one being played out against the panoramic narrative of politics, economies, and public patronage, while the other insulated to a larger degree within the confines of research, construction, and the transformation of industry bottom-up.

In the meantime, lacking the kind of competitions found in Europe that were the engine for the successes of many young firms, the more speculative firms of the United States retreated increasingly into the medium of installations as an avatar for architecture itself. The transformation of today's schools – their fab-labs, workshops, and architectural pedagogies – are also a reflection of this historical passage. The results are varied as some graduates enter into practice with an entrepreneurial lens, sometimes entering architecture through the construction industry (Mark West's fabric-formed concrete research being an early signal of things to come and Ensamble Studio's full-scale constructions becoming part and parcel of their normative practice), through the arts (Tomas Saraceno and Anne Holtrop, both demonstrating that the context of the museum enabling certain feats that the architectural discipline would never allow through its own constraints), or through the 1% clause (Ball Nogue and Iwamoto Scott, whose various architectural installations have become synonymous with mainstream academic practices); in turn, while some see the installation as a research conduit to a more immersive practice – engaging urbanism, complex building typologies, and programmatically charged projects, others have also seen the installation itself as the destination.[2]

The Mock-up Manifested: A Physical Form of Representation

The mock-up, as artifact, can also be seen against this immediate historical backdrop. As Gelpi brings panoramic nuance to the mock-up's longue durée by including varied manifestations and adaptations, he also offers a critical response to it by way of the unique historical moment of which he is a result. The last decade has seen radical transformations in both practice and the academy, in great part because of the way in which maker culture, fab-labs, digital printing, and DIY protocols have impacted ideas about manufacturing. Thus, while Gelpi probes into history with some depth, he is also deeply conscious of the instrumentality that this historical moment may yet bring: at once enabling us to adopt the research done in the academy to impact the building industry, while also imagining that the ability to make on one's own volition may not require the same reliance on a static definition of the construction trades.

Gelpi taps into the mock-up as the site of two very different historical subjects. On the one hand, he imagines the "unmediated" act of making as a craft that, through its own protocols, may engender invention, even if by accident; on the other hand, he is also deeply conscious that the advent of representation as a disciplinary precondition for the possibility of making architecture. In the latter, the intellectual predisposition of architecture as a discipline dispenses with craft altogether in lieu of a deeper investment in the possibility of radicalization of spatial, formal, and material protocols that do not require precision in labor as their basis for success. Moreover, Gelpi shrewdly braids together the idea that the process of construction – mock-ups in this instance – is in itself a design process that is the manifestation of a representational system; as such, he inverts the traditional temporal dichotomy between drawing and building, imagining that the physical mock-up is the basis for a new form of drawing, and thus a conceptual transformation about how we might see architecture as an intellectual construct.

Gelpi's conception of the mock-up as a medium is telling, especially given how it has been historically adopted in varied ways. If the sciences of the modern world did not always have the means to prove a structural theorem, the mock-ups of Antoni Gaudi, Frank Lloyd Wright, or Felix Candela would serve not only as a testing ground, but a process of re-calibration and its eventual proof. That these figures would radicalize the optimization of structures and the morphologies of architecture they imparted through the exploration of mock-ups become even more poignant when viewed in relation to the absorption of mock-ups in the corporate ranks of patronage today; most often, building mock-ups are now contracted as a confirmation of preconceived ideas, and often after it is too late to transform or revise them for the actual building in question – alas a futile act in the theater of the public approval process.

The Mock-Up as Performance

While all mock-ups involve testing certain performance criteria, we come to understand that the varied definitions of performance are the critical factor in their evaluation. It is productive to think through a set of instantiations where the mock-up has served to advance an idea about architecture that could not have been done through other means. The wood models of Antonio Sangallo, prepared for the Pope, were not mock-ups in the strict sense; the millwork did not rehearse actual construction techniques imagined for the building, but the sheer scale of the model served as headgear and viewfinder, so that the Pope could envisage what would otherwise have to be "mediated" through other representational inventions such as perspective. In this instance, the translation from the two dimensional to the third, via perspective, might have seemed more daunting for the Pope than the conceptual shift in scale and materiality as proposed through a mock-up. The mock-up, as a large model, would entail the meticulous handcraft of woodworkers that could anticipate its expansion and contraction, and the very movement it would undergo as a result of both temperature and humidity fluctuations; in this sense, as an act of building, the model was itself a feat, and an end product, with its own means and methods, completely independent of the building it was meant to represent.

As such, the colossal Renaissance models were primarily optical mock-ups, and the verisimilitude of the St. Peter's model only helps to radicalize the acceleration of optics as a field, something that is built into Palladio's Teatro Olimpico as a stage set, where the image of the city is materialized through a gradient scale, bridging the idea of a model and mock-up into confluence through the anamorphic fabrication of its various streets. The theater also connects the artifice of stagecraft to architecture as an indelible part of the discipline. Within this context, projects such as Teatro Olimpico, the mock-up of Potemkin Village, and the construction of EUR, all speak to the ways in which architecture is called on to construct perception, not only in the appearance of its streets, but in the ways that those very streets amount to a form of representation about power, presence, or urbanity. Gelpi's account helps us to better understand the fluid ways in which we can better understand the mock-up, as model, simulation, structural test, installation, or even building, underlining the speculative nature of building as research, no matter what scale or raison d'etre.

The tension between the actuality of buildings, and the perception they produce is, of course, an indelible part of one of architecture's main disciplinary characteristics: the theory of tectonics that establishes the tension between actual material performance and their requisite representational performance. The entasis of the Doric column has emblemized this theory for ages, but many of architecture's so-called necessities are fraught with design choices that, by rule, entail varied options in their execution, and each of which offer a slightly different form of surplus. As such, visual performance can be said to be a critical factor of even the mock-ups whose purpose is to test structural performance. Gelpi's passages on Mies Van der Rohe's Köller-Müller Villa and the Frank Lloyd Wright column mock-up for the Johnson Wax Building are apt examples of this argument, adopting these two buildings to demonstrate not only their structural, but so too their tectonic properties.

The Building as Mock-up

If performance were viewed from the perspective of an extended or deep history, then the systemic codification of architectural types can also be said to be construed around the idea of a mock-up. Not a mock-up in the strict sense of the term, the architectural type is rooted in an idea about a building's organizational, formal, or technological systems such that each iteration contributes to its overall contribution to the field. After all, it is in the context of Diocletian's Palace, the Escorial, and the Berlin Free University that we come to appreciate the transformations of the Rolex Center by Sanaa. Each conceived in a different era, in relation to varying social, political, and economic forces, their organizational makeup, between rooms, courts, and urbanistic layout, constitutes a type commonly referred to as a mat building. With a density and depth in plan that challenges the accessibility of light and air, all these buildings push certain limits to establish a meaningful relationship between part and whole; and yet, it is Sanaa's Rolex Center, whose introduction of the form active vaults that help give singularity to what would otherwise be an inaccessible mass, providing for a brilliant challenge to the many mock-ups that preceded it. In this sense, under the regime of typology, each building can be seen to serve as a mock-up for the next, building up a historical narrative of inventions along the way.

With the emergence of performance software, today there is a myriad of ways in which the idea of the mock-up has gained traction in the context of simulation. Beyond the reliance on the expertise of the consultant, designs are put under structural, environmental, and traffic engineering tests on a routine basis, if only to demonstrate their interiority to speculative design practices; digital mock-ups are part of the process, not just part of the proof. And yet, there is sometimes no substitute for the haptic, the physical, and the material. What can be more visceral than the plummet of a parabolic flight path to create an expanded understanding of weightlessness? In the architectural context, ironically, patronage rarely offers the space within which to research or advance innovations for their own purposes; that is assumed to be part of the responsibility of the architect's life commitments. Notwithstanding added pressures from the insurance sector, the idea of the production of new forms of knowledge through making remain academic in nature, and rarely underwritten by clients. For this reason, it is all the more awesome to understand those delicate historical moments when architects gained a different form of agency through making, if only to underwrite their own failures as a positive form of intellectual and professional advancement. In the article "Cheap and Handsome: The Cost of Efficiency in Mexican Development," Maria Gonzalez Pendas documents Felix Candela's calm reaction to the collapse of the Palmira Chapel after its first "decentering," effectively underlining its process of construction as a central part of building knowledge – and its requisite efficiencies – not only for that building, but for the very industry to which he and his brother had given birth in Mexico City. While this model of practice still remains rare, Gelpi's book offers a lens into what potentials might await architectural practice if viewed from this expanded perspective.

In revisiting the historic footage of the collapse of the Tacoma Narrows Bridge, I have been impressed by the thoroughness of its documentation. Seemingly the product of a special effects studio, the footage is exactly the opposite: real footage un-doctored by any sort of representational deceit. The documentary, with the voice of Professor Farquharson, presents a calm restraint as he narrates the unfolding of dramatic events, balancing out the scientific evaluation of vortex shedding and resonant oscillation with the personal account of his daughter's dog stuck in the car at midspan. Moreover, what this footage spectacularly presents is the tension that arises from the prospect of a sublime collapse, and unintended as it may have been, the fecundity of the full-scale mock-up as the basis for the production of new forms of knowledge.

Notes

1. Greg Lynn's article in *ANY* may serve as a good reference for this emerging debate. "Blobs, or Why Tectonics is Square and Topology is Groovy," *ANY* 14, May, 1996.
2. The established younger practices today are maybe too many to enumerate, but the research of studios like Ball Nogue, Situ Studio, Alibi studio, Matter Design, Matsys, or The Very Many have all contributed to the transformation of the thinking behind making as both a representational tool, while also advancing our conception of the building industry.

Introduction

Figure 0.1 Frank Lloyd Wright observing the full-scale mock-up of his column design. Frank Lloyd Wright, S.C. Johnson Wax Administration Building (Racine, WI, USA) 1937.

Courtesy of Wisconsin Historical Society – WHS-ID1911.

FROM REPRESENTATION TO REALITY

In 2013, as the new building for the Pérez Art Museum Miami was nearing the final stages of construction, a separate set of buildings were being demolished on site. These smaller buildings lined the western edge of the site and were more costly per square foot than the museum itself. The Swiss firm, Herzog & de

Meuron, designed these sacrificial buildings but the general public would never see these structures; the public would only ever experience their impact. What is striking about the Pérez Art Museum Miami, is the degree to which it had already been built before finally being built, albeit in fragments, but at full-scale. These full-scale fragments are mock-ups. The many mock-ups constructed in Miami were dress rehearsals, anticipations of the final building, like a negotiation intended to mediate the local conditions on the ground with imaginations from afar.

At its best, a full-scale mock-up does not lead to a reconsideration of the broad conceptions of design. Rather, mock-ups solidify and deepen conceptual approaches through a series of detailed fine-tunings, transforming drawn representations into sometimes surprising realities. Mock-ups represent a powerful opportunity to engage the unpredictable entanglements of representation and reality, entanglements which are difficult to anticipate.

Mock-ups represent a transformation, as the flat media of the drawing is translated into the thicker materiality of the building, resulting in a new negotiated reality. For the Pérez Art Museum Miami, Herzog & de Meuron productively employed such full-scale mock-ups as both a conceptual and practical extension of the design process. In fact, Herzog & de Meuron consistently utilize mock-ups to push the boundaries of practice, ultimately dissolving the borders between designing and building, extending the reach of design beyond the page. They are not the only ones.

While the architectural profession increasingly engages in the construction of full-scale mock-ups generally, a few practices are uniquely experimenting with mock-ups to redefine assumptions about the design process and architectural practice. These unique practices not only use mock-ups to prove the physical viability of design concepts, but also to extend the architect's creative possibilities.

Through mock-ups, the architect can better anticipate the interactions of matter and form, and the particularities of site, absorbing these empirical observations into deeper forms of design. Approaching design with or without mock-ups, suggests different outcomes for the resulting constructions, respectively, one which is generic to its material surroundings or, preferably, one which is specifically immersed in its physical context.

As a result of being constrained to the page and at small-scale, conventional representations do not allow a deeper consideration of material properties and behaviors which will exist at full-scale. Mock-ups, instead, require representation to exist in the material world, distorting ideal representations with the internal forces of physical matter.

Mock-ups test uncertain ideas, providing new opportunities for experimentation and failures. These failures exist as both cautionary tales as well as new opportunities for innovation through pre-meditation. These pre-meditations enable deeper engagements with physical reality, negotiating design intent with the camouflaged realities of building and practice.

PHYSICAL FORMS OF REPRESENTATION

Mock-ups are a more articulate convention of representation, because unlike drawings, they are constructed of the same physical matter as the material objects that they also represent. This consistency allows them to more smoothly embody representation, avoiding the unpredictable distortions of translating from two-dimensional to three-dimensional or from representation to reality. As physical forms of representation, mock-ups can provide new insights and feedback not possible when constrained to immaterial representations. Through mock-ups, architecture is in a unique position to encompass not only formal and aesthetic concerns, but also to define the degree to which the physical world is embodied or avoided.

While diverse in scope and technique, mock-ups fit into a different category of representation, as hybrid conventions which are simultaneously drawing and building and occupy the territory where representation blurs into reality. Seemingly paradoxical, in a mock-up, the reality *is* also the representation.

While the motivations of mock-ups are contingent on the particularities of each project, not predefined by a standardized set of conventions, what they all have in common is a necessary motivation by the diverse issues of matter and materiality. Within drawings, materials are represented graphically, constrained by flat convention to descriptions of their extensive properties such as dimensions and boundaries. However, it is the intensive properties and characters of materials which are unique, but beyond the capacity for what drawings can communicate. These intensive properties and characteristics of materials need to be mocked-up to be seen, building qua building.

THE IMAGE OF STRUCTURE

Figure 0.2
Contractor Ben Wiltscheck climbs a ladder to determine how much more sand can be added, 1937. Frank Lloyd Wright, S.C. Johnson Wax Administration Building (Racine, WI, USA) 1937.
Courtesy of S.C. Johnson.

Mock-ups are not new. An early and important modern example of mock-ups is the mock-up of Frank Lloyd Wright's column design for the S.C. Johnson Wax Administration Building in 1936 (see Figure 0.2). Wright represented his unusually designed column with the usual conventions of drawing. But having reviewed the design, the column was rejected by the Wisconsin Industrial Commission. Because of its flaring top and slender base, the building department believed it would fail as a result of its unusual shape. To prove the adequacy of his design, Wright challenged the ruling of the commission by building one of the columns at full-scale. This full-scale mock-up demonstrated that

Introduction

his unique shape not only functioned as designed, but also far exceeded the required structural load.[1] Simply stated, the physical realities of Wright's column could not be represented by drawing alone. It needed to be constructed to be understood. It needed to be built, to be built.

Here, the insufficiency of drawings highlights a shortcoming of our representational language. While drawings are sufficient for representing the image of form, or in this case the image of structure, they lack the capacity to communicate form's important relationships with matter. The flat drawing is an imprecise approximation of architecture. Only mock-ups successfully bridge that liminal space between drawing and physical building, that space between representation and reality.

FULL-SCALE REPRESENTATIONS

Whether or not they exist as monumentally as Wright's column, mock-ups are instrumental in solving constructability issues. However, these are not the only issues about which mock-ups can provide valuable insights. A central concern of mock-ups is the role of scale. Scale is not a passive condition, nor one which serves as a simple frame for zooming in and out. While the consequences of scale do impact constructability issues, they also serve a vital role in the experience of space and its effects.

An even earlier example of a full-scale mock-up highlights an alternative approach toward moving beyond small-scale representations. In 1912, Mies van der

Figure 0.3 Full-scale wood and canvas mock-up in the landscape. Ludwig Mies van der Rohe, Kröller-Müller Villa Project (Wassenaar, The Netherlands) 1912.

Mies van der Rohe: © 2016 Artists Rights Society (ARS), New York/VG Bild-Kunst, Bonn.

Rohe constructed a mock-up of one of his first commissions, the Kröller-Müller Villa. Unlike Wright's mock-ups, which consisted of only one piece of his building in isolation, a single column at full-scale, here Mies constructed the entire villa at full-scale. An additional but fundamental difference between Mies' and Wright's mock-up is one of materiality. While Wright utilized the actual materials of construction for his mock-up, Mies constructed this full-scale mock-up out of canvas and wood for a villa that he had designed to be built of stone. Mies's mock-up was intended to test at full-scale the effects of form and space, even landscape, without regard for the actual materiality of construction.

These two distinct examples exist at opposite ends of a wide spectrum of mock-ups, one which casts aside the limitations of drawing for what only can be represented in the material world itself, and one which disregards materials and only concerns itself with the consequences of space. Most contemporary examples of mock-ups function somewhere between these two extremes, to prove the constructability of certain designs, but also to incorporate full-scale considerations into the representational realm, and thus to extend the range of the architect's creative vision.

DRAWINGS AND BUILDINGS

If mock-ups exist between drawing and building, perhaps it is worth restating the terms of these boundary conditions. The terms "building" and "drawing" are categorically distinct but when placed in relation to architecture, they are framed side by side with unique interactions.

According to Oxford English Dictionary the term "drawing" is defined as "The formation of a line by drawing some tracing instrument from point to point of a surface; representation by lines, delineation; hence 'any mode of representation in which the delineation of form predominates over considerations of colour'";[2] and alternately as "*The arrangement of the lines which determine form.*"[3]

The term "building" has broad reference, but for comparisons to "drawing" its differences include being three-dimensional and physical. The definition of the term "Build" references the act of constructing by physically joining separate parts or pieces of material together, generally at a larger scale.

> BUILD, v ... To erect, construct (any work of masonry), and by extension, To construct by fitting together of separate parts; chiefly with reference to structures of considerable size, as a ship or boat, a carriage, an organ, a steam-engine (not, e.g. a watch or a piano).[4]

According to these definitions, several key differences can be gleaned. While drawings are assembled of lines on flat surfaces, buildings are constructed with three-dimensional parts. The definitions also highlight drawing as a mode of representation, which implies malleable scales, while building is the assembly of parts, at full-scale, and primarily of large scale format.

While drawings are a language of flat lines that delineate or determine form, building is the thick physical construction of that form. One describes and predicts form, while one embodies that description, or put another way, the drawing is virtual, while building is actual. These differences suggest that for architecture to exist both in the language of drawing and the language of building, one language must be translated into the other.

But building isn't always a predictable or routine act. In a subtle, poetic reconsideration of the term, Mike Cadwell pulls at the certainty of the definition, hinting at the elusiveness of building. To build, requires interpretation and judiciousness specific to its own procedures, separate from the distinct procedures of drawing.

> Building. Building is a good solid word. Not just a noun; an object spied in a distant field or an object perused in a magazine. Building is also a verb; a creative act with its own unpredictable unfolding in the physical world. Building as such is not finally determined by the machinations of language or the preconceptions of the studio but demands its own solid ground, its own insightful embrace.[5]

If "building" is a creative act, not simply a mundane translation from the imaginary to the physical, then it must be the architect's role to fill in the blanks, to guide an unpredictable process through the creative acts of translation. Cadwell argues for an embrace of building that exists outside of drawing. But what exactly is it that cannot be contained by drawing, and must be embraced through building aside from the generic differences between thick and thin?

The unique nature of that boundary condition is discussed in Robin Evans' essay, "Translations from Drawing to Building." In this insightful text, Evans elaborates on various types of translations, highlighting the unique qualities of translation between drawing and building within architecture.

Evans begins by defining translation in terms of translatory motion, in which he observes "to translate something in space is to move it intact without altering it."[6] This notion of translatory motion is different than the act of translating between languages, of which he states it is a myth to believe that nothing is altered as a result of translation, because "the substratum across which the sense of words is translated from language to language does not appear to have the requisite evenness and continuity; things can get bent, broken or lost on the way."[7]

Consistent with Evan's example of translating meaning between languages, translations between drawing and building, are likewise discontinuous as each representational language is different, lacking the same evenness and continuity. But how are they particularly different?

Evan's highlights the uniqueness of drawing within architecture that inevitably leads to the more significant distortions of translation.

Evans recalls his time teaching in an art department in which he states he assumed that artists and architects shared the visual medium of drawing as something in common. However, he later realized that the architects and artists engaged drawings in different ways, observing that while artists might spend a little time sketching or producing maquettes, it was only for a brief time before moving onto the actual thing itself which absorbed most of their attention and effort. In contrast, Evans notices a peculiar disadvantage under which architects work, "never working directly with the object of their thought, always working at it through some intervening medium, almost always the drawing."[8]

Evans also notes that within the arts, the most intense creative effort is in the construction of the final artifact not the preliminary drawings. This makes architecture unique in that it could be argued that the most creative design efforts are invested in the design drawings and not the process of building.

He states,

> Recognition of the drawing's power as a medium turns out, unexpectedly, to be recognition of the drawing's distinctness from and unlikeness to the thing that is represented, rather than its likeness to it, which is neither as paradoxical nor as dissociative as it may seem.[9]

Through this observation about drawings distinctness to building, we can foresee the significant task of translations which would be necessary to convert from one form of representation to the other. This uniquely widened gap seems to invite an architectural convention which exists between drawing and building, more mutually invested in the generative capacities of both. That convention is the mock-up.

BUILDINGS WITHOUT DRAWINGS

Mock-ups exist somewhere between drawing and building, not canceling out one or the other, but entangling one with the other, illustrating their tensions, strengthening their individual power through the feedbacks they allow. But if, as Evans argues, the distinction between drawing and building is what lends each its communicative power, then do mock-ups reduce that power by blurring the distinctions between the two conventions? It is worth considering what the logical extension of mock-ups would look like, as something which moves representation beyond drawings, to establish an architecture of buildings without drawings.

In an essay by Jim Lutz titled "Music Lessons: Improvisation in Four Movements," the author argues that improvisation, or the ability to be spontaneously creative, is more frequently established within music than architecture.[10] One example of achieving an architectural version of a spontaneous creative outpouring is the project of Michael Rotondi and Thom Mayne, the CDLT House. This spontaneous creativity achieved in the CDLT House, results from the architects removing drawings from the design process, providing us with a tangible example of building without drawing.

Lutz uses the example of the composer and the performer as an analogy for the architect and the builder. The composer represents music by generating notations for the musician to perform, as do architects represent buildings through drawing, which the builders translate into building. But what if architecture were more like jazz as a model for improvisation, in which the performer also composes in the moment, collapsing the two roles into a single form.[11] It is Mayne and Rotondi's uncanny CDLT House which seems to do exactly this.

In 1989, Rotondi and Mayne designed a house that attempted to incorporate the improvisational qualities of John Cage, who described his compositions as acts for which the outcome is not known. In the CDLT House, Rotondi and Mayne state, "This house resulted from an interest in working at full-scale, closing the gap between the moment of conception and the moment of occupation."[12]

They describe the house as resulting from ideas which "rather than being speculative, came out of direct experience."[13] For the house, the architects made no working drawings, producing only a series of sketches for the contractor to work with each day. At the end of each day, the contractor directed lights, illuminating areas that needed more input from the architects, allowing a type of architectural improvisation.

The radical act of constructing the CDLT House without drawings, in an effort to achieve a spontaneous creative expression, suggests that drawing actually may constrain the creative capacities of architects at full-scale.

DRAWINGS WITHOUT BUILDINGS

When we consider the typical separation of roles between the architect and builder, we can see the boundaries which prevent the type of creative improvisation present in the CDLT House. If Mayne and Rotondi's house is one extreme example of design through direct engagement with building, unencumbered by the negotiating effects of drawing, then what are the consequences of the inverse of that relationship in which drawings are separated from building? The impact of that separation is described in the essay "Murder in the Court," by Nader Tehrani.

> The architect is charged with the design; the builder is responsible for the means and methods of its construction-as long as it remains faithful to its "design intent." While this legal provision may seem a guarantor of design implementation in general, it significantly disempowers the architect and presents several theoretical predicaments. First, the law effectively severs the architect from the "specific" relationship she or he can construct between the technical specification of an artifact and its corollary effect-the assumption being that the architect's investment is in the image and its rhetoric, not in its constructive makeup. Second, it further problematizes the relationship between design intent and material construction … as if to suggest that any detail or any material will suffice, so long as the general effect is delivered.[14]

If the architect is separated from the physical considerations of building, then not only are the results of drawing not guaranteed and open to corruption, but the actual territory of the architect's creative vision is also greatly reduced. This is a boundary through which mock-ups provide new openings.

EXTENSIVE/INTENSIVE

The boundaries between building and drawing may be productive at times, but in addition to potentially severing the architect from the process of translating drawings into building, it is the convention of drawing itself which is limiting. If they are intentionally not the thing which they describe, then perhaps a third convention is required to shepherd the process of moving from reductive drawing to the complexity of things. In some cases, the reductive qualities of drawing determine a type of building that conforms to the limited capacities of drawing, but for some buildings, the normative conventions of representational drawing are not sufficient to understand what the built condition of architecture will be.

In the case of Frank Lloyd Wright's design for Johnson Wax, the image of the column's form was articulately represented in drawing; however, it was the material and mechanical properties of its form which could not be determined through drawing. This begs the question of when or for which buildings flat representational drawings are in fact sufficient to understand the built conditions, and what are the qualities or circumstances of some buildings that require more?

These separate properties of form could be categorized distinctly as "extensive" or "intensive."

Manuel Delanda highlights the distinctions between *extensive* and *intensive* properties as a difference that requires a fundamentally changed conceptual framework for understanding spaces, zones, and boundaries.[15] Extensive properties, including mass, volume, weight, and length, are directly proportional to the amount of material being considered. If you are to remove half of a 4-foot wooden board, you are left with a 2-foot board equal to half the original length, and (likely) half the weight of the original. However, the intensive properties of materials, such as temperature, pressure, tension, and compression remain unchanged as a result of the amount of material sampled, and are not divisible. If the same board had an ambient temperature of 80 degrees before being cut, the resulting pieces do not then, become 40 degrees or half the original temperature, even though the amount of material is now reduced by half. These intensive properties are not graphically scalable.

While extensive properties are visible because the size and quantity are visually noticeable, intensive properties remain hidden from view. Because one may be approximated visually, representational drawing can well describe extensive properties; intensive qualities remain invisibly present, elusive to drawings that represent the image of forms. These hidden properties require a different type of convention, one beyond the capacities of drawing.

This distinction is further highlighted by the Aristotelian notion of hylomorphism, in which matter and form are distinct. Historically between the two, form was considered more important, because it is rooted in the intellect. But by privileging the formal qualities of design, the meaningful contributions of matter are limited. Kiel Moe discusses classical hylomorphism in a more contemporary context. Motivated by the contemporary considerations of energy and performance, he observes that engaging material and form through the framework of extensive properties is limiting in that it assumes matter to be an inert receptacle for decision making. It is only through intensive considerations that deeper engagements with energy and material are enabled, engagements that inspire new motivations.[16] It is these deeper engagements that require a new form of representation.

If we as architects have become accustomed to considering the extensive bounds of form, without engagement with the intensive realm, perhaps that has occurred because we have privileged a representational convention that cannot capture these hidden forces. Mock-ups enable a bridge from extensive design tendencies to more intensive considerations of form.

REAL VIRTUALITY: MOCK-UPS AS THE STRUCTURE OF A SPACE OF POSSIBILITY

Mock-ups seem to exist in a paradoxical state of physically being built, without being buildings. It seems then, that a different conceptual framework for understanding mock-ups is necessary to resolve their status within the typical sequence of drawing and building. In consideration of this alternate sequence, I returned to Manuel Delanda. Delanda discusses how within the philosophy of Giles Deleuze, the distinctions between the *actual* and *virtual* become vital to understanding an alternative type of realist ontology. Perhaps these philosophical distinctions allow us to reconsider in a fundamentally changed way the relationship between architectural design as a process that ends in the final state of the building. Expanding on the distinctions between *extensive* and *intensive* properties, Delanda reveals how thinking intensively leads to a reconsideration of what is final or actual.

"Even in equilibrium thermodynamics scientists must face the fact that, given a system in which an intensive difference exists, the final state of equilibrium to which the system trends is somehow already present prior to its actualization."[17]

What is suggested as the "final state of equilibrium" by Delanda is what we might historically consider to be the *final building* resulting from the architectural design process. But perhaps then a reconsideration is necessary when viewed through the frame of mock-ups. As in this observation of thermodynamics, mock-ups might serve the purpose of assembling the extensive pieces of architecture, to allow their intensive differences to find equilibrium. It could be argued then that mock-ups reveal the consequences of the final building, prior to the construction of the final building.

It could then be argued that the mock-up represents a new spontaneous form of process, one which represents a type of final state, to which the final construction of the building simply trends. Instead of process leading to outcome, when reconsidered according to Delanda, "the final state acts as an attractor for the 'process.'"[18]

Delanda then suggests, that as a result of the final state guiding the process before even existing, we must redefine or reconsider what the concept of actual finality is. "But what ontological status does that final state have prior to its coming into actual existence?"[19]

> This suggests a continuity between the process and the final state instead of a break in the sequence where the virtual process leads to the actual final state as two separate phases. If the typical boundary between drawing and building represented the break where the virtual process ends with the actual final state, then mock-ups may represent a new concept of continuity between these two states.

> "States acting as 'attractors,' on the other hand, possess a certain objective efficacy even while not being fully actual, since they guide real processes towards a definite outcome prior to the latter's actualization."[20]

> Delanda further defines this paradoxical state, by titling this new continuity as "the structure of a space of possibilities."[21] Because of the fact that out of all possible outcomes, only a few ever become actualized, Delanda suggests that while possibilities are not real, the space for these possibilities to become realized has structure and is itself real. Mock-ups are not the final building but they are still real, and perhaps better considered not as drawings or buildings, but something altogether conceptually distinct. That conceptually unique consideration could likewise be described as the "structure of a space of possibilities."[22]

> Delanda goes on through Deleuze to describe the seemingly paradoxical state that this space represents, in fact real but not actual.

> > But if this reality is not actual (by definition) what is it? Deleuze's answer would be that it is virtual, not in the sense of a virtual reality (as exemplified by computer simulations or even cinema) but in the sense of a real virtuality.[23]

It is this space of *real virtuality* which may best describe the situation of mock-ups within architecture. Perhaps mock-ups could more productively be considered attractors, of some built condition, providing a deeper physical framework for a space of possibilities, not some flat pre-determined outcome.

MOCK-UPS AS THE CONSTRUCTION OF FALSIFIABILITY

An important aspect of mock-ups is that while they allow certain possibilities to become real, they also allow for certain possibilities to be disproven. If we consider mock-ups a productive place to affirm what is physically possible, then an additional capacity unique to mock-ups, is the formation of failures. If buildings represent a form that affirms permanence, function, and more generally "truth," then the opportunities to interrogate or undermine these truths don't exist in the form of the building itself.

While buildings must not fail or fall down, the ideal definition of building limits how and what architects can in fact design. Designs must avoid the potential for failures. But failures could be conceptualized to be equally as valuable as successes when considered in the pursuit of knowledge. In a way, mock-ups are also a stage to disprove as much as they prove, through critique and interrogation, allowing insights that are not possible within the conventional framework through which we view building.

The paradox of this situation for mock-ups seems to be referenced in the concept of falsifiability by Karl Popper. Popper's notion of falsifiability is a somewhat counterintuitive framework in that it seeks to prove by disproving: "The very refutation of a theory – that is, of any serious tentative solution to our problem-is always a step forward that takes us nearer to the truth. And this is how we can learn from our mistakes."[24]

Ultimately, the goal of falsifiability is not to define truth, but to define a method for eliciting the truth. Instead of waiting for the definition of truth to be fully formed, Popper proposes to make a false solution and critique it by demonstrating its failings, in order to move closer to the source of knowledge.

He states, "Criticism of our conjectures is of decisive importance: by bringing out our mistakes it makes us understand the difficulties of the problem which we are trying to solve."[25]

If the architectural process is limited by the conventional definition of buildings as its end goal, then perhaps we as architects miss a more creative approach toward a deeper source of knowledge, in favor of avoiding any potential form of failure. Popper's idea of falsifiability emerges out of the constraining debate between the two classical sources of knowledge, observation versus intellectual imagination.

"In this quarrel the British school insisted that the ultimate source of all knowledge was observation, while the Continental school insisted that it was the intellectual intuition of clear and distinct ideas."[26]

While one model limits knowledge to what is observable, the other exists in the imaginary realm of ideas. This duality could function as an analog for how we as architects represent our ideas. In order for our ideas to be observable, they must be instantiated in the world and physically built. In order for our ideas to be intellectual they must exist as intuitions, unconstrained and freed from the physical world; for architects these exist as drawings.

While drawings are not empirically observable in the world, instead, they are determinations of some future form, buildings are physical things and as such, they are less flexible than the imaginings of pen on paper. Nonetheless, mock-ups are at once observable because they are built, but also imagined physical versions of intellectual ideas. In a sense, they are physical representations, able to be refuted and questioned. Popper describes this as the method of trial and error.

> The method of trial and error is applied not only by Einstein but, in a more dogmatic fashion, by the amoeba also. The difference lies not so much in the trials as in a critical and constructive attitude towards errors; errors which the scientist consciously and cautiously tries to uncover in order to refute his theories with searching arguments, including appeals to the most severe experimental tests which his theories and his ingenuity permit him to design.[27]

Mock-ups allow something that buildings cannot, the opportunity to refute or critique their form of truth, while buildings are necessarily irrefutable and must not be critiqued to the point where they fail. The nature of this definition may characterize the way we as architects go about designing, by avoiding approaching the moments of failure. Mock-ups allow physical construction to embody both truth and falsifiability. "It gives us a chance to survive the elimination of an inadequate hypothesis."[28]

MODEL/MOCK-UP

The unique capacities of mock-ups to enable productive insights are most evident when considering the differences from the more traditional architectural model. Mock-ups are different from models in scale but also in ambition. Models are typically small-scale and built to represent other materials while mock-ups are large or full-scale and constructed of the actual materials they represent. Models are intended to suggest the future, by representing what's to come without material consequence, while mock-ups actually build that future in the present.

Despite an architectural model being physical, it has traditionally served more like the architect's rhetorical device, as the client presentation tool, typically built of small-scale representational matter and hypothetical in its definition.

While the model is a linear progression of scale, increasing from small to large scale in the process of design development, the mock-up represents a feedback, whereby full-scale tests can have a significant effect on the small-scale representations of form. Instead of functioning as a rhetorical device, mock-ups function as a new form of calibration and creative tests. These tests measure architecture's entanglements with reality, not only structural capacities, but also the full-scale effects of space. Mock-ups become most useful, as the process of translating representation into reality becomes uncertain, and unexpectedly difficult due to a number of factors encountered during the process of scaling up.

Mock-ups don't represent reality; they are reality. They are real and physical, but their reality is slippery. They aren't real buildings, even though they look nearly identical to the buildings they imitate, rather they are real representations. Models are about a future yet to come and mock-ups are about defining that representation in the present.

THE EFFECTS OF FULL-SCALE

When considering the differences between models and mock-ups, it is valuable to revisit the two historical case studies mentioned earlier; Mies van der Rohe's mock-up of the Kröller-Müller Villa from 1912, and Frank Lloyd Wright's 1936 mock-up of his dendriform column for Johnson Wax.

Upon closer inspection, we can consider both of these examples to be full-scale mock-ups, yet they go about mocking-up in two very different ways. Indeed both are constructed at full-scale, yet each gains feedback from the effects of scale with explicit attitudes toward materiality. Mies' mock-up is executed out of provisional materials, not the actual stone and mortar of its intended construction, but fabric and lightweight wooden scaffolding as substitutes. Wright's column failure test examines what Mies' mock-up ignored; it fully engages at full-scale the performance of form's relationship to materiality.

While one tests the performance of form at full-scale, the other tests its effects. These tests are only necessary because scaling up, or zooming in, is unpredictable. As things get bigger they often behave differently, and both of these tests were intended to provide full-scale insight into the consequences of their design subjects. Even though small-scale representations of both projects were available, each of these projects needed to be represented at full-scale, beyond the scope of conventional representations. This suggests that scale is critical.

In an important essay titled "On Being the Right Size," originally written 1928, the biologist J.B.S Haldane, gives many examples of how forms exist at specific scales. Through examples and dimensional analyses, Haldane illustrates how if animals were to change scale, their forms that we are familiar with, would fail in unexpected ways. He also discusses how little attention has been dedicated to the category of size for biological animals and how one cannot simply consider all objects a universal size, arguing the size of the animal is as important as its form, and those couplings are not interchangeable.[29]

> The most obvious differences between different animals are differences of size, but for some reason the zoologists have paid singularly little attention to them. In a large textbook of zoology before me I find no indication that the eagle is larger than the sparrow, or the hippopotamus bigger than the hare, though some grudging admissions are made in the case of the mouse and the whale. But yet it is easy to show that a hare could not be as large as a hippopotamus, or a whale as small as a herring. For every type of animal there is a most convenient size, and a large change in size inevitably carries with it a change of form.[30]

MOCKING PERFORMANCE AT FULL-SCALE

But what were the circumstances that demanded, for each of these case studies, a full-scale test? Frank Lloyd Wright's design for the dendriform column broke every conventional rule of the day. It tapered toward an extremely slender base, a mere 9 inches, where state codes of the time, required that a 21-foot high concrete column with a design load of 6 tons should have a cross-section at its base of a full 30 inches.[31]

In fact, according to the historical formulas which were applied, a column with a 9-inch diameter at the base could only support a maximum column height of 6 feet 9 inches, not the 21 feet proposed by Wright. Wright's column also dramatically flared at the top and was additionally designed to be hollow in the center, more like

Figure 0.4 Detail drawings for the S.C. Johnson Administration Building structural column. Frank Lloyd Wright, S.C. Johnson Administration Building (Racine, WI, USA) 1937.

The Frank Lloyd Wright Foundation Archives (The Museum of Modern Art | Avery Architectural & Fine Arts Library, Columbia University). All rights reserved.

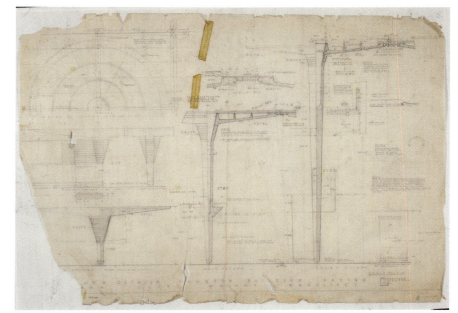

a thin shell structure reinforced with steel mesh. This unique materiality of construction arose from Wright's analysis of the giant saguaro cactus found in nature. When combined, these unconventional design decisions gave a form to the column, which seemed to ignore every structural convention at the time.

The Wisconsin Industrial Commission rejected the design and withheld approval of the structural elements, granting a series of conditional waivers allowing the construction of non-structural elements for the project.[32] Wright's design relied on technical innovations in construction for the fabrication and performance of the column, which had yet to be widely illustrated in building construction.[33]

Figure 0.5 Scaffolding for test column's forms (rear center) 1937. Frank Lloyd Wright, S.C. Johnson Administration Building (Racine, WI, USA) 1937.

Courtesy of S.C. Johnson

Insistent on the feasibility of the form, Wright attempted to explain the design to the commissioners, and later after much debate summarized his conversations in a letter stating,

> The commission being unable to say "yes" or "no" have virtually thrown up their hand and allowed us to proceed. I suggested in the first place that we would make any reasonable tests for them at any time during construction. So, so far as we are concerned this is a proper capitulation on their part.[34]

Wright convinced the commission to participate in a test where a full-size sample column would be mocked-up on site and if it could support 12 tons, twice the required 6 tons approval would be granted.[35] A full-scale mock-up was created to specifications and reported on in *The Milwaukee Journal* in an article titled, "Wright's Upside-Down Column Tips Over Theories," on June 4, 1937. The articles stated,

> Wisconsin's internationally famous architect Thursday (June 3rd) won the first round of an encounter with the Wisconsin Industrial Commission. He successfully loaded 24 tons of sand on the top of a test column which he designed for the new administration building of the S.C. Johnson & Sons Wax Co., at Racine without cracking the pillar.[36]

The commission was satisfied once the 12 tons had been applied as agreed, but Wright insisted on pressing his point further, instructing the contractor to continue adding weight until the column failed. At 30 tons and enjoying the drama, Wright directed the loading crew to "Keep piling," until a total of 60 tons had been added without room to add more.[37]

Figure 0.6 Wright, Johnson and Wiltschek watch as a crane dumps loose sand on the column, 1937. Frank Lloyd Wright, S.C. Johnson Administration Building (Racine, WI, USA) 1937. Courtesy of S.C. Johnson.

Figure 0.7 Column petal falling, 1937. Frank Lloyd Wright, S.C. Johnson Administration Building (Racine, WI, USA) 1937. Courtesy of S.C. Johnson.

Introduction

It is worth noting that Wright's imperial hotel in Japan was one of the few buildings to survive a devastating earthquake as a result of his particular considerations of structure. But for Wright, what existed as sufficient research through the familiarity of experience into the relationships between structure and form, simply wasn't trusted as a drawn representation because it had never been done before.

The novelty of Wright's design positioned the hylomorphic relationship of matter and form beyond what the two-dimensional drawing could communicate. The design of this structure was assumed to have pushed its form beyond the potentials of matter.

This representational unraveling suggested matter is not inert, but active and only capable of agreeing with certain forms, some which exist in drawing and others which can only be stitched back together through physical construction. This mock-up represents a critical moment of physical representation, one where the design couldn't be convincingly drawn, but simply had to be built to be believed. In fact upon successful execution of the full-scale mock-up Wright stated, "new precedents for reinforced concrete construction were established … This marks the end of rod reinforced columns."[38]

Figure 0.8 Inspectors examine a fallen shaft of the column, surrounded by spectators, 1937. Frank Lloyd Wright, S.C. Johnson Administration Building (Racine, WI, USA) 1937. Courtesy of S.C. Johnson.

MOCKING THE EFFECTS OF FULL-SCALE

We see the necessity to scale up and construct Wright's column to be able to observe the unpredictable performance of material at full-scale, but these were not the same motivations for Mies van der Rohe's full-scale mock-up for the Kröller-Müller Villa. In fact, the motivations for this unusual mock-up, built of fabric and wood, not stone, are less clear. Mies had both representational models and rendered drawings, and while the structural performance of the project was never in doubt, to the client, the merits of this project could only be understood when constructed at full-scale.

The clients for the Kröller-Müller Villa, A.G. Kroller and Helene Kröller-Müller commissioned Mies in 1912 to design the house with an art gallery on their estate.[39] Initially, the Kröller-Müller's had hired Peter Behrens to execute the design of this house, but Helene Kröller-Müller was never content with Behren's proposal.

Upon presentation of Mies' new design for the house with drawings, renderings and presentation model, Helene, was similarly unsure, and in January, 1912 her husband arranged for a full-scale mock-up of Mies' design to be built on-site.[40]

17

Introduction

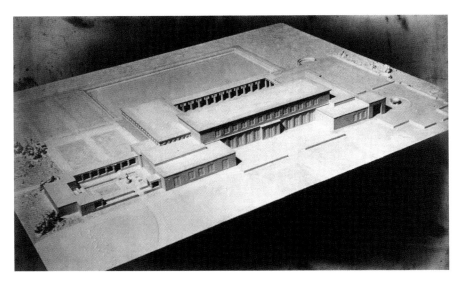

Figure 0.9 Small-scale presentation model of the Kröller-Müller Villa Project design. Ludwig Mies van der Rohe, Kröller-Müller Villa Project (Wassenaar, The Netherlands) 1912.

Mies van der Rohe: © 2016 Artists Rights Society (ARS), New York/VG Bild-Kunst, Bonn.

This mock-up was constructed at full-scale of wood and sailcloth, painted to match the intended final house color and set on a system of rails so that it could be moved around the site to find its ideal placement. Through the use of this full-scale mock-up, many of the usual design decisions were determined in unusual ways. Typically, determinations for the location of the building in relation to its landscape is conducted at the smallest of scales, as in a site map or in a site model small enough to represent the context of the landscape. But by constructing the villa at full-scale, the actual landscape itself is reframed conceptually as a full-scale representation, reframed as an inhabitable site model which allows its views to be observed without the distorting effects of translating between forms of representations.

In this case, the building did not need to be real but the effects of the landscape and its spaces did, in order to understand the full-scale impact of the building and its interactions. There is an unusual juxtaposition of representation here between the unreal full-scale object in the full-scale very real context. Much like Wright's mock-up, there exists a critical moment of scale, where the small-scale representational matter lacked the representational capacity to be trusted, and the project had to be built at full-scale to be understood. This mock-up was not motivated by the performance of material construction in relation to form, but had to be built at the exact size and placement in order to understand the actual interactions between its form and spaces.

Instead of the unpredictable performance of materiality, this mock-up engages another set of consequences of form, the unpredictable effects of its spaces. Mies' mock-up is unique in its subjectivity, in that there is hardly a measurable metric by which to evaluate the mock-up aside from the purely experiential, suggesting that the materiality is only a corollary of the project, and not a vital component of the experience. Effectively, this mock-up is a very large model or map, not the real or material territory but instead a full-scale representation which enables the user to inhabit the representation.

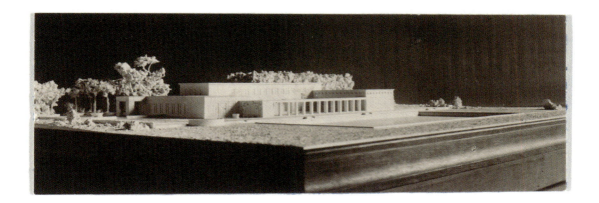

Figure 0.10 Presentation model view of the garden/pergola and large gallery. Ludwig Mies van der Rohe, Kröller-Müller Villa Project (Wassenaar, The Netherlands) 1912.

Mies van der Rohe: © 2016 Artists Rights Society (ARS), New York/VG Bild-Kunst, Bonn.

While the drawing as a flat form of representation could not sufficiently represent the intensive qualities of matter for Wright, so too, the idealized artificial perspectives of Birdseye, and orthographic projection, could not sufficiently represent the dynamic qualities of inhabiting the space in drawing for Mies. Instead of only appreciating the project's forms, through prescribed perspectives and projections, the inhabitants of this mock-up were able to witness the unpredictable impacts of their own interactions with its spaces, at full-scale.

While quite elaborate, this mock-up was not simply an extravagant gesture. This mock-up produced consequences, and we know it was consequential, because upon visiting and experiencing the mock-up, the clients were informed enough to ultimately reject Mies' design.

The Kröller-Müller Villa mock-up could be seen as an influence on Mies' future project, the Rezor House in which the architect makes a set of collaged drawings as if one is standing in the house at eye height, experiencing the site through the frame of the space.[41] For the Rezor House, Mies problematizes the position of the house in relation to the geological formations on-site, including the interactivity of the river and the mountain. These collaged drawings are unique in that they seem to represent the experience of this earlier mock-up, not the final building, more like a representation of experimentation. But in this case, instead of physically constructing a mock-up and moving it around in the landscape, the eye-level experiences witnessed in the Kröller-Müller Villa mock-up are represented by collaging drawing and photography, something Mies had not undertaken in the earlier project.

Figure 0.11 View of the full-scale wood and canvas mock-up in the landscape, with a shadow of the viewer in the foreground. Ludwig Mies van der Rohe, Kröller-Müller Villa Project (Wassenaar, The Netherlands) 1912.

Collection Kröller-Müller Museum, Otterlo, the Netherlands./Mies van der Rohe: © 2016 Artists Rights Society (ARS), New York/VG Bild-Kunst, Bonn.

Ultimately, the two case studies of Mies van der Rohe and Frank Lloyd Wright, delineate separate insights gained through the use of full-scale mock-ups. These insights are also found in other examples, but more often in combination. We could consider those two types of insight as being separately concerned with both testing performance and testing the effects of full-scale. These early precursors are something we will see later in contemporary contexts with mock-ups falling into separate categories, more commonly defined as either visual mock-ups (VMUs) or performance mock-ups (PMUs).

NEW ENCOUNTERS WITH REALITY

Despite the fact that this book is primarily interested in the influence of mock-ups on design and architectural practice generally, there exist extraordinary examples of mock-ups from outside which may help frame their definition within architecture. There is one example in particular which perhaps more simply illustrates the differences between representation and reality in stunning experiential terms.

In 1960 United States navy pilot Joe Kittinger was instructed to do something that had never actually been done before. As the national space programs of the cold war advanced, Kittinger was assigned the duty of testing the effects of this newly emerging reality. That reality was the danger of high-altitude bailout. As planes soared higher and manned missions to orbit the planet grew nearer, aircrafts became spacecrafts, and Kittinger was drafted to test the dangers of evacuation from new heights.

Kittinger boarded a helium-filled balloon and ascended over 19 miles into lower orbit. When he could no longer see blue in the sky, only the blackness of space beyond, Kittinger leaped out of the balloon, initiating a very long freefall before deploying a parachute back to the ground. But something went wrong.

To his surprise, upon jumping from the hot air balloon, Kittinger felt nothing. He felt no rush of air going by, no rippling of the spacesuit, he was unstable and without reference as he couldn't stabilize his position. His interpretation of this experience suggested he had gone too far, now caught between competing gravitational pulls. Kittinger was actually free-falling at a velocity nearly 600 miles per hour; he just didn't know it. In such high-altitude there is virtually no air pressure and to Kittinger, what was simply a mechanical property of the environment radically altered his perception of space.[42]

He was the first to occupy this territory, and in so doing, Kittinger experienced the unexpected physical effects of a high-altitude reality. While the terms of the experiment were to test his equipment and the mechanics of his spacesuit, what's most remarkable about his test was his unpredictable experience of it.

This experiment encompasses the ambitions of both Wright's and Mies' mock-ups, testing both the performance of materiality and also the effects of that space. Here, Kittinger's experience of space is beyond the predictive capacity of calculation. The most advanced engineers of the time possessed everything needed to predict through their own disciplinary conventions what would happen to Kittinger, but in fact what was required was a physical test, not a simulation. What was required, was the actual construction of an event to verify predictions as a series of observations. In architectural terms, Kittinger was acting as a type of scale figure, placed into an undefined space to give reference, defining scalar relationships, except that in this case rather than a representational graphic figure, he is an actual vital figure.[43]

AN ARGUMENT FOR MOCK-UPS: ORGANIZATIONAL CONCEPTS

There exist many unique forms of mock-ups, and as such the projects included in this book document a variety of unique approaches toward engaging the potentials of full-scale mock-ups. These case studies do indeed have some similarities between them, but each also illustrates a particular type of engagement, presenting a wide variety of approaches and insights gained through full-scale mock-ups in architecture.

When considering how to best organize the content of this book, two organizational strategies initially seemed most appropriate. Both strategies considered the fact that the various architects presented here are influenced by a range of conditions in which they practice and build, including economics, cultural influences, technological capabilities and creative processes. With these factors in mind, it seemed appropriate initially to consider organizing the sequence of mock-ups as a progression from low-tech to high-tech. This structure could allow full-scale mock-ups to be considered in relation to the technological platforms which support them, ranging from the purely physical and low-tech, to the purely virtual and high-tech. This is an important discussion to have given the advancement of technological capacities today.

In some ways, these technological advancements question the necessity of full-scale mock-ups as a result of digital computation becoming increasingly capable of simulating certain physical performances. To arrange the case studies from the low-tech to the high-tech, or from primarily physical to primarily virtual, would illustrate the influence that digital technology has on the capacity of full-scale mock-ups. While this seems an appropriate and insightful framework for engaging this broad range of examples, it also lacks in that it too narrowly positions mock-ups as something primarily technological. While technological considerations are important, they are ultimately focused on the question of "how," instead of the more nuanced conversations about utility, or the question of "why" certain architects rely on full-scale mock-ups.

This second approach suggests a more expansive organizational scheme that incorporates the role of technology without reducing mock-ups to mere instruments. Questions of utility reveal the diverse motivations for constructing mock-ups which suggest a range other than the purely technological. This other range of motivations is defined by two ends of a spectrum. At one end, full-scale mock-ups are commissioned to demonstrate that certain construction issues can be resolved, while at the other end of this spectrum full-scale mock-ups become part of the architect's creative capacity.

In both cases the mock-up defines the translation point between how an idea is imagined and how that idea is constructed. These translations become the mediator between the demands of reality and the architect's creative vision. If an architect's design process is sometimes constrained to the realm of the two-dimensional page, then the utility of mock-ups extends that reach, creating a continuum between drawing and construction.

Many mock-ups focused on resolving construction details, fit into prescribed formulas for testing. These mock-ups are highly standardized processes often defined by ASTM standards for measuring air and water infiltration among other performance criteria intended to demonstrate that a given design will perform as intended. The process for these standardized mock-ups is predefined, and the architects adapt their designs to the format of these given procedures to see if they will perform as prescribed. But at the opposite end of this spectrum exist mock-ups which are themselves creatively invented for an improvised utility. In this family of mock-ups the architect does not simply design solutions for a standardized mock-up, but invents new forms and procedures as mock-ups. This type of improvised mock-up, is unique, not standardized and incorporates the act of making and building into the creative process of the architect. In a way, these mock-ups acknowledge that certain designs need to be built to be built.

At this end of the spectrum, mock-ups are defined by the creativity that goes into the design of the mock-up itself. These mock-ups become playful and inventive, sometimes embodying a stronger creative vision than what is visible in the final building. While standardized mock-ups are formal and recognizably distinct from the final building, the mock-ups of the architect's creative process are at times difficult to distinguish from the actual building, and in some cases they are the building itself. These examples pull on the definition of the mock-up expanding it to incorporate new models for creative process.

LEGIBILITY OF MOCK-UPS THROUGH PRACTICE

While recognizable forms of mock-ups are discussed, each chapter highlights additional, less conventional methods of design decisions that anticipate the consequences of physicality in the design process. These unusual forms of experimentation are not immediately evident as mock-ups; however, upon closer investigation, it can be seen as situated within a discourse of experimentation enabled through mock-ups.

There exist many potential definitions for the term "mock-up," and more interesting than the varying meanings of the term, are the individual motivations for becoming physical. Instead of focusing on arbitrary types and categories like a catalog, each chapter investigates the circumstances of each design which leads the architect to experiment through physical representations.

The various case studies presented here will highlight practices where experiments are translated into building, and not experimentation outside the context of a constructed building. As such, much contemporary installation and fabrication work may remain outside the scope of this book. I am interested in those cases where physical mock-ups are instrumental in the translation of architectural representation into the various realities of architectural practice.

MOCKING MATERIALITY

Many of the projects documented in this research were selected for their diversity of material application. In general, projects document a diverse range of focus on a certain material or process of negotiating the physical consequences of form at large or full-scale. Particular materials include wood, copper, steel, concrete, brick-masonry, and light. Through the unique capabilities of mock-ups, deeper integrations and creative applications of these materials are seen.

While mock-ups have clear utility in studying the particular effects of material performance in construction, there are many opportunities for mock-ups in design that should not be limited to projects with only a limited material palette. In fact, when the clarity of given material is well known and understood, often that certainty becomes indeterminate once it is combined with other materials. As different families of materials are brought into combination, they begin to interact with one another, in often unforeseeable and undesirable ways. Mock-ups serve an important role in determining these reactions, but they are illustrative beyond only material interactions.

CORE PURPOSES: PHYSICAL MOTIVATIONS

Architectural representation has the paradoxical task of promising an un-witnessed future while relying on the familiar conventions of the present. When we experiment with architecture, we experiment with architectural representation. Ordinarily, experimentation occurs at the beginning of a project, as a small-scale concept model or graphic study in the form of an experimental representation of an idea.

Typically, that idea is free from the consequences of reality, existing as something virtual, which is possible, but not yet real.

But some projects utilize mock-ups earlier in the process of design for their greater capacities of representation than that which drawings can provide. For these projects, early design experimentation is not free from the consequences of reality, and while drawings do exist, ultimately the complex relationships between material, scale, and form, require a physical type of representational convention, one that must be physically built to be understood. These are buildings that must be built to be built.

The projects collected in this book broadly represent a range of mock-ups that exist as strange physical representations in relation to the buildings which they impact and enable. They exist as strange because they cannot be comfortably fit into previously established categories of representation or into a singular format. These projects are certainly not the only examples of mock-ups, but articulate a range with an intention to present a broad approach toward a study of their motivations and potentials.

There are several core purposes of mock-ups. While mock-ups are useful in anticipating problems, and coordinating the various trades of construction, they can enrich the architectural process by presenting new opportunities for the architect, often absent or passively incorporated within the creative design process. Mock-ups expand the territory of the architects' creative visions beyond the limitations of drawing, extending their reach into the realm of construction. This book presents examples of pulling on the boundaries of drawing to allow new processes. Through these examples, the goal is to articulate a broad multivalent argument for the value of mock-ups, one which not only results in better quality buildings, but also one which suggests new practices and processes of design.

THE NOVELTY AND CREATIVITY OF FALSEWORK

"Let us be quite clear: these grey, hollow, spiritless mock-ups in which we live and work, will be shameful evidence for posterity of the spiritual descent into hell of our generation, which forgot that great, unique art: architecture."[44]

Under completely different circumstances, Walter Gropius argued that a mock-up is not real architecture. A mock-up is instead a type of fake architecture or architectural false work. Not only an imposter of practice, but a missed opportunity to engage in the unique capacities of architecture as a creative art form. This statement finds new contemporary resonance when considered in the context of today's expanding palette of architectural representations and the tools which enable those representations. To Gropius, the mechanical acts of technical mocking-up represented a divorce from the connections of architectural experimentation as an artistic practice.

I would argue Gropius is referring to the translation of existing conceptions of architecture into built form without questioning the merits of previously established conceptual frameworks of architecture. In his admonishment against the un-thoughtful production of form, the term "mock-ups," is employed as a pejorative, describing something fake, technical indeed but not new, an architecture which doesn't question itself.

Ironically, mock-ups are exactly the place where a new type of novelty in architecture and building are found. Mock-ups more fully than any other device enable precisely that fusion of architecture and art for which Gropius cared. This book is focused on precisely those examples of architecture, where gaps between contemporary conceptions of architectural representation and the practice of building must be bridged. Mock-ups in fact do become a necessary part of a creative practice which as a result of these unusual conventions are newly enabled to question and ultimately reinvent itself.

MOCKING WHAT

As we find ourselves in a contemporary context in which the design processes of making, prototyping and fabricating seem to have renewed priority in architecture, we must acknowledge that the various motivations for translating representation into physical forms are not uniform. In this present context, while we certainly cannot consider all physical constructions to be buildings, we likewise cannot consider all of the other physical forms of architecture to be mock-ups. But exactly what it is that constitutes a mock-up is difficult to delineate without example. The questions of what architectural mock-ups are, and how they are executed, are practical but also deeply conceptual.

Sometimes mock-ups have the power to move our subjectivities beyond what was previously thought, and other times they simply reinforce what was already suspected. Regardless of which, what they all have in common is that they confirm something unpredictable through their physicality at full-scale. If new possibilities for building have become so abundant and if any of the forms we imagine can be built, then I would argue that the flat representations of architecture, typically assigned to the processes of drawing, are no longer sufficient to capture a more complex contemporary discourse of material. In some cases these flat drawings are not sufficient to represent what is imagined beyond form, and must be reinforced with mock-ups. While drawings could previously be defined as determinations of what will be built, in some cases mock-ups now take priority reversing that process by first determining what we draw. Instead of only designing what we build through drawings, through mock-ups we can also creatively design how we build.

The ambitions of this book are to function as a theoretical and practical introduction to the historical and contemporary relevance of mock-ups in architecture. Building upon the early examples highlighted in this introduction, the remainder of the book will present the embodiment of mock-ups' influence in seven contemporary case studies of building. Present in these examples are the precise but malleable embodiment of mock-ups, physically built, but without an agreed-upon definition. The evidence of the mock-ups influence found in these diverse examples will map a contemporary context, through which a more precise definition can be approached.

The approach to this subject is a hybrid type of journalistic and forensic study, reporting on the documentation retained by the individual architects, engineers and other consultants and collaborators. The text will rely as much on photographic evidence, as first-hand interviews and wherever possible site visits. The ambition is to examine the discursive categories for mock-ups, which allow new processes for architecture to more fully engage in physical forms of representation. These new processes ultimately expand our presumptions of building and drawing, redefining each within new hybrid combinations.

Mock-ups are not new, but certainly something which finds renewed relevance today. As a result of this re-emergence within practice, it is worth reconsidering where they come from and the potentials that they present. What were once historical conventions, are now reinvented through their interactions with new contemporary forms and procedures that accompany them.

As a hybrid form of physical representation, mock-ups can empower new forms of collaborations between drawings and building, representation, and reality, and in the process perhaps they also momentarily allow architecture to reimagine and reinvent itself.

If mock-ups are the physical representation of translation, then perhaps a more expansive application of mock-ups is appropriate. This broader application of mock-ups not only allows new translations between drawing and building but also perhaps the translation of architecture itself into something new, something which gets bent and broken into new negotiated realities and practices.

Notes

1. Jonathan Lipman, *Frank Lloyd Wright and the Johnson Wax Buildings* (Chicago: Rizzoli, 1986), 62.
2. Oxford English Dictionary, s.v. "Drawing," Oxford University Press, www.oed.com.ezproxy.fiu.edu/view/Entry/57552?rskey=E7fyQi&result=1&isAdvanced=false.
3. Oxford English Dictionary, s.v. "Drawing," Oxford University Press, www.oed.com.ezproxy.fiu.edu/view/Entry/57552?rskey=E7fyQi&result=1&isAdvanced=false.
4. Oxford English Dictionary, s.v. "Build," Oxford University Press, www.oed.com.ezproxy.fiu.edu/view/Entry/57552?rskey=E7fyQi&result=1&isAdvanced=false.
5. Mike Cadwell, *Small Buildings: Pamphlet Architecture 17* (New York: Princeton Architectural Press, 1996), 6.
6. Robin Evans, *Translations from Drawing to Building and Other Essays* (London: Janet Evans and Architectural Association Publications, 2011), 154.
7. Robin Evans, *Translations from Drawing to Building and Other Essays* (London: Janet Evans and Architectural Association Publications, 2011), 154.
8. Robin Evans, *Translations from Drawing to Building and Other Essays* (London: Janet Evans and Architectural Association Publications, 2011), 156.
9. Robin Evans, *Translations from Drawing to Building and Other Essays* (London: Janet Evans and Architectural Association Publications, 2011), 154.
10. Jim Lutz, "Music Lessons: Improvisation in Four Movements," in *IMPROVISATION, 2005 ACSA SW Regional Proceedings*, ed. Corey Saft et al (Lulu: American Collegiate Schools of Architecture, 2005), 1.
11. Jim Lutz, "Music Lessons: Improvisation in Four Movements," in *IMPROVISATION, 2005 ACSA SW Regional Proceedings*, ed. Corey Saft et al (Lulu: American Collegiate Schools of Architecture, 2005), 9.
12. Thom Mayne and Michael Rotondi, *Morphosis: Buildings and Projects 1989–1992* (New York: Rizzoli International Publications, 1994), 153.
13. Thom Mayne and Michael Rotondi, *Morphosis: Buildings and Projects 1989–1992* (New York: Rizzoli International Publications, 1994), 153.
14. Nader Tehrani, "A Murder in the Court," in *Strange Details*, by Michael Cadwell (Cambridge: The MIT Press, 2007), IX.
15. Manuel DeLanda, "Space: Extensive and Intensive, Actual and Virtual," in *Deleuze and Space*, ed. Ian Buchanan and Gregg Lambert (Edinburgh: Edinburgh University Press, 2005), 81.
16. Kiel Moe, "Energy and Form in the Aftermath of Sustainability," in *Production: Journal of Architectural Education, 71:1* (London and New York: Routledge on Behalf of the Association of Collegiate Schools of Architecture, 2017), 89.
17. Manuel DeLanda, "Space: Extensive and Intensive, Actual and Virtual," in *Deleuze and Space*, ed. Ian Buchanan and Gregg Lambert (Edinburgh: Edinburgh University Press, 2005), 83.

18   Manuel DeLanda, "Space: Extensive and Intensive, Actual and Virtual," in *Deleuze and Space*, ed. Ian Buchanan and Gregg Lambert (Edinburgh: Edinburgh University Press, 2005), 83.
19   Manuel DeLanda, "Space: Extensive and Intensive, Actual and Virtual," in *Deleuze and Space*, ed. Ian Buchanan and Gregg Lambert (Edinburgh: Edinburgh University Press, 2005), 83.
20   Manuel DeLanda, "Space: Extensive and Intensive, Actual and Virtual," in *Deleuze and Space*, ed. Ian Buchanan and Gregg Lambert (Edinburgh: Edinburgh University Press, 2005), 83.
21   Manuel DeLanda, "Space: Extensive and Intensive, Actual and Virtual," in *Deleuze and Space*, ed. Ian Buchanan and Gregg Lambert (Edinburgh: Edinburgh University Press, 2005), 83.
22   Manuel DeLanda, "Space: Extensive and Intensive, Actual and Virtual," in *Deleuze and Space*, ed. Ian Buchanan and Gregg Lambert (Edinburgh: Edinburgh University Press, 2005), 83.
23   Manuel DeLanda, "Space: Extensive and Intensive, Actual and Virtual," in *Deleuze and Space*, ed. Ian Buchanan and Gregg Lambert (Edinburgh: Edinburgh University Press, 2005), 83.
24   Karl Popper, *Conjectures and Refutations: The Growth of Scientific Knowledge* (London and New York: Routledge, 2002), xii.
25   Karl Popper, *Conjectures and Refutations: The Growth of Scientific Knowledge* (London and New York: Routledge, 2002), xi.
26   Karl Popper, *Conjectures and Refutations: The Growth of Scientific Knowledge* (London and New York: Routledge, 2002), 4–5.
27   Karl Popper, *Conjectures and Refutations: The Growth of Scientific Knowledge* (London and New York: Routledge, 2002), 68.
28   Karl Popper, *Conjectures and Refutations: The Growth of Scientific Knowledge* (London and New York: Routledge, 2002), 69.
29   J.B.S. Haldane, "On Being the Right Size," in *On Being the Right Size and Other Essays*, ed. John Maynard Smith (Oxford University Press, 1985), 1.
30   J.B.S. Haldane, "On Being the Right Size," in *On Being the Right Size and Other Essays*, ed. John Maynard Smith (Oxford University Press, 1985), 1.
31   Jonathan Lipman, *Frank Lloyd Wright and the Johnson Wax Buildings* (Chicago: Rizzoli, 1986), 59.
32   Brian Carter, *Johnson Wax Administration Building and Research Tower: Frank Lloyd Wright* (London: Phaidon Press Limited, 1998), 11–12.
33   Brian Carter, *Johnson Wax Administration Building and Research Tower: Frank Lloyd Wright* (London: Phaidon Press Limited, 1998), 11–12.
34   Jonathan Lipman, *Frank Lloyd Wright and the Johnson Wax Buildings* (Chicago: Rizzoli, 1986), 59.
35   Jonathan Lipman, *Frank Lloyd Wright and the Johnson Wax Buildings* (Chicago: Rizzoli, 1986), 59.
36   "Wright's Upside-Down Column Tips Over Theories," *The Milwaukee Journal*, June 4, 1937.
37   Jonathan Lipman, *Frank Lloyd Wright and the Johnson Wax Buildings* (Chicago: Rizzoli, 1986), 62.
38   Jonathan Lipman, *Frank Lloyd Wright and the Johnson Wax Buildings* (Chicago: Rizzoli, 1986), 62.
39   Terrence Riley and Barry Bergdoll. *Mies in Berlin* (New York: Museum of Modern Art, 2001), 166.
40   Franz Schulze, *Mies van der Rohe: A Critical Biography* (Chicago: University of Chicago Press, 1985), 59–60.
41   Michael Cadwell, *Strange Details* (Cambridge: The MIT Press, 2007), 101–103.
42   Capt. Joseph W. Kittinger, Jr., "Inside the Original Space Dive: Joseph Kittinger on 1960 Record Jump," *National Geographic*, https://news.nationalgeographic.com/news/2012/10/121008-joseph-kittinger-felix-baumgartner-skydive-science/.

43 Capt. Joseph W. Kittinger, Jr., "Inside the Original Space Dive: Joseph Kittinger on 1960 Record Jump," *National Geographic*, https://news.nationalgeographic.com/news/2012/10/121008-joseph-kittinger-felix-baumgartner-skydive-science/.
44 Walter Gropius, Exhibition Pamphlet for "Exhibition of Unknown Architects" quoted in Gooden Mario, *_orm is a Four Letter Word (That Starts with "F")*, in *PERSPECTA 43, TABOO: The Yale Architectural Journal*, ed John C. Brough, Seher Erdogan and Parsa Khalili (Cambridge: The MIT Press, 2010), 92–93.

Bibliography

Cadwell, Michael, *Small Buildings: Pamphlet Architecture 17* (New York: Princeton Architectural Press, 1996).

Cadwell, Michael, *Strange Details* (Cambridge: The MIT Press, 2007).

Carter, Brian. *Johnson Wax Administration Building and Research Tower: Frank Lloyd Wright* (London: Phaidon Press Limited, 1998).

DeLanda, Manuel. "Space: Extensive and Intensive, Actual and Virtual." in *Deleuze and Space*, edited by I. Buchanan, G. Lambert (Edinburgh: Edinburgh University Press, 2005), 80–88.

Evans, Robin, "Translations from Drawing to Building." in *Translations from Drawings to Building has been Produced through the AA Print Studio*, edited by P. Johnson, M. Crolla, D. Crompton, J. McIvor, S. Prizeman, M. Sparrow (London: Janet Evans and Architectural Association Publications, 2011), 153–193.

Gooden, Mario, *_orm is a Four Letter Word (That Starts with "F")*. in *PERSPECTA 43, TABOO: The Yale Architectural Journal*, edited by J. C. Brough, S. Erdogan, P. Khalili (Cambridge: The MIT Press, 2010), 90–104.

Haldane, J.B.S. "On Being the Right Size." in *On Being the Right Size and Other Essays*, edited by J. M. Smith (Oxford: Oxford University Press, 1985), 1–8.

Lipman, Jonathan, *Frank Lloyd Wright and the Johnson Wax Buildings* (Chicago: Rizzoli, 1986).

Lutz, Jim, "Music Lessons: Improvisation in Four Movements." in *IMPROVISATION, 2005 ACSA SW Regional Proceedings*, edited by C. Saft et al (Lulu: American Collegiate Schools of Architecture, 2005), 1–10.

Mayne, Thom and Rotondi, Michael. *Morphosis: Buildings and Projects 1989–1992* (New York: Rizzoli International Publications, 1994).

Moe, Kiel. "Energy and Form in the Aftermath of Sustainability." in *Production: Journal of Architectural Education*, 71:1 (London and New York: Routledge on Behalf of the Association of Collegiate Schools of Architecture, 2017), 88–93.

Popper, Karl. *Conjectures and Refutations: The Growth of Scientific Knowledge* (London and New York: Routledge, 2002).

Riley, Terrence and Bergdoll, Barry. *Mies in Berlin* (New York: Museum of Modern Art, 2001).

Schulze, Franz. *Mies van der Rohe: A Critical Biography* (Chicago: University of Chicago Press, 1985).

Tehrani, Nader. "A Murder in the Court." in *Strange Details*, by M. Cadwell (Cambridge: The MIT Press, 2007), VII–XII.

1 An Alchemy of Bricks

The Teletón Children's Rehabilitation Center and Quincho Tía Coral, Asunción, Paraguay

Solano Benitez and Gabinete de Arquitectura

Figure 1.1 The surprisingly thin, triangulated brick canopy in the form of something constructed of steel. Gabinete de Arquitectura, Teletón Children's Rehabilitation Center (Lambaré, Paraguay) 2010.

Courtesy of Gabinete de Arquitectura.

THE TREACHERY OF FORM: PAINTING WITH BRICKS

One of Rene Magritte's best-known works is a painting of a tobacco pipe, with the statement painted below which states, *Ceci n'est pas une pipe*; or translated to English, *This is not a pipe*. The painting, titled "The Treachery of Images," illustrates the paradox of representation, where a painting of a pipe will never be more than the painting itself, yet there exists an in-between state where one is realized in the form of the other. The physical materials which construct the pipe, wood and horn, are translated into constructive brushstrokes of paint.

> And yet could you stuff my pipe? No, it's just a representation, is it not? So if I had written on my picture "This is a pipe," I'd have been lying![1]

Paraguayan architect Solano Benitez is renowned for his innovative and experimental approach toward building, and he creates structures that are consistently constructed out of surrealist arrangements of bricks. The forms of his buildings are surprising, more closely resembling steel or thin-shell structures despite their counterintuitive construction out of brick and mortar. It might be appropriate to consider each of Benitez's buildings through the conceptual tensions of Magritte's painting, because like the paradox of representation in Magritte's pipe, one could argue that while each of Benitez's buildings are actually constructed of bricks, they are representations of some other form of construction. These other forms are not simply constructed, but actually seem to be conceived of differently, not built, but painted from bricks. Saddled with the economic reality of the region where he practices, Benitez transforms these abundant and mundane elements from something pre-programmed, into arrangements of something suggestive, representative of other forms of possibility.

BRICK CONSTRAINTS

Brick and mortar may be considered the most primitive of construction materials. There is a clarity and an order to the way bricks ought to be assembled. In fact, Louis Kahn's infamous observations from the perspective of the brick itself, aptly capture what is innate about their nature, which is that brick has a pre-programmed logic to it, suggesting how it ought to be used.

There are generally six ways to lay a brick based on its three sides: the face, the edge, or the end, combined with their orientations in space. A "*stretcher*" is a brick laid horizontally on its face with the edge exposed, while a "*header*" is laid horizontally on its face with the end exposed. A brick laid horizontally on its edge with the face exposed is a "*shiner*" or "*bull-stretcher*," while laid horizontally on its edge with the end exposed is known as a "*rowlock*." Two vertical orientations are called "soldier" and "sailor." A "soldier" is a brick stood up vertically on its end with the narrow edge exposed, while a "sailor" is stood vertically with its wider face exposed.

These various orientations of brick are laid into repetitive patterns titled "*bonds*." One of the most basic bond patterns is the "*running bond*" or "*stretcher bond*." "Running" bond is a pattern of bricks laid horizontally on their face in rows called courses, which overlap the course below by half the dimension of the brick. If you add a course of headers after every five or six courses of stretchers, you get an arrangement knows as an "American bond" or "common bond." Alternating headers and stretchers in the same course, with headers centered on stretchers above and below, are known as a "Flemish bonds." There is an established set of brick-bond patterns, including "English," "English cross," "Dutch bonds," "stack bonds," and "vertical bonds." There is also "corbelling," which projects individual bricks beyond the flush face of the wall surface giving it a toothed appearance; if you add this, you have nearly the complete vocabulary of brick masonry construction. Solano Benitez uses none of these established configurations.

BEYOND CONSTRAINTS

Brick construction in Paraguay is common. While bricks are typically used for the construction of masonry walls, in Paraguay they are applied more widely because of their abundance, such as in the construction of floors and ceilings. The primary reason is economic. Because labor is cheap, and the cost of materials is high, there exists more opportunity to creatively invest in labor than in better materials. According to Benitez, in order to build in such a scarce environment, a tactic of austerity is required, focused on the essentials. This acceptance of reality is not a surrender of creative approach; paradoxically, these constraints serve as a catalyst for surprising inventiveness and experimentation.

> Where there is not much, austerity is required, and the tactic to get it, is to operate only from the essential. Ceramic brick is the cheapest construction material in our country and it is used to the limits of its capacity as floors, walls, and even ceilings.[2]

Benitez has earned the regard of many of his contemporary colleagues who practice in more privileged settings. According to Brazilian colleague Angelo Bucci,

> The early works by Solano Benitez … clearly announced that he could accept conditions and resources available in Paraguay as a point of departure, to achieve a result that didn't seem possible given the circumstances. Since that time he has been creating a repertoire by building prototypes with bricks, load testing them and analyzing structural schemes by isolating the role of each resistant element.[3]

While consistently constructed of bricks, the various projects of Gabinete de Arquitectura are each unique in their construction. Taken as a body of work, the designs span the range of an unorthodox trial and error approach to building, each instance building upon the last, inventing new unexpected roles for the brick to play. This approach is not based on conventional norms, but grows out of empirical evidence and observation, only enabled by abandoning conventions. Freed from conventions, the architect begins anew with a single brick, imagining new configurations that defy its typical bonds, coursing, and orientations. It seems in this work that being constrained to an orchestra of only bricks has emboldened the architects to conduct new ways of playing the same instrument. These reconsiderations of instrumentation reveal an unexpected and surprisingly rich diversity of new sounds and qualities (Figure 1.1).

EXPERIMENTAL APPROACHES

Much of the way that we understand the role of the brick in construction is by applying it in ways that are pre-defined. But what occurs in the architecture of Solano Benitez, is that bricks are radically reconsidered, mortared end to end into linear elements, cast as broken fragments into thin-shell concrete structures, and stacked at rotated angles into toothed slabs of brick and mortar which seem to defy gravity and logic. These radical transformations emerge out of the particular combination of the architect's creative approach against the backdrop of a constraining context. Out of this combination, two particular ambitions are formed: the desire to expand creativity, beyond the narrow window implied by the imposing constraints of brick; and to have a practice that is conceptually rooted in irreverent experimentation.

According to Benitez, "an architecture that is not experimental, is useless."[4] These motivations combine into surreal formations, by asking the brick to do something it does not seem to want. These projects enable bricks to do things we did not know they could do, often resulting in buildings which more closely resemble the forms of steel trussed structures, rather than the traditional forms of their actual brick construction.

ALCHEMICAL RECONSIDERATIONS

This depth of experimentation is surprisingly transformative, because despite being constrained to building with bricks, the architects still conceive of a wide range of structural types, abandoning the typical associations of materials and structures. Being constrained to masonry creates a consistency of materiality in their approach, allowing the differences between structural types to be observed in their distortions of the normative arrangements of brick. It is through this compelling consistency that brickwork seems capable of much more than we thought, seeming to defy expectations as they give form to the invisible demands of structure with new unexpected arrangements. This approach requires not only a tacit understanding of engineering and construction, but also subtle reconsiderations of the typical frameworks for engaging materials and structures.

> If you ask a priest, "Father, can I smoke while I am praying?" he will say "Of course not!" … However if you ask a priest, "Father, when I am smoking can I also pray?" he will say, "Yes of course you can!"[5]

> Likewise, if you ask an engineer, "Can we construct a brick wall, a mere 4 centimeters thick, made of broken brick fragments, mortared on their ends?" the answer would be an enthusiastic "No!" however if you ask the engineer "Is it possible to cast a concrete wall, 4 centimeters thick, using brick pieces as aggregate," the engineer would say "Yes, of course!"[6]

By asking the engineer the same question in two different ways, the hidden possibilities of brick are unlocked by conceptually reframing the approach, almost echoing Magritte's surrealist statement that "These are not bricks." It is this malleable defining of matter, and fluid categorization that allows Benitez to coax unexpected behaviors from the bricks that Paraguay offers.

STRENGTH THROUGH VOIDS

In one of Benitez's earliest buildings, he designs the walls to be constructed of bricks stacked on their narrow side, creating a brick wall which is thinner, and thus utilizes less material and labor (a point of economy). While the bricks stacked on their long edges, known as a shiners or bullstretchers, do achieve a thinner wall-section and conserve material, they also inadvertently create problems of stability when cutting windows. Benitez's early reconsiderations of brick first emerged when reconsidering the relationship of the window to the wall. Considered one way, windows erode the stability of the wall, but if reconsidered then they potentially transform the wall by reinforcing it. Because the wall is thinner, the window openings create unsupported edges which tend to warp. Benitez conceived of a solution: simply rotate the bricks in the other direction at the edges. A typical stretcher orientation, building them up in thickness and depth, to produce a deep horizontal frame, which stabilized the wall where it contacted the window. Within the deep frame, thin supporting walls were placed, and rotated for stability and views.

> The problem is inertia … if you have a wall, then every place you put a hole, is a weak place, but if you think of the window as a beam, then the holes are not points of weakness …[7]

This unconventional window transforms the idea of the opening as a moment of weakness, reconsidering it as a structural element that strengthens and stiffens the thin wall into which it is placed (Figure 1.2). While the wall and window are constructed of the same material parts, each element is now behaving in a unique way as a result of these particular rotations. This reconsidered window splits the definition of the brick into two. While stacked on edge, the brick satisfies the requirement

Figure 1.2 A void in the brick wall, constructed by rotating bricks to form a void, which is strong not weak. Gabinete de Arquitectura, First Office (Asunción, Paraguay) 2003.

Courtesy of Gabinete de Arquitectura.

Figure 1.3 The volumetric window beam wraps around the corner, and its rotated thickness can be seen in relation to the single brick edge thickness of the vertical wall. Gabinete de Arquitectura, First Office (Asunción, Paraguay) 2003.
Courtesy of Gabinete de Arquitectura.

of a façade in that it creates a thin boundary that works well in compression while conserving material. When stacked on its face, the brick produces thickened elements capable of stabilizing.

The result of these two different orientations are optically unique but also deeply rooted in physics. While the resultant deep horizontal window defines a moment of unique expression, it is there out of physical necessity, and achieves a central ambition of Benitez's work: how to build in an environment of scarcity. As a result of breaking the wall into specific aggregations, each of which accomplishes different goals, greater economy is achieved by a more nuanced consideration of the bricks' unique capacities in relation to different demands.

STRENGTH THROUGH THINNESS

According to Benitez, when you want to reduce the budget, you have only two paths: the first is to reduce the quantity of material, and the other is to reduce the labor itself. In another early house project, the Esmeraldina House, a large supporting wall was constructed with the thickness of only a single brick. This wall was assembled of broken brick fragments a mere 4 centimeters thick, but was given additional structural capacity by introducing folds into the surface of the wall. This folded form broke down the single expanse of the wall into smaller facets, allowing the craftsmen to construct the wall in a series of interlocking panels. Benitez observed that when you introduce a panel, you can focus less on laying each brick, and expedite the work by only coordinating the edges of each panel.

An Alchemy of Bricks

Figure 1.4 A structural material mock-up testing the strength of brick fragments mortared together into a thin folded wall, for the Esmeraldina House. Gabinete de Arquitectura, Esmeraldina House (Paraguay) 2004.
Courtesy of Gabinete de Arquitectura.

Figure 1.5 The folded brick wall in the Esmeraldina House constructed of broken brick fragments at large scale. Gabinete de Arquitectura, Esmeraldina House (Paraguay) 2004.
Courtesy of Gabinete de Arquitectura.

For the triangular folds of this thin ceramic surface, a single-layer plywood scaffolding was assembled in space, on top of which the brick fragments were placed and cemented together with trowels, reducing the double layer formwork which is typical of concrete construction. A small fragment of this folded wall was attempted as a mock-up before constructing the larger wall. This mock-up allowed the workers to fine-tune the amount of mortar, also allowing the architect and engineer to inspect it for stability before executing improved versions in the construction of a house (Figures 1.4 and 1.5).

"How can the labor work fast, and how can the labor produce more?"[8]

When looking at the panel surfaces, there is a playful randomness that exists between each of the brick pieces. They are not intended to bear directly on one another; they rather take up space and reduce the amount of concrete. As observed in the different roles of the thin façade surfaces and deep window frame, as a result of introducing triangulated folds into this thin surface a different behavior is achieved, while the materiality remains unchanged. The deep window frame and folded wall become important departure points for reconsiderations of brick. These early projects are mock-ups, offering proof of some new potential which is further developed and built upon in two later projects.

TWO PROJECTS

In the work of Gabinete de Arquitectura, geometry and structure redefine the material, as bricks seem to spring into new forms of matter, like the spontaneous phase transitions from solid to liquid. Benitez seems to suggest that brick has only been considered in its solid-state, and by reconsidering it as other phase-states of matter, the brick is able to take on new qualities and capacities. These deep relationships between matter, structure and geometry evolve further into more exotic constructions in two building projects which demonstrate their approach toward imagining an architecture of empirical craft.

The first is a single project, but defined by at least five individual brick constructions; each one, a thoughtful evolution of the role of the brick. This project, titled the Teletón Children's Rehabilitation Center, is remarkable in that it is composed of what could be considered a series of permanent mock-ups. Ordinarily, mock-ups are only temporary, demolished and rebuilt with the final construction. At the Teletón, the mock-ups are left in place, as elements of the final building. Here, we can most clearly see the experimental approach to design itself which is thematic in the work of Gabinete de Arquitetura. While the second project that follows, the Quincho Tía Coral, is a separate project altogether, it is one which clearly fits into the uncanny evolution of the brick established in the design of the first.

Each of these experimental constructions builds upon the last, with each serving as a mock-up for the next. What is unique about these projects is that in most other cases, when a material is selected, it leads itself uniquely to a certain structural system. But in the case of these two projects, the material remains constant, and yet it is the structural ideas that are plastic, able to give new forms to brick, seeming to evolve into different families within the same species of material. In this way, the structural material selection is reversed, and the important variety is not in the form, rather in the structural capacity of bricks to do work. In these two projects structure, geometry and matter blur into one form, through empirical testing and experimentation, which also blurs drawing and building into a single process of mock-ups.

Project 01: Teletón Children's Rehabilitation Center, Lambaré, Paraguay, 2010

The Teletón Children's Rehabilitation Center project was a renovation and series of additions featuring several thin-shell vault structures, each one uniquely constructed of brick and cement. The project began on the interior, with a renovation of a very large warehouse space. The existing metal roof was replaced with another that was redefined geometrically to transform the symmetrical roof to an asymmetrical shape which begins high on one side, allowing natural light to flood into the room, dropping down near the ground on the other side, placed in contact with its young users (Figure 1.6).

This move sets the stage for a series of new interventions built under this rolling surface, and marks an important tendency in the designs of Gabinete de Arquitectura (GdA): the conceptual reconsideration of existing norms. Here, we see this reconsideration of an existing condition, which is not altogether replaced, but simply modified subtly. The roof is still structured the same, built of thin trusses and metal panels, but is now shaped like a vault, animating the roof and the space it covers, serving as anticipation of what is next to come.

To subdivide the grand scale of the space, a smaller row of cubicle-like rooms was constructed along the perimeter of the highest wall, tucked under a newly constructed thin-shell vault. From the main space of the rehabilitation room, this thin-shell vault conceals the presence of these rigid offices. This new addition alters the definition of the rehabilitation room from something static, existing between walls, to something dynamic, now existing as the space between two gently swooping surfaces.

Figure 1.6 Workers on scaffolding installing a new ceiling for the modified roof which now is asymmetric, high on one side and low on the other. Gabinete de Arquitectura, Teletón Children's Rehabilitation Center (Lambaré, Paraguay) 2010.

Courtesy of Gabinete de Arquitectura.

Brick Shell

The thin masonry vault on the interior is constructed of thin broken brick fragments cemented together at their edges, and stabilized by a series of diagonal ribs, which cross in the center of each section. A scaffold of bent plywood was constructed on rolling formwork; beginning from the bottom, a single thickness of brick fragments are laid face down, cemented with trowels. Since the bricks are broken fragments, the arrangement is organic, without a legible bond pattern, echoing the dynamic instability of the room. Once a complete section is finished, the formwork is released and then transferred in line where the process is repeated.

As the bricks are laid onto the plywood vault-form flat on their face, diagonal ribs are built up of bricks rotated on edge, to stiffen the thin-shell surface. Diagonal lines are drawn on the formwork, and as the bricklayers construct the vault beginning at the bottom, the rotated bricks are stacked end to end, tracing the diagonal lines, crisscrossing in the center of the vault's face (Figures 1.7 and 1.8). This simple rotation of the brick is important, since the brick is not rotated in service of a decorative bond pattern, but rotated to change the performance of the brick structurally. The ribs formed through this rotation on edge crisscross the face of the parabolic vault, stiffening the thin surfaces like a triangulated framework.

Figure 1.7 A thin plywood form is bent into shape, on top of which workers mortar together brick fragments to form individual sections of a vault. Gabinete de Arquitectura, Teletón Children's Rehabilitation Center (Lambaré, Paraguay) 2010.
Courtesy of Gabinete de Arquitectura.

Figure 1.8 Workers assembling the thin surfaces of the masonry vault by mortaring broken brick fragments together. Gabinete de Arquitectura, Teletón Children's Rehabilitation Center (Lambaré, Paraguay) 2010.

Courtesy of Gabinete de Arquitectura.

Upon releasing the formwork, the initial vault section was inspected for stability by testing the surface with a tension cable and strain gauge to measure the amount of deflections. After empirically observing these deflections, this initial vault span was approved and left in place with modified recommendations to further improve subsequent sections of the vault. The engineer manually pushed and pulled on the individual sections, even kicking the surface to test for its durability to simple human interactions (Figures 1.9 and 1.10).

Figure 1.9 The underside of the first thin-shell masonry vault section, after the plywood formwork has been shifted from below. Diagonal ribs can be seen crisscrossing to provide stiffness to the vault. Gabinete de Arquitectura, Teletón Children's Rehabilitation Center (Lambaré, Paraguay) 2010.

Courtesy of Gabinete de Arquitectura.

As the rolling formwork was repositioned and additional sections of the vault were constructed in sequence, several were redesigned to have the diagonal rib structure connect higher along the parabolic section. The new layout of diagonal ribs first crossed and then extended to the edges of each individual section at the top of the vault where they could contact the neighbor, allowing each section to interconnect with the others along the length of the entire vault.

When viewing the sequence of vault sections together as one interconnected surface, the initial vault section (which was a mock-up) is visible in its constructed differences (Figure 1.11). The slight corrections and variations of each section become apparent when viewing the completed vault, identifying certain individual sections, which are to remain as mock-ups for the next. Toward one end of the vault, the ribs were dramatically thickened to provide additional rigidity. In the original mock-up section, the diagonal ribs can be seen to not even make contact with the ground.

Figure 1.10 The engineer evaluates the mock-up by kicking and pushing to empirically observe its strength and determine if additional stiffness is required. Gabinete de Arquitectura, Teletón Children's Rehabilitation Center (Lambaré, Paraguay) 2010. Courtesy of Gabinete de Arquitectura.

This original vault section was a mock-up, and it is unusual to see that this original mock-up remains in place and is made permanent, not replaced and reconstructed, but presented. This is a recurring theme in the work of Benitez, in that generally the experimental constructions are proof of concept that remain in place, not discarded as is common practice for mock-ups. Here the mock-up is the building, and the process is adapted to accommodate the lessons of each step, representing this evolution of feedback in the construction of these surprising surfaces.

Figure 1.11 The individual sections combined to form a deeper vault. The diagonal ribs can be seen to vary over the course of the vaults construction, as improvements are made based on empirical engineering observations. Gabinete de Arquitectura, Teletón Children's Rehabilitation Center (Lambaré, Paraguay) 2010. Courtesy of Gabinete de Arquitectura.

Off the Ground

Upon completing the construction of the first thin-shell vault to conceal the office spaces behind, a second set of brick enclosures were constructed in the grand space of the rehabilitation room. In the original brick vault, the surface as a whole is structural, but the stiffening provided by the diagonal ribs, locates a difference in structural role as a result of simply rotating the orientation of the brick. Drawing upon this difference, Benitez exaggerates this by constructing two more unique brick enclosures at either end of the space. These simple but experimental structures further evolve the structural formations of the brick, based on transformed rotations in space. In these two rounded rooms, the same dichotomy of structural surface and rib exists. Here, Benitez further illustrates the difference by lifting the wall surface above the ground, allowing it to hover between diagonal ribs which are constructed of brick rotated end to end. The clarity of this move is explicit, as one element is now clearly spanning, while the other is supportive. In this dichotomy, one is a surface while one is a frame; yet they are each made from the same material, differentiated only through configuration of parts, which completely transforms their form and behavior.

In the case of these enclosures, it is as if the original thin-shell sections of the vaults themselves are rotated parallel to the ground, while the structural ribs remain in place supporting them vertically. This transformation of space allows the users to further experience these spaces in new ways observing the difference in structural roles of the same material. Again, the flat brick fragments are mortared together along their broken edges, constructing thin-shell wall surfaces (the thickness of a single brick). What is most unusual about these surfaces is that they are lifted above the ground, utilizing their deep, yet thin section to span. As in the original vaulted structure, which experimented with the thickening of the ribs to stiffen and strengthen the surface, the diagonal ribs are further thickened, sandwiched together as a double layer (Figure 1.12).

Figure 1.12 Bricks are stacked end to end, diagonally to form triangular supports, which lift the single thickness surfaces above the ground like columns. Gabinete de Arquitectura, Teletón Children's Rehabilitation Center (Lambaré, Paraguay) 2010.

Courtesy of Gabinete de Arquitectura.

This grand room which functions as the main rehabilitation space of the building seems malleable, subtly warped to interact with light and gravity in unique ways. The structural surfaces and systems at work are like gymnastics, suggesting a progression of phases, as strength and structure are accomplished by working the material in a disciplined approach (Figure 1.13).

It is perhaps this constructive logic that fits the program of a rehabilitation center, more so than any formal idea. The space is warped in section and plan, eliminating any orthographic space on the interior, suggesting a space in formation instead of something static. Benitez conceals the static arrangement of cubicle rooms behind the interior vault and then wraps smaller pockets of space with hovering brick walls, which still flow freely into the whole. This warping breaks down the hard institutional edge of these types of clinical spaces, and is repeated with a new novelty on the exterior of the building, transforming its entrance.

Figure 1.13 A view of the large space and the suspended brick walls which form smaller protected areas of space open above and below. Gabinete de Arquitectura, Teletón Children's Rehabilitation Center (Lambaré, Paraguay) 2010. Courtesy of Gabinete de Arquitectura.

Triangulated Brick Canopy Vault

These interior interventions are technical achievements of material and engineering, but also reinforce a larger conceptual relationship between the building and its occupants. Having transformed the interior of this main space through subtly warping surfaces, Benitez next focuses on the hard boundary between the interior and exterior. Here, the architects propose a transition space that bridges between indoor and outdoor, within the space of the building, but still outside like a type of inhabitable brise-soleil. Typical for this tropical environment, this new space takes the form of an open canopy, which much like the thin-shell vault on the interior of the building, transforms the space on the exterior of the building from static to dynamic (Figure 1.14).

Figure 1.14 On the outside of the building a thin triangulated brick canopy vault was constructed, creating a new threshold between inside and out. Gabinete de Arquitectura, Teletón Children's Rehabilitation Center (Lambaré, Paraguay) 2010. Courtesy of Gabinete de Arquitectura.

An Alchemy of Bricks

Figure 1.15 An initial piece of rough lumber was erected forming the geometry for the edge of temporary scaffolding. Gabinete de Arquitectura, Teletón Children's Rehabilitation Center (Lambaré, Paraguay) 2010.
Courtesy of Gabinete de Arquitectura.

Figure 1.16 Triangular brick modules are placed on top of the temporary scaffolding. Gabinete de Arquitectura, Teletón Children's Rehabilitation Center (Lambaré, Paraguay) 2010.
Courtesy of Gabinete de Arquitectura.

This porous, effervescent structure, functions as both a sun-shading device and a folly, creating a soft informal zone between building and landscape through a thin triangulated vault. The addition of this structure blurs the definition between the hard boundaries of the existing square building and the organic gardens outside. This structure's form marks a transformation occurring, and the constructive logic of the vaulted canopy echoes that transformation in its unexpected application of brick construction.

In the design of this vaulted canopy, Benitez continues the transformative evolution of the brick from surface to frame, constructing a new rib like vault, as an open framework instead of a closed surface. This uncanny brick structure draws upon the stiffening potentials of the diagonal ribs used in the interior thin-shell vault, multiplying and overlapping them into a triangulated brick structure which strangely resembles the formations of steel truss construction upon first impression.

To construct this entry vault, scaffolding is first built from rough-hewn lumber, beginning at the top of the existing roof and springing up to a height of 5 meters, before returning to the ground. Three vertical posts at fixed distances from one another are used in the construction of the scaffolding sections to define the geometry (Figure 1.15). These stick members provide a template for translating linear measurements of overall length with discreet points along the bend to verify heights. This allows a few fixed points in space to be verified, while the lumber gently bends between each point to produce a parabolic arch. With these consistent points established, this section of scaffolding is spaced, repeated, and connected with planks of wood, upon which the brick canopy vault will be assembled (Figure 1.16).

VOID AS STRENGTH: BRICK MODULAR FRAMES

The parabolic shape of this exterior canopy is consistent with the shapes of the interior brick structures, but while the interior brick vaults conceal and subdivide space, this vault is intended to reveal what is beyond. To construct it, Benitez could have echoed

 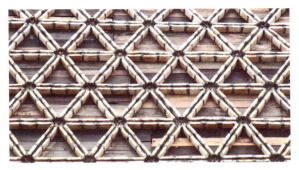

Figure 1.17 The bricks are pre-assembled into triangular modules, by joining the bricks end to end into lengths of three and at the corners using mortar. Gabinete de Arquitectura, Teletón Children's Rehabilitation Center (Lambaré, Paraguay) 2010.
Courtesy of Gabinete de Arquitectura.

Figure 1.18 The individual triangular brick modules placed together with an initial layer of cement in-between and steel reinforcing placed on top. Gabinete de Arquitectura, Teletón Children's Rehabilitation Center (Lambaré, Paraguay) 2010.
Courtesy of Gabinete de Arquitectura.

the procedure utilized on the interior, which tracked thin steel reinforcing members diagonally and built them up with bricks rotated on edge for structural thickness, the way gothic rib system works. On the exterior, however; tracing enough independent ribs to achieve a density would produce many overlapping intersections that require an inefficient precision to the work, difficult to achieve.

As in the Esmeraldina House, where Benitez observed that by breaking the folded wall into smaller panels coordination was only necessary at the edges, and thus a more efficient form of labor was utilized, here a similar logic is applied. Instead of considering the ribs as elaborately constructed lines in space, Benitez breaks down the definition of the whole into individual triangular modules of the vault. These modules are pre-assembled before being cemented together to define the entire canopy (Figure 1.17).

The structural ribs are defined incrementally through the addition of each triangular brick module, affording a highly efficient process of construction. The brick triangles simultaneously act as structure and voids, but also as formwork between which ultrathin steel reinforcing and cement are poured to tie the entire structure together. Because the individual brick triangles are not fully structural until they are cemented into place, they can be minimally mortared together when pre-assembled. The mortar used to assemble the triangles is applied at the ends of the bricks, temporarily holding them in place until they are interconnected with the others, locked together by force. The individual triangular units are defined by laying nine bricks on edge, three on each side, and then mortaring the ends together at the corners (Figure 1.18).

As a result of these pre-assembled modules, the work of installing the brick is simplified and expedited. These triangles can then be stacked in rows, beginning at the bottom of the formwork with minimal reinforced concrete between. The brick is playing multiple roles, reinforcing the concrete by replacing the aggregate, and taking up space thus reducing the amount of concrete used, but also becoming a new structural building block that is mortared together utilizing the edges of this new module as a template. The individual triangles were dry-stacked on the temporary scaffolding, and locked into place by placing thin reinforcing bars in the thin space between before

Figure 1.19 The first section of scaffolding is removed, with temporary posts placed beneath to stabilize the thin structure. Gabinete de Arquitectura, Teletón Children's Rehabilitation Center (Lambaré, Paraguay) 2010.

Courtesy of Gabinete de Arquitectura.

Figure 1.20 An additional course of bricks are added every sixth line of diagonal structure, in order to selectively stiffen the structure creating new hierarchy out of the same matter. Gabinete de Arquitectura, Teletón Children's Rehabilitation Center (Lambaré, Paraguay) 2010.

Courtesy of Gabinete de Arquitectura.

Figure 1.21 The view from beneath the brick vault with certain members evidently thickened. Gabinete de Arquitectura, Teletón Children's Rehabilitation Center (Lambaré, Paraguay) 2010.

Courtesy of Gabinete de Arquitectura.

filling with concrete, resulting in a brick framework, not much thicker than the edges of two bricks. Once the scaffolding was released, the structure of triangulated bricks was free spanning, distributing force between the diagonal lines which connected the modules (Figure 1.19).

Once again, a strain gauge was installed after construction, and tensioned to measure displacement on the overall structure. The engineer determined that the vault structure was too flexible, and as a result, an additional layer of bricks was installed on top and bottom of every fifth diagonal member, thickening up these intermittent members to produce a subtle hierarchy of structure. This new hierarchy utilizes these discreet moments of stability, despite the structure functioning more like a continuous meshwork (Figures 1.20 and 1.21).

Instead of treating this structure as a failed mock-up, which is demolished and rebuilt, it is simply improved upon, strengthened in place. In this way the building is a mock-up, able to represent the process of empirical observation in its final state. The addition of the thickness successfully stabilizes the structure and stiffens it. Instead of constructing a structure that is overdesigned, this structure is constructed minimally, and then by mining the built artifact for weakness and capacities, it is operated on, strengthened through a process of thickening and physical verification. The structure seems impossibly thin for a brick construction and, except for the thickened ribs, the entire structure is a mere 7 centimeters thick (Figure 1.22).

This minimally structured vault contrasts with a second vault built adjacent to it on site.

This second vault is based on the first thin frame vault, and in a sense the first acts as a mock-up for the second. This second vault, however, was not designed by Solano Benitez, it was designed by an engineer, who over-structures it by thickening it beyond what Benitez demonstrated is necessary. This over-structuring represents a more typical process of prediction through calculation and building to resist all forces acting on it with an applied factor of safety to account for anything missed in the prediction.

In the design of the second vault, the bricks can be seen rotated with their ends facing down, like soldiers, mortared edge to edge, instead of end to end. In addition to this increased structural depth, is an additional layer of brick between each brick module, also increasing the amount of cement to join them, and thus increasing the dead load of the structure itself (Figure 1.23). The thinness of the original is lost in this second iteration, and while the two resemble each other, they highlight two fundamentally differences in approach. One is based on physical construction and observation, allowing the matter of material to play a role, generating feedback in

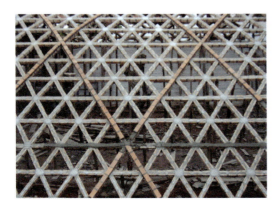

Figure 1.22 Mortar can be seen added in a continuous length with reinforcing before another course of bricks are added end to end, in order to form a stiffer network of deeper diagonal structure. Gabinete de Arquitectura, Teletón Children's Rehabilitation Center (Lambaré, Paraguay) 2010.

Courtesy of Gabinete de Arquitectura.

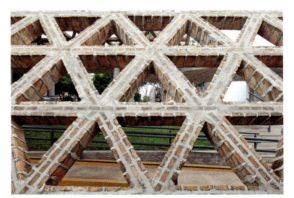

Figure 1.23 A second vault was constructed adjacent to the original, but designed by the engineer. While the original is surprisingly thin, here the members were oversized in the design. Gabinete de Arquitectura, Teletón Children's Rehabilitation Center (Lambaré, Paraguay) 2010.

Courtesy of Gabinete de Arquitectura.

An Alchemy of Bricks

Figure 1.24 A deeper triangulated flat canopy constructed of brick fragments and cement. Gabinete de Arquitectura, Quincho Tía Coral (Asunción, Paraguay) 2015.
Photo by the author.

the overall design; the second treats matter as an inert receptacle for form. Benitez strips down this dichotomy between form and material to the point of near collapse, both physically and conceptually, blurring the hierarchy between the form and material of the building.

Project 02: Quincho Tía Coral, Asunción, Paraguay, 2015

A Quincho is a Paraguayan term for a gazebo or barbeque. In 2015, Gabinete de Arquitectura completed construction of a Quincho built of bricks, situated behind an existing single-family home in a residential neighborhood in Asuncion. This small building, titled the Quincho Tía Coral, served like an annex to the main house, built adjacent to the home's existing swimming pool. The project once again blurs categorical boundaries. It is an extension of the house, but separated from it, structured by a thickened slab but with a strangely cantilevered beam overhanging the pool. Built a few years after the completion of the Teletón building, the Quincho Tía Coral empirically builds upon the conceptual reconsiderations of brick established in the earlier project. The design of this simple space is defined by two new and highly experimental formations of triangulated brick structures. Both of these new forms could be considered mock-ups, constructed on-site, and developed physically before finally being left in place, to be occupied and reconsidered. These various mock-ups are the building itself, one which results from this highly experimental approach to architecture.

Flat Canopy Slab of Bricks

The Quincho Tía Coral is a simply shaped enclosure consisting of a single story, open floor plan with two small enclosed bathrooms, and a built-in barbeque tucked between brick walls. The roof of the Quincho is similar to that of the Teletón's entry canopy, except that it is not vaulting, it is flat and constructed of deeper brick modules, spanning uniformly over the entire space of the interior. There are some structural gymnastics happening in this Quincho, which are not noticed upon first impression.

The springing form of the thin triangulated brick vault at the Teletón is transformed into a flat slab which now relies on additional depth to provide structural spanning capacity. In addition to this evolution of form, the flat slab canopy is transformed in its structural definition, no longer defined by a singular structural system. It is, instead, composed of four separate contributing structures, revealed and concealed, brought together in a seemingly unstable arrangement. The horizontal brick

47

canopy, which spans overhead, is actually hung below three parallel cast concrete beams. Counterintuitively, while there are three beams whose ends are exposed, there are only two supporting columns.

While the two outer beams are supported by columns at each end, the middle beam is missing a support on the end, facing the backyard seeming to hover in place. This unsupported end is instead held above the ground by a separate structural member which blends in with the surrounding bricks in space, gathered together into a thickened brick spanning member which resembles a truss.

Figure 1.25 A cantilevered brick beam, constructed of pre-assembled triangular brick modules. Gabinete de Arquitectura, Quincho Tía Coral (Asunción, Paraguay) 2015.

Photo by the author.

This brick truss, extends out beyond the outer supporting column, cantilevered and acting as a fulcrum for the unsupported beam, springing it into place. This structural diagram is hardly noticeable at first, becoming apparent upon closer inspection of what seems to be an underlying concrete post and beam system left incomplete, to be stabilized by the addition of bricks; a reversal of the typical brick and concrete hierarchy. The building is defined structurally and spatially by two unusual brick elements: the deep horizontal triangulated slab, and the spanning triangulated brick cantilevered truss (Figure 1.26).

When ceramic bricks are made, a certain amount break during the production process of firing and handling. The brick factories retain this by-product and grind the fragments into ceramic dust which is added back to the fresh mix before again being extruded.

Figure 1.26 Broken brick fragments are manually placed into preformed frames before being cemented together into panels. Gabinete de Arquitectura, Quincho Tía Coral (Asunción, Paraguay) 2015.

Courtesy of Gabinete de Arquitectura.

Figure 1.27 An excessive amount of mortar is applied to the bricks as the workers themselves don't trust the strength of the thin panels. Gabinete de Arquitectura, Quincho Tía Coral (Asunción, Paraguay) 2015.

Courtesy of Gabinete de Arquitectura.

The factories also retain a certain amount of this by-product to sell as a cheap building material, which is typically utilized in construction as a type of cheap subflooring. In Spanish it is called "*contra-piso*," or under the floor. This is a standard base for finish flooring, packed tightly and then cemented together to receive the finish floor surface on top. These fragments are much cheaper than intact bricks, typically sold by the truckload, without even knowing the quantity of brick fragments, instead measured by volume.

For this project, intact bricks were not required for each application, and only used where exposed on the surface. To construct the horizontal thickened slab, the architects specified assembling the deep triangular coffers out of these broken bricks, which possess a uniform depth.

A base layer of sand was laid and leveled on-site, on top of metal frames which served as the molds for the flat brick panels to be formed. Broken brick fragments were placed within these frames and then filled with mortar between their broken edges (Figure 1.28). Initially, the workers did not trust the thinness or integrity of the brick fragments, as the material seemed flawed in some way, simply because it was broken. But according to Benitez, the idea of the panel is to use less quantity of concrete, by replacing volume with these fragments as filler, and after allowing the panels to cure for seven days, they transform chemically and you can lift the panel. It is not the quantity of cement that provides strength because as you add more and more cement, the dead load is increased and the material must waste its structural capacity supporting itself. The heavier something gets the stronger it needs to be.

This logic is somewhat counterintuitive, and because the workers were initially skeptical about the strength of the panels, the first panels they built were heavily mortared (Figure 1.28). After a few weeks, the workers gained familiarity by handling

Figure 1.28 The pre-assembled panels are stacked on-site, with the heavy amount of mortar in these early pieces. Gabinete de Arquitectura, Quincho Tía Coral (Asunción, Paraguay) 2015.

Courtesy of Gabinete de Arquitectura.

the panels and started to believe in what they were doing. In fact, the workers learned from their early mistakes, observing the difficulty of working with these heavy panels after they had cured. This is typical of Solano Benitez's buildings; there is disbelief on the job site initially, and through early mistakes everything ends up being invaluable lessons and moments of knowledge that inform the process later in the project (Figure 1.28). The design phase is more like an opportunity to conceive of a strategy, and the design is really only completed once it is built.

Figure 1.29 The panels are assembled into triangular modules, joined at the edges and held together with steel tension wires. Gabinete de Arquitectura, Quincho Tía Coral (Asunción, Paraguay) 2015.

Courtesy of Gabinete de Arquitectura.

After the panels were cast on-site, the process of assembling the triangles began. They were initially held together simply with a thin steel wire wrapped around the three sides to pull the panels together, forming deep triangular modules. It was apparent in the assembly of the individual triangular modules how excessive the amount of concrete was, and how difficult these modules became to work with (Figure 1.29).

Once pre-assembled, the modules were arranged on a temporary platform of scaffolding, with space left between to run steel reinforcing and concrete (Figure 1.31). Finally, the cavity between the modules was filled with concrete and the entire structure was cemented together. The idea of the panel is a Roman idea from the Pantheon; where you look at the admirable construction of brick, but in fact the walls are many meters thick, and a thin layer of bricks only exists on the exposed surface. This is actually ancient concrete construction, not brick construction. It is a humble, not heroic work for the brick, which is simply used to contain the concrete.

The design problem here is the problem of the Pantheon; which is not a problem of bricks, but a problem of concrete being heavy, not strong. By using brick, the architects begin the process of developing the concrete, and between one

Figure 1.30 The triangular modules are again placed atop a temporary scaffolding with sufficient space between for steel reinforcing and cement. Gabinete de Arquitectura, Quincho Tía Coral (Asunción, Paraguay) 2015.

Courtesy of Gabinete de Arquitectura.

Figure 1.31 The steel reinforcing assembled above the modules continuously tied together before being dropped into place. Gabinete de Arquitectura, Quincho Tía Coral (Asunción, Paraguay) 2015.

Courtesy of Gabinete de Arquitectura.

An Alchemy of Bricks

brick face and the other, they start the process of reducing the distance between the two bounding surfaces, to reduce the amount of material.[9] Bricks are not as strong as stone, but they are much lighter, and the brick panels are a way to cover the concrete serving as a lost formwork which remains in place. The broken brick fragments in the Quincho are efficient both structurally and economically because the material is both lighter and cheap.

Figure 1.32 The gaps between modules are filled with cement tying the entire canopy together. Gabinete de Arquitectura, Quincho Tía Coral (Asunción, Paraguay) 2015.

Courtesy of Gabinete de Arquitectura.

Triangulated Brick Beam

The Quincho Tía Coral is constructed of two interlocking structural pieces: the flat spanning canopy slab and a massive brick truss to support the canopies' unsupported edge, picking up the slack for a missing column. This unique truss-like beam is supported at one end by a load-bearing brick wall, and unsupported at its other end, cantilevered beyond its midpoint which rests on a steel column. The truss-like beam flares toward the ground, forming another open triangle, which allows one to walk beneath the brick truss uninterrupted. While this brick truss is necessary to support the unsupported edge of the horizontal slab, it is itself unsupported at one end, yet through the confluence of both seemingly incomplete structures, complete stability is achieved.

Figure 1.33 The cantilevered brick truss which supports the ends of beams, without the use of additional columns at the end. Gabinete de Arquitectura, Quincho Tía Coral (Asunción, Paraguay) 2015.

Photo by the author.

Figure 1.34 A few modules demonstrate the stacking method with spacers to leave a cavity for concrete to be poured between for the construction of the brick beam. Gabinete de Arquitectura, Quincho Tía Coral (Asunción, Paraguay) 2015.
Courtesy of Gabinete de Arquitectura.

Figure 1.35 The bottom chord of the triangulated brick beam, assembled by stacking bricks edge to edge in three courses. Gabinete de Arquitectura, Quincho Tía Coral (Asunción, Paraguay) 2015.
Courtesy of Gabinete de Arquitectura.

Figure 1.36 Diagonal steel reinforcing is assembled on top of the bottom chord, before the brick modules are arranged between. Gabinete de Arquitectura, Quincho Tía Coral (Asunción, Paraguay) 2015.
Courtesy of Gabinete de Arquitectura.

To construct this massive structural member, a second set of triangular brick modules were pre-assembled; only in this case, they were to be stacked vertically to form this very deep truss (Figure 1.35). Temporary shoring was constructed to support a platform, at the edge of the horizontal canopy, on top of which a single layer of brick was laid face side down in three rows (Figure 1.36). These bricks would form the exposed underside of the beam, and on top of this layer, the first course of triangular brick modules were placed oriented vertically.

Between these triangular modules, steel reinforcing bars are inserted in the diagonal gaps between the faces of the equilateral triangles. This thin system of reinforcing spans the full height of the beam, overlapping at each intersection point, creating a woven reinforcement cage that also serves as a template for the placement of modules. The reinforcing from the three canopy beams which run perpendicular to the large truss is extended and woven into the reinforcing of the massive brick beam, interlocking them before being poured (Figure 1.37).

The brick modules were dry-stacked into rows the entire length of the beam, after which the gaps between modules were capped with temporary formwork before being filled with concrete locking them together. After each row was completed, the next horizontal course was stacked on top and again cast together with concrete (Figure 1.38). Areas of

An Alchemy of Bricks

Figure 1.37 Triangular modules are placed within the reinforcing members and capped at the edge with plywood formwork as the cavities are filled with cement. Gabinete de Arquitectura, Quincho Tía Coral (Asunción, Paraguay) 2015.
Courtesy of Gabinete de Arquitectura.

Figure 1.38 Where the perpendicular concrete beams intersect with the brick truss, the surrounding area is filled solid with concrete. Gabinete de Arquitectura, Quincho Tía Coral (Asunción, Paraguay) 2015.
Courtesy of Gabinete de Arquitectura.

smaller triangles and solid infill can be seen where moments of intersection occur, such as where the truss rests on the steel column at mid-span, and where the three individual canopy beams interlock with the brick webbing of the larger truss. These smaller triangles selectively strengthen the areas of intersection points, providing additional support only where necessary (Figure 1.39).

Figure 1.39 The fourth row of brick modules were placed on top of the third, based on the drawings, but were ultimately removed, and excluded from the design. Gabinete de Arquitectura, Quincho Tía Coral (Asunción, Paraguay) 2015.
Courtesy of Gabinete de Arquitectura.

The process of building up this brick beam continued by stacking the first three complete courses of modules, until the fourth course of brick triangles were added, and the architects encountered a new moment of reconsideration. Solano Benitez's son, Solanito, supervised the construction of the design on-site, and began to notice that the proportions of the beam were beginning to differ substantially from the drawings. The design as had been drawn called for four rows of stacked modules; however, due to differences of tolerance and craft, the proportions were off, and the beam became significantly taller. Observing this, the architect approached the engineer to determine if the beam could function based upon the three courses which were already constructed.

The architects were not dismayed by this variation from what they had drawn or imagined. In fact, Solano Benitez considered this difference a new opportunity for the process to inform the design. The 5-centimeter difference between the drawn dimensions of the brick modules and the built reality resulted from the workers adding too much mortar at the ends and in between each module. This difference built up incrementally over the course of construction causing substantial shift between the drawing and building.

These differences become moments to think and develop other strategies. In fact, there is a legible lack of precision in the constructed buildings, one which is clearly present in service of experimentation. By relaxing the precision and opening the process, the architects are able to guide the process by interacting with the sequence. In place of absolute determinism, what is most important to Gabinete de Arquitectura are the larger spatial objectives and proportions, and that the conceptual behaviors and qualities of the building remain intact.

This particular construction predicament presented two options: either to remain true to the drawings, and construct the beam with the same amount of brick triangles; or to keep the spatial proportions and accept fewer rows of structure, improvising the design. The engineer recalculated based on differences in the field and once he had verified what was built was structurally sufficient, the architects determined to remove the top row, maintaining the proportions of space, capping off the brick beam above the third (Figure 1.40).

The translation of the design from drawings to the material realities of the building was a journey opened up to incorporate the workers and the engineer. Unlike other processes of translation where the architects' drawings must not be changed at all costs, this approach invites the feedback of the workers involved in the crafting of the

Figure 1.40 A top chord is formed on top of the third row of brick triangles. Gabinete de Arquitectura, Quincho Tía Coral (Asunción, Paraguay) 2015.
Courtesy of Gabinete de Arquitectura.

project on-site, acknowledging that the materials will contribute to the design. Like the physical process of the drawing, this is the process of mocking up.

Journey vs Instruction

Solano Benitez states that the Quincho project is not his work; it is the work of his son, Solanito, who is a partner in his office. Solanito personally supervised the construction and design decisions made on site. It was Solano who initially designed the Quincho, but his design drawings which established the conceptual ideas, were not yet solidified, and intentionally left malleable to feedback from the process of building.

The design was drawn, sketched and then even constructed in the computer; but here, Solano points out that the drawings are only a reference, merely a suggestion which will take on new inertia once established on site. For Solano, the project was about allowing his son, Solanito, to guide the project along a journey. A journey is understood to be unpredictable.[10]

This acknowledgment of the journey presents the multiple reconsiderations that are thematic in the work of Gabinete de Arquitectura. While most architects demand respect for

Figure 1.41 Solano Benitez' original sketch of the Quincho, showing four rows of brick modules stacked up. Gabinete de Arquitectura, Quincho Tía Coral (Asunción, Paraguay) 2015.
Courtesy of Gabinete de Arquitectura.

Figure 1.42 A view of the completed triangulated brick beam/truss, with a triangulated steel stiffener added to reduce lateral flexibility. Gabinete de Arquitectura, Quincho Tía Coral (Asunción, Paraguay) 2015.
Courtesy of Gabinete de Arquitectura.

Figure 1.43 The view beneath the flat canopy, with diagonal steel columns supporting the beam at a midpoint beyond which it cantilevers in the distance. Gabinete de Arquitectura, Quincho Tía Coral (Asunción, Paraguay) 2015.
Photo by the author.

the authorship and first gesture as an absolute truth, Solano points out that this approach has nothing to do with the process and experience of workers doing what they do. This insistence prohibits the workers and the process of construction itself, from contributing to the project as a collaboration.

This primary reconsideration asks whether the main priority in the process of building is to privilege the exact design as drawn by the architect no matter the consequences, or to allow the capacity of the worker to influence the ideal state. To Gabinete de Arquitectura, this question is open-ended; and when everything is in conflict, the architects, through negotiation and interaction, must guide the journey.

What Can't a Brick Be?

While drawing bricks in new orientations is typically attempted to create decorative brick-bond patterns, the work of Solano Benitez and Gabinete de Arquitectura illustrates that those simple rotations contain tremendous potentials. This body of work builds empirically from one experiment to the next, revealing through its physical proofs of concept that the capacities of matter cannot simply be drawn to be understood.

The triangulated brick slab of the Quincho has some remarkable similarities to the tetrahedral concrete ceiling of Louis Kahn's Yale University Art Gallery. Kahn's ceiling is concrete but is in fact precast, much like the brick modules of Benitez' Quincho. In addition to the differences of material composition and geometric patterning, there is a more fundamental conceptual reconsideration, and Benitez is well aware of the consistencies. While Kahn's famous questions of "what does the brick want to be?"

Figure 1.44 Where the horizontal canopy meets the vertical structural member, both constructed from the same repetition of triangular brick modules. Gabinete de Arquitectura, Quincho Tía Coral (Asunción, Paraguay) 2015.
Photo by the author.

is well worn; Benitez approach is unique in transforming the nature of the question itself from "what does it want to be," to "what can it not be?" The difference is subtle, but the approach is a provocation, opening up new forms and potentials that were previously overlooked. By constructing these full-scale mock-ups, bricks are not accepted as bricks, but more broadly interpreted as matter, and according to Benitez, "The only relation we have with matter is the possibility to imagine a different condition for it."[11]

CONCLUSION

It is tempting to compare Solano Benitez and the work of Gabinete De Arquitectura to other building practices with formal similarities; however, there is a fundamental difference in approach which is unique. By consistently beginning with bricks, Benitez suggests a counterintuitive indeterminacy in an approach to design concepts that are crafted from scratch by reconsidering the potentials of a single brick. These empirical concepts aren't borrowed from other contemporary practices, rather they emerge out of a deep re-reading of how we act, beginning with the brick and its overlooked capacities. Only once these ideas begin to develop and come into focus, do we find the consistencies that tie various disciplinary practices together.

There is some regional precedent for this experimental work, and Benitez acknowledges learning early in his education from the Uruguayan master, Eladio Dieste. While the influence of Dieste is unmistakable in the suggestions of new approaches, the actual approaches emerge from contexts that are quite different. While Dieste invented his own bricks, Benitez assumes them as a material condition he is constrained to, which comes from an outside process that he is not involved in. While Dieste was able to know the precise performance of each brick, Benitez does not, and is thus forced to engage bricks and their fragments as a field condition of averages, which much be engaged through empirical testing and observation.

Because he certified both the making of his bricks and the processes. That is why he could approach the calculation. I, on the other hand, strive to work with inertia and brick in a structural way, but not at the maximum capacity of compression as he did. What we do share is the structural point of view, that is, the ability to visualize when there is traction, compression, twisting, cutting, etc. It is a training, just as you learn to look and understand spaces, you can see how the forces are distributing and finally reaching the ground.[12]

It is in this way that Benitez is most unique. By assuming the Paraguayan brick as his palette, he must find a new method of speculation which accounts for the physical capacities of bricks, not by imposing his will upon them, but by extracting new insights and tactics from his observations and interactions. This is a representational language of matter and forces, visualized through physical mock-ups. Instead of determining a form, and investigating how to structure it, the designs of Gabinete de Arquitectura begin anew with the brick, pulling on their traditional arrangements, building up forces and new ways of building. "It's the way to build, not the shape, that interests me."[13]

There is perhaps a more relevant example that better illustrates Benitez's transformative reconsiderations of bricks from outside of architecture. In the 1980s, an illustrator named Russell Mills cataloged the variety of strange and creative lyrical combinations from the music of composer Brian Eno. He set about illustrating scenes that he composed based on the lyrics from Eno's songs, assuming them as a narrative structure. What emerged is an extraordinary set of illustrations, which collapse the strange storytelling of Eno's words into a visual form of representation. In fact, these strangely illustrated forms emerge because of a simple misreading. Brian Eno never cared about the meaning of the lyrics, rather he only cared about singing, and he simply needed words to produce song. Eno used words to construct his music, not much caring about the meaning of the individual words themselves; simply using them to articulate larger conceptual forms, which emerged from their surprising aggregations.

> Between 1973 and 1978 Brian Eno composed and sang thirty-nine songs; but he is not, and never wanted to be, a songwriter; … With Eno, the writing of lyrics has always been a by-product of his desire to sing, and the need for a vehicle for his voice, rather than an expression of an inherently literary sensibility.[14]

Eno's approach to music is similar to Benitez's approach to bricks in that neither arise out of an allegiance or embrace of language, but simply out of necessity. The unique work of Solano Benitez, and Gabinete de Arquitectura, achieves something much more than bricks. It may be appropriate to consider that Benitez does not care more about bricks than any other material, but it is available to him and therefore a necessity for building. He uses bricks as a vehicle for producing architecture, the way Eno produces songs, which is far more than any pile of bricks can hope to achieve. Throughout these diverse and surprising forms, the bricks become the connective tissue that ties all of the various experiments together. It is these subtle manipulations with drastic implications which create the alchemical transformations of bricks into buildings, distinguishing the work of Gabinete de Arquitectura.

Notes

1. Rene Magritte quoted in Harry Torczyner, *Magritte: Ideas and Images* (Harry N.Abrams, Inc.First Edition, 1979), 71.
2. Solano Benitez, "This House," in *The O'Neil Ford Duograph Series, Volume 5 – Paraguay, Abu & Font House, Surubi House*, (Austin, TX: The University of Texas at Austin, 2013), 35.

3   IBID
4   Davide Tommaso Ferrando. "The Plentifulness of Scarcity," www.zeroundicipiu.it/wp-content/uploads/2016/04/VV04_ENG_10.pdf, Accessed July 7, 2016, 86.
5   Solano Benitez (Paraguayan Architect), in discussion with the author, March 10, 2016.
6   Solano Benitez (Paraguayan Architect), in discussion with the author, March 10, 2016.
7   Solano Benitez (Paraguayan Architect), in discussion with the author, March 10, 2016.
8   Solano Benitez (Paraguayan Architect), in discussion with the author, March 10, 2016.
9   Solano Benitez (Paraguayan Architect), in discussion with the author, March 10, 2016.
10 Solano Benitez (Paraguayan Architect), in discussion with the author, March 10, 2016.
11 Davide Tommaso Ferrando. "The Plentifulness of Scarcity," www.zeroundicipiu.it/wp-content/uploads/2016/04/VV04_ENG_10.pdf, Accessed July 7, 2016, 86.
12 *Cita: UFT. "La Poética del ladrillo o la arquitectura de Solano Benítez" 05 nov 2009. Plataforma Arquitectura. Accedido el.* www.plataformaarquitectura.cl/cl/02-30850/la-poetica-del-ladrillo-o-la-arquitectura-de-solano-benitez
13 *Cita: UFT. "La Poética del ladrillo o la arquitectura de Solano Benítez" 05 nov 2009. Plataforma Arquitectura. Accedido el.* www.plataformaarquitectura.cl/cl/02-30850/la-poetica-del-ladrillo-o-la-arquitectura-de-solano-benitez
14 Rick Poynor, "The Words I Receive," in *More Dark Than Shark*, eds. Eno Brian and Mills Russell (London: Faber and Faber Ltd, 1986), 120.

2 Drawing without Paper and Building without Buildings: Large Representations in the Field

Copper House II, the House with White Net and Saat Rasta, Mumbai, India
Bijoy Jain/Studio Mumbai

Figure 2.1 The courtyard of the Studio Mumbai office where many models, details, and mock-ups are first constructed. Studio Mumbai (Mumbai, India) 2011.
Courtesy of Studio Mumbai.

REFORMULATIONS: STRANGE CONVENTIONS

Often mock-ups exist as a bridge between the process of drawing and building. This characterization suggests that mock-ups are a means to an end. But throughout the work of Studio Mumbai, in particular, the relationships between the means and the ends are reformulated. These reformulations lead to an architecture which is not revolutionary in its outcomes, but more subtly and significantly destabilizing in its embrace of strange conventions as the ends themselves.

Instead of an architecture of novel forms which are executed by any means necessary, the buildings of Studio Mumbai are in fact conventional at their ends, but arrived at through exceedingly creative, yet unconventional means. When reconsidered, these unconventional means reformulate the typical processes of design, suggesting an uncommon shift in the design focus of the architect from the outcomes to the process of arrival.

Studio Mumbai engages architecture by subtly re-orchestrating the many micro-processes and conventions that converge to create buildings. This subtle reengagement shifts the mock-up as a directional bridge from drawing to building onto an ambiguous path, allowing reverse flows and overlaps across boundaries. It is in these overlaps where new relationships, unique to each project, are allowed to take shape, often in the form of physical mock-ups. These full-scale mock-ups function as a generative design tool, fusing physical materiality and intangible ideas in new ways, through an active process of building. This overlapping zone of practice and convention is not only a virtual one for critical thought, but it is a physical one as well.

As the name suggests, Studio Mumbai, is an architecture firm based in Mumbai, India, and led by architect Bijoy Jain. The studio is not structured like a typical design office composed primarily of architects; the firm is more like a village, consisting of a community of skilled carpenters and craftsmen, together with architects. This village eschews the typical roles of a design office; whereas here, architects build, carpenters draw, and together they build the buildings they have designed, fusing the act of building with the process of design in an open exchange. This fusion results in projects which seem both familiar and peculiar, resolved but not settled, finalized yet still in the process of conversation as an indeterminate dialog (Figure 2.1).

Bijoy Jain describes his interaction with mock-ups as an opportunity to engage in a new type of practice, one he describes as "work-place." In his definition, he observes that mock-ups allow a more active role for the "observation of real life conditions, into a process existing between idea and reality."[1]

> Work-Place is an environment created from an iterative process, where ideas are explored through the production of large scale mock-ups, models, material studies, sketches, and drawings. Here projects are developed through careful consideration of place and a practice that draws from traditional skills, local building techniques, materials, and an ingenuity arising from limited resources. Inspired by observation of real life conditions, these architectural studies are vital tools that enable us to look at the complexity of relationships within each project and to respond and adapt freely through the practice of making. They are ambiguous, exciting as part and whole, between idea and reality …[2]
>
> Bijoy Jain

Design at Studio Mumbai is not a formulaic process where duties and responsibilities are conventionally assigned. Instead, they are contingent on the peculiarities of each project becoming mixed up in a process of reformulation.

> While the phrase "means to an end" typically describes an action carried out for the sole purpose of achieving something else, in the work of Studio Mumbai, it is the architectural means themselves which are creatively embraced, situating design within the processes of actions … Not simply the results of those actions.

UNCONVENTIONAL PROCESS OF ARRIVAL

This new blurring of the architectural ends can be seen in the structure of the office itself. The firm consists of a working community of over 100 professional craftsmen and architects, which has reformulated the design process into a method based on materials research, full-scale mock-ups and unusual drawings, which more actively engages collaboration. Much of this collaboration occurs in a collective workplace that combines the typical architectural studio with a construction site in a laboratory setting. This combination allows for a new process to emerge at Studio Mumbai, one which fuses conceptual thinking, design and craftsmanship into a single sphere of action.[3] The results of these overlapped activities are that the architects are not merely designers but also builders, and the craftsmen themselves play a more active role in the design of the project.

> The fusion of these roles produces a setting for an expanded architectural practice in which the zone of ideas: theories, lessons and skills, become a set of actions or acts of engagement, realization and practicing the application of ideas.[4]

The work of Studio Mumbai emerges out of this application of ideas, as an iterative and empirical process, where ideas are translated into actions through the production of large scale mock-ups, material studies and peculiar drawings, which fuse the means with the ends, potentially relocating architecture from something residing in the finality of "building," to the acts of making beyond the simple outcomes of practice.

DRAWINGS

If drawings could be considered as the means and the building as an end, wherein the flat media of drawings predict the thick physicality of the building, then a reformulation of the ends and the means would suggest a transformation in characteristics of the media which embody architecture, resulting in strange new hybrid representations.

It is unclear in the work of Studio Mumbai whether this reformulation causes or is caused by a more frequent engagement with material mock-ups, but their work also produces unique shifts in the typical processes of drawing. These shifts occur through a variety of substitutions, either by removing paper and drawing directly on the site at full scale, or removing the pencil and sketching by building, or by shifting authorship of the drawing from the architect to the craftsmen.

If architects have traditionally invested their design efforts in producing drawings, then that tendency is transformed in the work of Studio Mumbai into an active process of making and building, where drawing is not abandoned but transformed into peculiar new forms.

These strange conventions can be seen particularly in the transformation of the design process in the design of two houses by Studio Mumbai: the House with White Net and Copper House II.

THE HOUSE WITH WHITE NET/HOUSE ON KANKESHWAR HILL (KANKESHWAR, MAHARASHTRA, INDIA) 2011

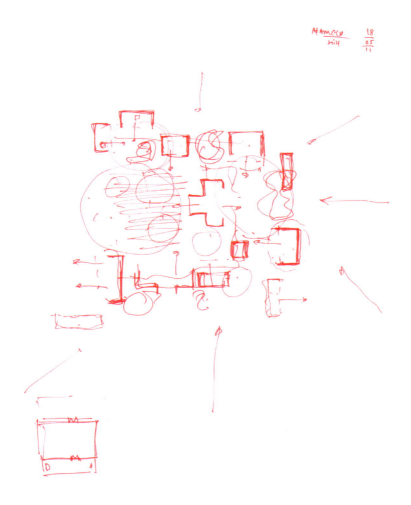

Figure 2.2 Bijoy Jain's sketch of a site plan for the House with White Net, illustrating the arrangement of living volumes positioned in relation to the existing dense foliage. Studio Mumbai, the House with White Net/House on Kankeshwar Hill (Kankeshwar, Maharashtra, India) 2011.
Courtesy of Studio Mumbai.

DRAWING ON SITE: SETTLING THE LAND

The House with White Net is a house on a hill, fitted tightly into an existing grove of mango trees. Unlike most houses the organization of rooms seems to be on the edge of unraveling, and with the landscape so tightly distributed throughout the plan of the house it appears the house is being invaded by the surrounding grove. While site planning operations might ordinarily establish a clearing in which to push back the surrounding landscape and construct a building free of conflict, for this house the existing landscape is inhabited by the plan, surgically inscribed between the trees, sometimes coming within mere inches of their trunks (Figure 2.2).

This close proximity creates a surprising entanglement between the neutrality of the plan as a representation and the unpredictable organic qualities of the field. The existing site is preserved and embraced, established as the plan itself, casting the organic arrangement of trees into architectural elements from which to develop a plan. These landscape elements are thrust into dialog with the other elements of the house such as the walls, rooms, and openings. The individual rooms are not arranged within an ideal container, rather distributed throughout the site as a scaffold in which to construct a type of settlement.

SITE IMPRESSIONS

In general, before beginning the design of a project, Bijoy Jain spends time on the site, surveying a variety of conditions: the slope, the vegetation and trees, the sun, the wind, and the views, conceiving of a three-dimensional impression of the site. This arrangement of impressions attempts to understand the site through all of its material qualities, not only what it looks like on a map. These impressions are lost by reducing the site to a two-dimensional plan, and it is only after a deeper impression of the site that a design considered.

After many visits to the site, observing site conditions in person, Jain sketches an idea for the plan, not a plan itself; rather, suggestions of a plan which brokers the qualities of the site. From this sketch, and before a plan was finally drawn, a site mock-up was constructed out of inexpensive agricultural net, materializing the initial sketch, testing it in relation to the conditions of the site.

The initial studies test how and where to place the rooms, without a diagram or conceptual sketch other than the site itself. The sketching started by placing rooms in the site as someone in a village would do, considering how to occupy the landscape, based on where rooms feel safe, where they have a view, where the water is. Based on these conditions, the architect began placing the house like planning a community, sketching lines in the sand on-site as someone in a nomadic village might do, finding a new place to construct a shelter. The plan began organically in this way, based on how the site feels and varies environmentally. Instead of the complete neutrality of drawing on a representation of the site, these plans are situated within the actual qualities of the place. From this organic sketching, a site model was constructed, yet still not conceived of as final, just a different approximation based on architectural conventions.

One of the first decisions established through this integrative approach was where to locate the center of the house. This was established by finding a clearing to occupy, and here the center of the house was defined as an open plaza around which the functions of the house would be arranged. This clearing in the site signaled a central outdoor plaza that was re-emphasized through the organization of the surrounding rooms. This plaza was absorbed from the landscape into the space of the house without yet making plans.

Once established, low stone walls were dry-stacked to retain the contours of the site, creating levels for the house emanating from this central plaza space. Offset elevations began to indicate where rooms would exist, like archaeology in reverse. These site levels prepared the site for the house, independent of the plan, but not without regard for the scheme. In this way, a plan is subconsciously there, but not fixed. The plan only emerged after the architects began manipulating the site, negotiating the contours, with the clearings and shade of the trees. These site leveling interventions began and then served as reference points from which the architects slowly started redrawing a plan and model of a house absorbed by its landscape.

FABRIC MOCK-UP: AGRICULTURAL NET

After the first small scale model, the architects realized the plans were becoming disengaged from the site, responding to approximations, not the actual entanglements of the site as intended. So the decision was made to model the house on-site, effectively building a full-scale model between the trees. This marks a departure from decision making based on the abstraction established through the small scale site model, and one which requires the actual feedback of full scale.

The design was constructed on-site out of inexpensive agricultural netting, which was ordinarily used to cover plants. The walls were constructed of rough wooden frames, simply nailed together before white netting was stretched to represent the surfaces of the walls (Figure 2.3).

The netting was cutout to locate the windows, revealing in the process the actual views which would be the result (Figure 2.4). In a sense, this mock-up was like building a placeholder for a house; not an actual house, but something which gave form to the actual encounters with the site.

Here, the architects began working with the carpenters directly on the site, modifying the size of the rooms, adjusting the heights and widths to site conditions. These fine-tunings were not possible in the model of the site, which served only as a generic approximation, not an active design tool because it lacked the feedback of the site. While the small scale site model pictorialized the site, it lacked the corollary effects of its spaces and forces, which needed to be engaged with at full scale to allow for its influence and interactions.

Figure 2.3 The Studio Mumbai, the House with White Net/House on Kankeshwar Hill (Kankeshwar, Maharashtra, India) 2011.
Courtesy of Studio Mumbai.

Figure 2.4 Openings in the walls of the mock-ups were constructed by inserting framing members above and below and then cutting out portions of the netting to reveal views of the landscape and other portions of the house. Studio Mumbai, the House with White Net/House on Kankeshwar Hill (Kankeshwar, Maharashtra, India) 2011.
Courtesy of Studio Mumbai.

Figure 2.5 The walls of the mock-up constructed within inches of the existing vegetation and framing views to the trees. Studio Mumbai, the House with White Net/House on Kankeshwar Hill (Kankeshwar, Maharashtra, India) 2011.
Courtesy of Studio Mumbai.

Figure 2.6 Separate volumes of the fabric mock-up which are connected through their mutual engagement with a single tree. Studio Mumbai, the House with White Net/House on Kankeshwar Hill (Kankeshwar, Maharashtra, India) 2011.
Courtesy of Studio Mumbai.

The architects would go to the site, inspect the quickly framed rooms, and instruct the carpenters to shift a wall 3 feet out or squeeze a room 2 feet in, and then move on to other rooms of the house. The design was modified not through drawing but by instruction to the carpenters and physical manipulations. After walking through the false construction site and giving direction, Bijoy Jain would return to the beginning and start again, in a series of editorial loops, adjusting things as he progressed (Figures 2.5. and 2.6).

This entire fabric mock-up took place over the course of a week, not the many months required for constructing a building. Bijoy Jain would visit the site continuously, alternating time spent with the stonemasons as they mocked up the paving details, the carpenters as they mocked up the pine frame and fabric walls, and the excavators as they determined on-site where to remove material and where to build up with a balance of cut and fill."

Visible in the photographs of the mock-ups, the pavers are cut from the ground and then chiseled to pave the central plaza court. From this central space, the mock-up boxes are constructed to represent the spaces of the house, scattered throughout the trees of the site.

REORGANIZATION OF SITE

All of the site pavers came from the site, nothing was imported from outside, and nothing went out. Instead, what occurred was a simple rearranging of what was already there in an elemental approach that avoided major changes to the existing conditions. This is important, since the approach for the design is to use what is there, to formalize what is already present into architecture, utilizing the site as a space within which to design.

The manipulations are subtle and sensitive to existing conditions, developed out of an understanding of how the site has always worked organically and simply formalizing these actual qualities into architecture, instead of imposing a plan. This layout respects the topography of the site, maintaining how water flows through it, and manipulating while preserving. The design is more like a subtle shift in the site, coaxing it out of the landscape itself, extracting and exaggerating a plan which already exists. Through the course of the mock-ups, the workers were instructed to gradually compress the ground, making it a floor, to formalize it into a subtle transformation of what was really just mud.

The openings cut through the fabric net revealed new views, framing views of the trees outside. This process reveals the landscape and architecture equally, creating an equivalency between natural and artificial. Eventually, the fabric would be replaced with stoic blank masonry walls, resembling the white netting itself (Figures 2.7, 2.8, and 2.9).

While the first moves were to locate the retaining walls on-site, they were initially dry-stacked lines of brick, so that if necessary they could be moved many

Figure 2.7 As the ceiling is added to the mock-up, the views revealed frame individual trees in the landscape, cropped out their context. Studio Mumbai, the House with White Net/House on Kankeshwar Hill (Kankeshwar, Maharashtra, India) 2011.
Courtesy of Studio Mumbai.

Figure 2.8 The central clearing around which the spaces of the house are arranged, paved with hand-chiseled stones excavated from the site. Studio Mumbai, the House with White Net/House on Kankeshwar Hill (Kankeshwar, Maharashtra, India) 2011.
Courtesy of Studio Mumbai.

Large Representations in the Field

Figure 2.9 A volumetric opening into the courtyard of the house, which seems to blur the distinction between the living spaces of the house and the exterior spaces of the site. Studio Mumbai, the House with White Net/House on Kankeshwar Hill (Kankeshwar, Maharashtra, India) 2011.
Courtesy of Studio Mumbai.

Figure 2.10 A long wall of the house beyond a line of mango trees through which an opening can be seen to reveal additional trees beyond, creating overlapped layers of built and natural spaces. Studio Mumbai, the House with White Net/House on Kankeshwar Hill (Kankeshwar, Maharashtra, India) 2011.
Courtesy of Studio Mumbai.

times as a result of the mock-up manipulations. Once confirmed, these bricks became the first course of a retaining wall making them concrete by permanently inscribing them in place (Figure 2.10).

Once mortared and backfilled with earth around them, they become fixed and their location is decided, not to be revised in the future. There is no coming back to the site to re-evaluate or need to survey the locations of where to build once construction starts. On top of these foundations, the walls are finally made of brick and then lined with pigmented plaster. The materiality of the final construction is reminiscent of the materiality of the mock-up itself, and even referenced internally by the name given to the project by the office, "the House with White Net" (Figures 2.11, 2.12, 2.13, 2.14 and 2.15).

Figure 2.11 A photo of the entry to the house beyond the first row of trees. The blank materiality of the house resembles the original qualities of the netted mock-up. Studio Mumbai, the House with White Net/House on Kankeshwar Hill (Kankeshwar, Maharashtra, India) 2011.
Courtesy of Studio Mumbai.

Figure 2.12 Openings lined with wooden framing, similar to the openings of the original fabric mock-up. Studio Mumbai, the House with White Net/House on Kankeshwar Hill (Kankeshwar, Maharashtra, India) 2011.
Courtesy of Studio Mumbai.

69

Figure 2.13 The volumes of the house, built around the central clearing in the locations of the original pine wood and fabric mockup, integrated into the dense vegetation of the site. Studio Mumbai, the House with White Net/House on Kankeshwar Hill (Kankeshwar, Maharashtra, India) 2011.
Courtesy of Studio Mumbai.

Figure 2.14 A volume of the house constructed where the mock-up first existed seems to solidify the netting into a more stable material. Studio Mumbai, the House with White Net/House on Kankeshwar Hill (Kankeshwar, Maharashtra, India) 2011.
Courtesy of Studio Mumbai.

Figure 2.15 The interior spaces of the constructed house resemble the spaces of the original mock-up, replacing the provisional fabric surfaces with solid masonry. Studio Mumbai, the House with White Net/House on Kankeshwar Hill (Kankeshwar, Maharashtra, India) 2011.
Courtesy of Studio Mumbai.

THE COPPER HOUSE II, CHONDI, MAHARASHTRA, INDIA, 2009

While the House with White Net challenged the capacity of the plan to represent the deeper realities of the site, a second house challenged the capacity of drawing to represent closer entanglements with construction. This house, titled the Copper House II, was similarly constructed within an orchard of mango trees. The house was similarly developed out of an exploration of the site, but it also engaged in an unusual process of drawing and constructing in which the carpenters were themselves drawing many of the details to better collaborate with the architects. As the title of the house suggests, there was an explicit use of the material copper in the construction, and because of this extensive full-scale mock-ups were constructed to test the integration of this material into the design and construction process.

The Copper House II is situated within a dense grove of trees, and while the setting appears to be scenic and pastoral, passively embedded within nature, the relationship here is more active as a result of the density of the surrounding forest and the seasonal flooding of the site. The trees on this site grow closely packed together, constricting the site and the amount of sunlight that reaches the ground. The site for the house previously housed a rice paddy which created a clearing in the dense canopy, where the architect determined to locate the house.

FULL SCALE LINEOUTS

Bijoy Jain began designing the project as he begins most projects, by visiting the site before drawing a plan. He went to the site and observed the constrictive qualities of the trees, the scarcity of sunlight in the ground, and the evidence of annual flooding. Developing a complex idea of the site as a series of these interactions, the architect walked the site with an assistant accompanying him with a bucket of chalk powder. Bijoy Jain's first sketch of the plan for the house was drawn on the site itself. As he walked through the clearing in the trees, he indicated to his assistant where to scatter chalk, outlining the footprint of the house at full scale (Figure 2.16).

These markings are not the plan, rather the primer of a plan, marking desired interactions of the house with the site. These lines were established based on the site conditions, which the architect interpreted as a site of extreme pressures. Pressure is exerted from the sides by the density of the trees, and from below the ground

Figure 2.16 Drawing the Plan at full scale on site, using chalk. Studio Mumbai, Copper House II (Chondi, Maharashtra, India) 2011.

Courtesy of Studio Mumbai.

Large Representations in the Field

due to the seasonal flooding of the site. What results is a rectangular donut-shaped house with a central courtyard, which is conceived of to absorb the pressures and anxieties of the site. A formal plan will later document this relationship in a more precise, yet less accurate, approximation.

CUT AND FILL

The architect walked the adjacent land and determined the location for a vast well to be excavated. The cut earth removed from the excavated void served as fill to build up an elevated plinth on which to construct the house (Figures 2.17 and 2.18).

This plinth elevated the house several feet above the surrounding land which routinely floods. During monsoon season, the entire site floods. The trees, the pools, and the paddy fields all flood, but not the footprint of the house, which sits just high enough above the waterline like an island (Figure 2.19).

Figure 2.17 The location of a well to be excavated, drawn at full scale. Studio Mumbai, Copper House II (Chondi, Maharashtra, India) 2011.
Courtesy of Studio Mumbai.

Figure 2.18 Studio Mumbai, Copper House II (Chondi, Maharashtra, India) 2011.
Courtesy of Studio Mumbai.

Figure 2.19 Site Section indicating the balanced cut and fill of the ground. Studio Mumbai, Copper House II (Chondi, Maharashtra, India) 2011.
Courtesy of Studio Mumbai.

After fully marking the site with chalk lines, the architects measure and survey the large scale markings using surveying techniques like triangulation to translate into formal plans and models. This idea of surveying the sketch, complete with existing interactions of site, reduces the dissonance which results from the process of scaling up. By drawing at a large scale on the site itself, the drawing takes into account the site phenomena, such as the wind, the light, and the impressions of the physical realities of site, which are difficult to represent as small scale representations. Here, there is no loss of information, as the initial sketches are already interacting with the larger scale phenomena present in the land.

Once drawn and formalized as plans and study models, the architects have established a bridge between the real conditions and a conceptual representation of the house. This bridge is precise, and yet malleable; at this point, Jain engages a team of carpenters with the study models to further develop the design. The way the architect and carpenters collaborate is itself a creative intervention into the more typical methods of drawing. While this scaling-up roots the realities of the site more intrinsically than traditionally flat media, the architect likewise innovates the translation from drawing to building by shifting the carpenters into more active roles in the design process.

CARPENTERS' SKETCHES

In the design of the Copper House II, each carpenter involved in the project maintained an exclusive sketchbook for the project. The carpenters' sketchbooks contain multiple drawings and detailed sketches of various elements of the Copper House, each dated and titled. This cataloging of sketches allows them to be followed noting how the design has evolved over time, how it was built, and ultimately recording the conversations which occurred.

Several of the sketches in the carpenters' sketchbooks are signed by Bijoy Jain, and these indicate a confirmation of approval by the architect. All carpenters do multiple sketches for the same detail and then they discuss together with the architect, ultimately approving one which is marked in the sketchbook as a way to confirm that what has been discussed and confirming what gets built.

It is not unusual for craftsmen to draw and sketch, but the drawings in these carpenters' sketchbooks are not typical. What is evident in the sketches of the carpenters is not a simple shop drawing solution, but an obsessive process of experimentation and problem-solving. These sketchbooks are very specific to Studio Mumbai's practice. In India, carpenters are typically highly skilled; however, most of the time they are given a set of drawings to follow and not involved in the process. Bijoy Jain recognized a shortcoming of that system, where the carpenters themselves knew more about the detailing and joinery of wood than the architects and the contractor, but were excluded from the conversation about their work. While the architect typically deals with one person, acting as the contractor, it is usual that the contractor does not know as much about craftsmanship (such as carpentry) and is effectively a middleman for distributing labor. This intermediary effectively divorces the architect from the craftsmen and the deeper entanglements that could result from these absent conversations.

Within this context, Jain decided to work directly with the carpenters and the craftsmen building the projects, not as a radical manifesto for design, rather simply as a result of an organic process of engaging carpenters directly. It is typical for Bijoy Jain to develop a design concept or thematic framework and then engage the carpenters discussing the ambitions of the project, after which the carpenters begin drawing themselves. These sketches become a scaffold for the architect to more closely collaborate with the craftsmen, in some cases even resulting in the carpenters sketching spatial perspectives. This act of empowering the carpenter in the design process changes the way the architects relate to the carpenter and the contractor, more deeply engaging the outcomes with the process of design, entangling the means with the ends (Figure 2.20).

PRACTICING WITH MOCK-UPS

At one point, Studio Mumbai employed 200 staff, including carpenters, plumbers, and masons in house; somewhat like a design-build operation where the architect was also the general contractor. The office has since downsized and their collaborations happen earlier in the design phase before construction begins on site. Now the conversation typically occurs earlier during the design process, and as a result the office builds many large scale mock-ups offsite in the courtyard of the Studio Mumbai office as a way of exploring and experimenting, combining design and construction into physical artifacts.

COPPER MOCK-UPS

For the Copper House II, the lead carpenter and his team were familiar with the architects, having previously worked with Bijoy Jain on several earlier projects. As the design commenced, the concept was presented to the carpenters with the architects' suggestions for construction details, but not yet confirmed or resolved. As the conversation progressed, the carpenters began slowly developing the architect's suggestions for key details through drawings of their own.

The carpenters were asked to communicate at each stage, and finer grain resolution and their communication primarily took place through the sketches they would draw. Over time, the carpenters become skilled at drawing, and rigorous about not only building, but also designing and thinking about construction conceptually.

FABRICATING PERSPECTIVES

The drawings from the carpenters' notebooks contain not only details, as you might expect from a craftsman, but also perspectives in space, sketched as you might expect

Large Representations in the Field

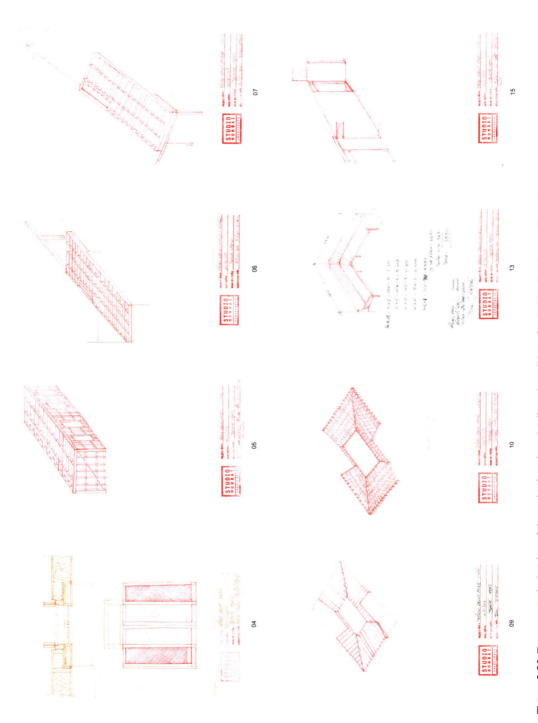

Figure 2.20 The carpenter's sketches of the project's various details and conditions. Studio Mumbai, Copper House II (Chondi, Maharashtra, India) 2011.
Courtesy of Studio Mumbai.

from the design architects' more conceptual imagination of space. The carpenters would not only sketch a key moment in detail such as a corner joint, but they would simultaneously sketch a perspective to illustrate how the space will receive those details.

But these drawings are not typical and must be learned. When a new carpenter begins, through conversations with the architect, they will be asked to sketch their ideas for how to put something together. While they may struggle initially, they slowly develop their own drawing craft over time, because it is insisted on in a way that the carpenters become like architects, representing their ideas in drawing, allowing for further considerations before building.

Examining the sketchbooks of the carpenters from the Copper House, a few sketches can be seen to demonstrate remarkable content. On one page, the entire structural framing system for a room can be seen, drawn as a three-dimensional axonometric, with calculations for the sizes of wood and quantities of nails and screws in a particular area of the house. These drawings visualize a combination of calculations and details mixing both into one large illustrated document (Figure 2.21).

While calculating quantities and precise dimensions is not unusual for a craftsman, present in another set of sketches is something far less typical. On one page two sketches can be seen stacked, allowing the carpenter to test two different designs for how his wall with interface with the floor. The floor in this case is to be constructed by a different craftsman than the carpenter constructing the wall, so the carpenter is exploring opportunities for interaction between the two trades. The two options illustrate an ability to execute what is necessary but also a creative capacity to absorb small scale influence into the larger-scale spaces as a result of these sketches.

In one option, the carpenters suggest a simple threshold and casement detail, which covers the edges of the flooring with standard rectangular trim pieces. In another, the carpenter is suggesting something more opportunistic. Here, the carpenter suggests a wall base detail in which the flooring rolls up and seems to seamlessly merge with the surface of the wall. While one of the options suggests a typical detail for masking the transition between floor and wall, with a baseboard, the other is conceptually distinct, not simply solving the detail within a familiar set of constraints, but designing a new solution and imagining the problem as a design opportunity, something typical in the realm of architects (Figure 2.22).

Another important detail is pictured in a set of sketches where four different materials are meeting at the same corner. The sketches show within the wall section the location of the window and an overhanging eve constructed of wood. The wood can be seen studied as two options for transitioning as the wall folds at the top and transitions from a vertical wall to a horizontal roof.

In one sketch, a layer of plywood can be seen wrapping up and over, with a small joint at the top; while the other illustrates plywood above and below, with a solid structural member located flush, serving as a transition piece. Ultimately, each of these would be wrapped on the outside with a folded copper sheet, which serves as a type of rain jacket to protect the interior wood framing. One of the details is circled and the exterior copper sheathing can be seen drawn in blue ink; this is the approved option agreed upon by the architect and carpenter (Figures 2.23a and 2.23b).

Large Representations in the Field

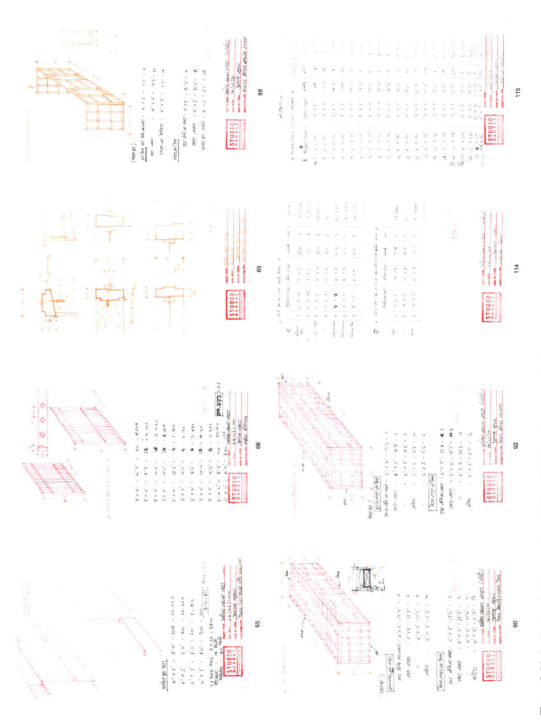

Figure 2.21 Studio Mumbai, Copper House II (Chondi, Maharashtra, India) 2011.
Courtesy of Studio Mumbai.

Large Representations in the Field

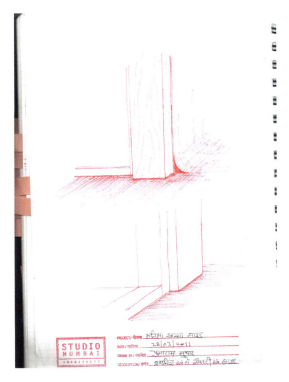

Figure 2.22 Carpenter's sketch of the floor to wall connection. Studio Mumbai, Copper House II (Chondi, Maharashtra, India) 2011.
Courtesy of Studio Mumbai.

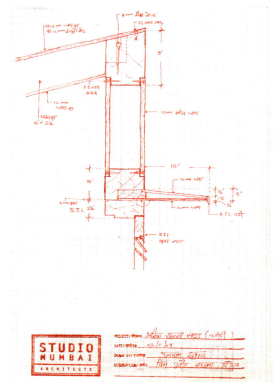
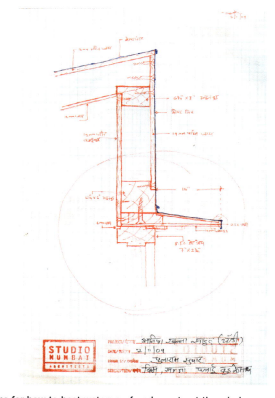

Figures 2.23a and 2.23b Carpenter's sketch testing options for how to best waterproof and construct the window header and visor. Studio Mumbai, Copper House II (Chondi, Maharashtra, India) 2011.
Courtesy of Studio Mumbai.

DRAWING IN COPPER: FULL SCALE MOCK-UPS

The Copper House is diagrammatically a wood building wrapped in copper. The copper is not simply decorative, but acts as a rain jacket for the house, which is otherwise constructed exclusively of wood and plywood, as are many of Studio Mumbai's buildings. Wood is a well-known material for Studio Mumbai, one which is predictable, and extensively engaged by the carpenters and architects alike. Copper, on the other hand, is understood but not in the familiar terms of hands-on collaboration and improvisation.

While the carpenters are able to understand the craftsmanship of wood construction and its impact on the outcome of design concepts, the interface between wood and copper was understood with less certainty. In order to address this lack of familiarity, many full-scale material mock-ups were constructed, which not only tested the relationship between design and construction, but also the interface between wood and copper.

COPPER TRAINING MOCK-UPS

Studio Mumbai had previously constructed a house which utilized copper, but in the earlier project, copper was limited in scope, and constructed by an outside consultant. This limited application of copper as a roofing membrane required only a limited catalog of details for the architects to generate and these details did not impact the rest of the building.

The Copper House, however, was a much more comprehensive application of copper which folded down the vertical wall surfaces from the roof, and around corners, encasing the wood framing details behind its thin surfaces. Because of the scale of this application, the carpenters had to engage copper consultants, who trained the carpenters to do this work themselves.

Studio Mumbai hired consultants from their previous project to train the carpenters over the course of a few months to oversee the construction of many mock-ups that tested these areas of uncertainty. While the carpenters were fully capable of rolling out copper sheets and generally possessed high levels of craft, that craft couldn't simply be applied to this. The detailing of the copper involves folding the seams and interacting with a variety of joints specific to sheet forms of metal materials Figures 2.24 and 2.25.

The architects and carpenters first identified the areas of uncertainty and constructed full-scale mock-ups which allowed these obscure moments to become defined physically. These mock-ups allowed the design team to not only learn how to represent this new material in drawing but also immediately witness the connection between these drawn details and their physical construction.

Part of this training involved purchasing the equipment necessary for the carpenters to learn to do this work themselves. The Studio Mumbai workshop acquired the cutting and folding equipment necessary to perform this work, ultimately setting up their workshop on-site to construct and finish the house themselves.

Because the copper was the rain jacket for the house, fundamentally tasked with keeping the wooden construction dry, the corners are where the most care needed to be taken, as these are the points where water was most likely to seep in. The mock-ups illustrate a variety of conditions, from flush walls with window openings, where the copper must be broken to allow the window, to simple seems between lapped layers of sheeting.

Other areas that were mocked-up included where a variety of conditions overlapped and needed to be coordinated, including window openings, overhangs, and the transition between wall and roof, where the material must either fold or be joined at the transition points of the wooden framing behind. In a sense, this was like tailoring a piece of clothing, achieving a tailored fit to a specific form within.

Figure 2.24 A mock-up fragment with a small piece of aluminum folded over the plywood joints. Studio Mumbai, Copper House II (Chondi, Maharashtra, India) 2011.
Courtesy of Studio Mumbai.

Figure 2.25 Many mock-ups can be seen in the courtyard, some with thin aluminum metal sheets folded over the exterior in place of copper. A scale model sits in the foreground. Studio Mumbai, Copper House II (Chondi, Maharashtra, India) 2011.
Courtesy of Studio Mumbai.

Studio Mumbai actually monitored the rate of copper over the course of many months, waiting for the right time to purchase the material for the house when it was at its cheapest. In the interim, the carpenters utilized aluminum sheets for many of the mock-ups, as it proved a more affordable substitute, which can be seen in photos of the mock-ups.

Initially, the mock-ups progress as design decisions are made, beginning generically with a framework, and with each subsequent layer, resulting in a finer level of detail and understanding. As the finer-scale details suggest conflicts, the mock-up is reassembled to merge the layers into a better alignment. The initial framework is constructed and erected in a concrete base that duplicates the conditions on-site. Next, the framework receives the first layer of wooden framing, and once resolved another layer; the sheet metal is applied to the exterior.

Each time a detail changed or became unique, the carpenters would construct a new mock-up to verify what difficulties may follow. Once all of these moments were verified, the final designs were confirmed and the same carpenters who constructed the mock-ups in the courtyard of Studio Mumbai traveled to the site to construct the house. In the courtyard, each framing member for the house, was precut, numbered, and laid out in the workshop, before being taken to the site for assembly (Figure 2.26).

In a unique mock-up which demonstrates the complexity of the design, an outstretched window header meets the vertical wall which folds over to form the roof. This mock-up demonstrates the construction of the wood framing before being wrapped in an aluminum cladding. Because it is difficult to design the process of folding and working with the material, this complex condition is mocked up, allowing the design to be verified through physical experimentation (Figure 2.27).

Within the many mock-ups constructed, an assortment of custom framing profiles are constructed to demonstrate the subtle differences in their shape, and also to consider how they will receive the metal cladding. These samples demonstrate the range of conditions, beginning with a wood screen mock-up, followed by framing mock-ups: one tapering toward the outside, with the other notched on both sides for window placement, followed with other framing profiles (Figure 2.28).

Figure 2.26 Mock-up of a complex framing condition which must be clad with copper to avoid water penetration. Studio Mumbai, Copper House II (Chondi, Maharashtra, India) 2011.
Courtesy of Studio Mumbai.

Figure 2.27 An assortment of custom framing profiles are constructed to demonstrate the subtle differences of shape. Studio Mumbai, Copper House II (Chondi, Maharashtra, India) 2011.
Courtesy of Studio Mumbai.

Figure 2.28 A mock-up of a hip joint which requires complex metal folding. Studio Mumbai, Copper House II (Chondi, Maharashtra, India) 2011.
Courtesy of Studio Mumbai.

ROOFING

In two of the many mock-ups, the metal skin is applied at difficult transition points in the roof where moisture will have a tendency to penetrate. In one, the overhanging window visor is constructed, which wraps horizontally around a corner meeting at a diagonal transition point (Figure 2.28). The aluminum wraps up from the thickness of the edge and folds over to receive the next layer of aluminum from above. This metal which wraps the edge of the overhang must also negotiate the hip joint between the adjacent diagonal slopes, and is folded with a more complex overlap to prevent moisture from permeating at that point. A second mock-up constructs the roof valley demonstrating standing seams where the individual sheets of aluminum are joined to prevent water infiltration. The mock-up illustrates how the seams will merge at the diagonal valley where both roof slopes meet (Figure 2.29).

CORNERS

Two mock-ups explore how the copper skin will accommodate the corner conditions of the wood framing behind. One mock-up shows the detailing of a corner condition, where a continuous strip profile runs vertically, sealing the joint between two plywood sheets. The long ends of this vertical strip are folded out to interlock with the adjacent sheets of material folded in, forming a water-proof seam that wraps around the corner (Figure 2.30).

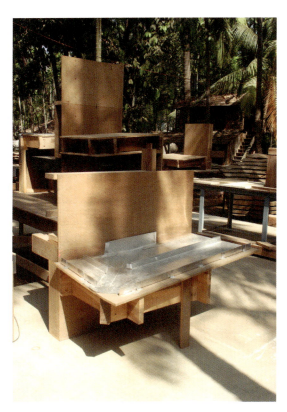

Figure 2.29 A mock-up of a diagonal roof valley with standing seems. Studio Mumbai, Copper House II (Chondi, Maharashtra, India) 2011.
Courtesy of Studio Mumbai.

Figure 2.30 A mock-up which locates the seam between separate pieces of the metal at the corner. Studio Mumbai, Copper House II (Chondi, Maharashtra, India) 2011.
Courtesy of Studio Mumbai.

Large Representations in the Field

A second mock-up demonstrates another corner condition where the copper sheet maintains the same dimensions as the adjacent vertical sheets but folds around the vertical corner overlapping the joint between the wooden framing with a continuous copper surface to better shield it from moisture. In this mock-up, the aluminum skin is also seen to wrap around the roof transition point. This detail shifts the seams from the corner, which is ordinarily where water would penetrate. The repetitive seams between strips can be seen to be folded flat against the vertical surface (Figure 2.31).

These extensive mock-ups illustrate an intention in the work of Studio Mumbai, which opens up the process of design to specific forms of material and craft. That process is opened up as a result of these physical tests, paradoxically loosening the process by making it physical, and allowing the opportunity to build sketches, rooting their intentions in the capacities of unique materials. The processes of drawing and building here become combined, which provides the opportunity to build better, with care, not by speeding up, but by opening an otherwise closed process. Through this physical practice new potentials are realized as a result of redesigning the process itself and ultimately bridging representation and reality.

Figure 2.31 A mock-up that wraps the corner with a continuous piece of metal. Studio Mumbai, Copper House II (Chondi, Maharashtra, India) 2011.

Courtesy of Studio Mumbai.

Mock-Ups and Other Conventional Mutations

Figure 2.32 A large scale detail drawing constructed of tape on plywood. Studio Mumbai, Saat Rasta (Mumbai, Maharashtra, India) 2010.

Courtesy of Studio Mumbai.

CONVENTIONAL MUTATIONS

In the two houses I've discussed there are subtle but significant shifts in practice and convention in an active process of design.

In the House with White Net, the site plays a more interactive role in the generation of the design scheme, and the architect is required to invent, not new forms, but new conventions of representation to allow these new interactions to occur.

These large scale site drawings incorporate actual site impressions that generate the plan without reducing the complexities of the site to a flat drawing or an empty environment.

In the Copper House, the introduction of copper as a new material causes the architects and carpenters to elaborately mock-up the built conditions to address the uncertainties presented by this new material. These physical fragments solidify and ultimately transfer new forms of knowledge, as the uncertain implications of a new material are able to be better understood in-between drawing and building.

Both projects orbit strange conventions of representation, uniquely fusing creativity with pragmatism. The designs ambiguously define an edge condition, where they both emerge out of these strange situations but also create a unique environment that enables conventional procedures to mutate.

TAPE DRAWINGS

It is within this ambiguous zone that another set of unique conventions emerge out of an otherwise seemingly typical project. Saat Rasta is a project which required the renovation of an abandoned warehouse building in Mumbai previously damaged in a fire.

Out of a combination of factors, the building was designed and drawn by the carpenters on site with tape on very large panels of plywood.

The building needed to be quickly fortified to prevent demolition by the local authorities, and in a matter of days new columns and enclosure were constructed. Because this occurred so quickly, there was not adequate time to prepare drawings, and as such new columns were placed intuitively where they made the most sense on the perimeter.

The existing roof was replaced, inverting a single outward sloping roof into a series of inward sloping ones which brought the water into interior courtyards around which the spaces of the old warehouse were subdivided and arranged. While the existing walls and footprint of the building were required to be retained out of heavy masonry, the interior partitions of each space were thin, constructed of a 4-inch thick wood frame. This thinness suggests a temporary structure with an inherent fragility.

As the interior courtyards were framed out to create individual courtyard spaces, Jain began working with carpenters directly on-site during the rainy months of the monsoon season.

On-site, Jain would make a sketch, give parameters, and then the carpenters would respond by making their own detailed drawings. They invented a new way of doing this because it was extremely damp and wet during monsoon season, and as a result paper drawings would become soggy like a sponge, swelling and tearing. The carpenters began cutting masking tape at large scale and applying the tape to plywood panels where they would draw. These tape drawings allowed them to retain the drawings without them tearing because of the excess moisture. Instead of this becoming a marginal moment for the project, Jain engaged this new medium itself, temporarily abandoning the architects' drawing sets in favor of these large scale drawings on-site (Figures 2.32, 2.33, and 2.34).

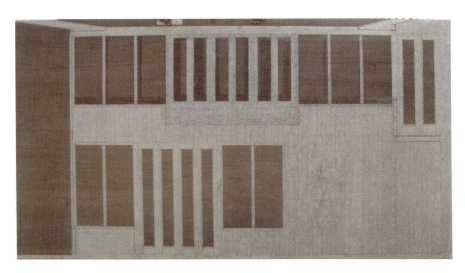

Figure 2.33 A large scale drawing of an interior elevation constructed of tape on plywood. Studio Mumbai, Saat Rasta (Mumbai, Maharashtra, India) 2010.
Courtesy of Studio Mumbai.

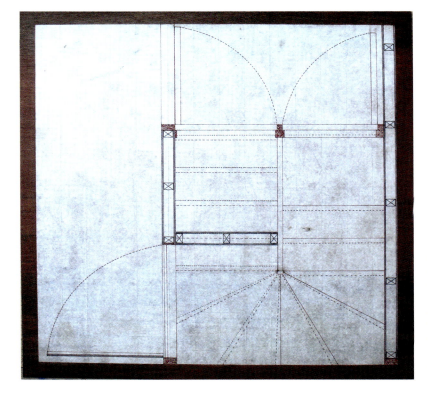

Figure 2.34 A large scale plan of a stair and door, drawn on tape applied to plywood. Studio Mumbai, Saat Rasta (Mumbai, Maharashtra, India) 2010.
Courtesy of Studio Mumbai.

Jain would discuss the designs of elements in these drawings with the carpenters, and as development occurred the tape drawings would be cut and repasted to reflect changes. Development occurred in these drawings and because the subject walls and building elements were actually constructed of the same plywood as these drawings, translation occurred somewhat seamlessly. These tape drawings were drawn at large scale to closely approximate their final positions in space, and because they were rigid and planar it was easy to make quick models from them, translating between the drawing and the models. What became a simple suggestion on-site as a way to negotiate the rain, became a new instrument for developing design and an opportunity for collaboration (Figure 2.35).

In fact, in the final photos of the completed spaces for the Saat Rasta, the walls can even be seen to be painted a similar color to the tape drawings which so closely approximated their design (Figure 2.36).

Figure 2.35 Bijoy Jain reviewing large elevation drawings taped to plywood panels. Studio Mumbai, Saat Rasta (Mumbai, Maharashtra, India) 2010.

Courtesy of Studio Mumbai.

Figure 2.36 Interior elevations under construction, which once painted resemble the tones and materiality of the tape used to represent them. Studio Mumbai, Saat Rasta (Mumbai, Maharashtra, India) 2010.

Courtesy of Studio Mumbai.

What we see in the design work of Studio Mumbai is not a preoccupation with mock-ups, but a recognition of the unique circumstances that this practice enables. It is within these unique circumstances that standard conventions are modified and evolved, enabling mutations in order to represent new capacities. These mutations create a unique approach to design, which once again re-engages the means of design, and creates new conventions for mock-ups.

Notes

1   Bijoy Jain, Spirit of Nature Wood Architecture Award 2012, Rakennustietoi, p 16.
2   Bijoy Jain, Spirit of Nature Wood Architecture Award 2012, Rakennustietoi, p 16.
3   Workplace/Studio Mumbai Archizoom, p 12.
4   Bijoy Jain, Spirit of Nature Wood Architecture Award 2012, Rakennustietoi, p 12.

3 The Impossibly Real: In Pursuit of New Translations

The Physical Motivations of Round Room and La Voûte de LeFevre

Matter Design/Brandon Clifford and Wes McGee

Figure 3.1 A dry fit, zero tolerance, compression-only, vault-structure, assembled from digitally fabricated plywood voussoirs without glue. Matter Design, La Voûte de LeFevre (Columbus OH, USA) 2012.

Courtesy of Matter Design.

LOST AND FOUND IN TRANSLATION

In 2012, Brandon Clifford and Wes McGee, together as Matter Design, completed the construction of a large scale structural vault, for which no representational drawings were prepared. The design was conceived of utilizing advanced computational tools, constructing a virtual model of the project in its three-dimensional entirety, while also anticipating its structural performance. Based on this highly sophisticated digital model, the architects already knew that this structure could stand, that it could indeed be built, and what it would look like; yet they built it anyway (Figure 3.1).

Between languages, there exist words which are not possible to translate with complete accuracy. There is something in the message which is lost in the translation of words between different languages. It is this phase transition from one form of language to another which redefines the received message. While these distortions are generally referred to as "lost in translation," the same distortions exist in the translation from the virtual to the actual, or from the drawing to the building.

Throughout the work of Matter Design, the tensions of translation are embraced by revealing these moments of distortion which exist between virtual and physical forms of representation. It is within this dissonance that mock-ups allow for the unique architecture of Matter Design.

The built works of Matter Design are not quite buildings; they are more like mock-ups in pursuit of becoming buildings. If mock-ups are intrinsically rooted in the physicality of the real, over the virtual forms of representation, then much of contemporary digital technology seems to question the necessity for actual constructions. Indeed, computation has allowed greater virtual reach, connecting the physical behaviors of materials with virtual forms, coupled with highly accurate techniques for physical fabrication. Given this power of new digital tools, some might question the relevance of physical mock-ups at all. While digital models allow greater formal capacities and control, there is a necessary and disruptive phase change in the translation from the virtual to the physical, which is not formal and not controllable. It is this process of translation, from one form of representation to another, which is unpredictable and must be negotiated. It is this realization that frames the work of Matter Design.

Their approach is deeply immersed in the virtual world. However, their work is not immune to reality because it is not an abstraction of it. Intriguingly, what seems accidental at first is revealed as a deliberate intention to avoid the use of digital technologies to idealize the material world, instead expanding one to foster deeper engagements with the other.

NEW TRANSLATIONS IN PURSUIT OF ARCHITECTURE

Advances in computation have enabled designs to take on more complex and precise forms. Counterintuitively, it is because of this hyper-precision that new obstacles are encountered and revealed even though it seems that these obstacles should not exist.

In fact, they are often revealed to exist as a result of translating the high precision of the virtual representations into the low-tolerance-reality of construction. The work of Clifford and McGee not only negotiates the obstacles of translation, but also seems to suggest that the distortions between the two forms of representation should be revealed and embraced, not avoided.

This subtle shift within their work represents a significant departure in their approach, where forms are utilized not in service of themselves but rather to provoke new interactions through translation. The significance of this shift is important since these interactions elude the typically shallow and flat forms of representation. What is required is a thicker convention that allows these unpredictable interactions and obstacles of translation to be revealed. Perhaps, computation allows Clifford and McGee a deeper form of drawing, but categorically these thicker conventions of representation seem to describe mock-ups.

There is a necessary process of translation where drawings must be translated into built forms. Predictably, there will be some distortions or loss of information. Some have argued that new digital technologies have enabled a more seamless interface between drawing and building through the process of digital fabrication. This argument suggests that there is nothing lost in translation, which is a myth pursued by the work of Clifford and McGee.

In his recent writings, Bernard Cache considers the obstacles of translation in digital terms. Seeming to allude to precisely the challenge of translating from the virtual to the actual, he states, "whereby the possible cannot become real without something of the virtual becoming actual … That is why … the reality cannot be anticipated in the possibility."[1]

Instead of drawing and building, Cache defines these categories as the differences between virtual and actual, possible and real, and the frequency and the membrane, arguing that it is not possible to translate from one form to another without producing change. He states, "the virtual cannot become real unless it undergoes a change in the nature of the membrane in which it is incarnated or the frequencies that animate it."[2]

Cache argues these changes are not only unavoidable, but also unpredictable. It is in this acknowledgment that he also seems to imagine a third state between the virtual and actual. This third state serves as a mock-up, where negotiations are not obstacles to be avoided but rather reconsidered and embraced for their productive tensions, as each redefines the other.

> How will the phase difference of an electron ripple relate to the texture of a predetermined membrane? Solutions to these problems cannot be anticipated, for in each case the actualization differs in nature from all others, and in no case can the selection be optimized.[3]

These observations suggest a significant conceptual reconsideration of perceived outcomes. If phase changes are accepted to be necessary and unpredictable, Cache seems to realize an untapped potential for new translations. As a philosopher, he considers a new approach as a shift from philosophy to what he calls "the pursuit of philosophy by other means."[4] "The 'pursuit of philosophy' refers to philosophy engaged as a mode of production – and not as a contemplative activity, and even less as an instrument of communication."[5]

Perhaps, this new approach in philosophical terms suggests a re-definition of architecture through mock-ups; moving beyond an architecture of buildings to buildings in pursuit of architecture. This architecture is motivated by the tensions between drawing and building. It does not rely on the physical to verify the physical, but rather uses the virtual to extend the physical to recalibrate the virtual. This new approach seems to be an adequate description of the work of Clifford and McGee.

BY OTHER MEANS

This shift in priority from the ends to the means is coupled with a shift in the mode of production itself. Cache recognizes and acknowledges in his argument the distortions revealed by pursuing familiar aims through unfamiliar means. By shifting the modes of production, the necessary step of translation is introduced. It is this vital step of translation in which Cache notes the potential to change the outcome in novel ways. "Our aims can easily be distorted by the means we use to achieve them."[6]

These vital shifts illuminate the utility of physical mock-ups even in the midst of advances in computation. It is the distortions, encountered in the translation from the virtual to the physical, that are always present and must be negotiated. While drawings and buildings are each individually predictable, it is the relationship between these different representations which is unknown, and must be built to be understood.

> On the other hand, what we will never be able to predict is the relation between a frequency and a membrane. Selecting a still image requires us to assign a value to the parameters of our periodic functions in order to manufacture singularities in a series of objects in a specified material.[7]

In architecture, the assignment of any material to the construction of a representation will always produce subtle distortions. Through a shift in our focus, it is these distortions that illuminate new relationships between drawing and building. This reconsideration serves as a useful framework for understanding mock-ups not as buildings but as a unique form of representation in the pursuit of buildings. It is with this reconsideration in mind that the architecture of Matter Design is most relevant and illustrative of mock-ups power to transform. Their work is not only novel in the sophisticated development of forms, but also reimagines new possibilities for building.

BEYOND EFFICIENCY: THICKER FUNICULAR

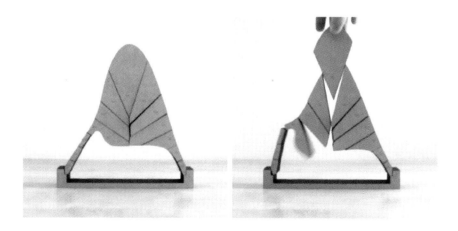

Figure 3.2
A prototype of a two-dimensional arch, dry-stacked and stable without glue. Matter Design, Thicker Funicular (Cambridge, MA, USA) 2010.
Courtesy of Matter Design.

The complex relationships between the real and the virtual found throughout the work of Matter Design were first approached in a series of experimental structural models. Existing on a small-scale these experiments were constructed of typical model making materials such as chipboard.

These models were actually more like small mock-ups, stacked into shape without glue. These forms were testing the interaction between structure and form while expanding the formal possibilities without losing structural performance. A central belief of the International Association of Shell Structures states that "Thinner is better." But in order to be thin, the form needs to be structurally ideal, and therefore less receptive to the many design demands other than gravity (Figure 3.2).[8]

Titled "Thicker Funicular," these stacked forms were first generated digitally in the computer by substituting thickness in place of the underlying thin structural diagrams. By utilizing interactive definitions within the coded environment of the computer the forms could be manipulated with a visualization of the overall structural performance. Because these forms were rooted in structural performance, physical models were constructed to demonstrate the virtual forms as physical structures.

These new hybrid forms maintain the same type of compression as thin shell structures, but allow for a new playful variety of forms to be explored by defining the zone between formal representations and structural performance.

This exploration demonstrates greater flexibility for design, enabling the architect to respond to the many other concerns which exist outside of structural stability. Concerns such as acoustical, formal, and programmatic, while still maintaining the structural identity of compression within each experiment. In this case, the formal thickening allows each structure to become more malleable to formal desires. These new formal manipulations transform the efficiency of structural flows, yet retain structural behavior as a reference, utilizing one to define the other by different means.

SKETCHING WITH PHYSICS: REPRESENTATIONS WITHOUT DRAWING

Three small scale prototypes were constructed to illustrate the structural behavior of these thickened forms. The shape of the material through which this force flows is manipulated, stretching the form away from thin efficiency, allowing a new formal definition without losing the same underlying structural basis. The process is a balancing act, manipulating the form while remaining constrained to the structural behavior of the initial definition.

Utilizing the powers of the computer, Clifford reverses the process by defining a base geometry which is inherently not structural, and by allowing the computer to thicken the vertical distance above to allow for the necessary thrust vectors to flow. The resulting form is one that is based on the original profile yet subtly transformed above and below based on structural stability (Figures 3.4 and 3.5). There is a key difference between a representation model and these prototypical models. While both may be constructed of similar materials, in a representational model, the form is privileged over the material. While these small prototypes are constructed of model making materials, the behavior of the material verifies the form by demonstrating structural stability. The performance of the structural principle is demonstrated by removing a key unit and recording the failure of the system (Figure 3.3).[9]

Because the calculations in the computer were conceived of without a particular scale or material, and without a specific material in mind, they can be constructed from a variety of materials at a small-scale, so long as the material does not deflect under the compression loads.[10] Even though the physical behavior

Figure 3.3 A prototype of an asymmetrically loaded arch, utilizing an isolated load for stability, which once removed causes the entire structure to become unstable and collapse. Matter Design, Thicker Funicular (Cambridge, MA, USA) 2010.
Courtesy of Matter Design.

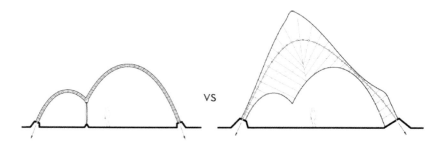

Figure 3.4 A comparative drawing of the difference between a thin shell vault, and the same bottom geometry constructed with a thicker structurally stable stack of voussoirs. Matter Design, Thicker Funicular (Cambridge, MA, USA) 2010.
Courtesy of Matter Design.

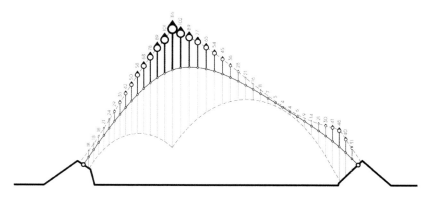

Figure 3.5 An overlaid diagram demonstrating the increase in vertical thrust based on the varying thickness of the material. Matter Design, Thicker Funicular (Cambridge, MA, USA) 2010.
Courtesy of Matter Design.

of the materials would be more influential on the structure at larger scales, they are still appropriately utilized with provisional materials such as paper, chipboard, and basswood.

Each of the forms in this series not only transforms the section from thin to thick, but also transforms the material thickness from uniform to variable. The third model/mock-up demonstrates how this variable thickness contributes to the compressive flows of force by factoring in an isolated external load. Removing this isolated load alters the location of thrust vectors causing the structure to collapse (Figure 3.6).[11]

These small prototypes establish an early interest in representation through building the interactions of forces and forms. There exists a reciprocity where forms are translated into structural flows, and flows are filtered through the medium of matter. While formally similar, it is clear how the physical behavior of each is different, something not normally evident in representation models. These early prototypes are not models at all, they are mock-ups, and they have the capacity to represent the interactions of more than one subject.

THICKER FORMS OF DRAWING

There is a difference between the ways architects and engineers draw, perhaps one is in pursuit of a formal idea, while the other diagrams the internal forces of form. While Clifford and McGee seem to combine the information of both types of drawings, their work is unique in that it could be argued that they do not produce drawings at all.

In older forms of representation, such as hand drafting with a "mayline," the architect or draftsperson was required to choose the scale of their representation. Typically, those scales were formal and representational, not material. Instead of drawing on paper, by designing in the virtual environment of the computer, many scales are considered simultaneously, and as a result the architect or designer can be involved in structural principles as well as formal and organizational strategies. Computation seems to allow the opportunity for deeper engagements with materials, allowing greater collaboration and opportunity for feedback.

For Clifford and McGee, the utility of the drawing seems to share similarities with traits utilized in stereotomy. In his essay "Drawn Stone," Evans discusses the cutting of solid stones through the guidance of these complex drawings.

> Traits were layout drawings used to enable the precise cutting of component masonry blocks for complex architectural forms, especially vaults. Thereby accurate fabrication of parts could be achieved prior to construction. Traits are not illustrations and yield little to the casual observer. They are orthographic projections, but they are not like other architectural drawings.[12]

In key ways, the virtual models of Clifford and McGee are similar in that they are not illustrative. To them, they are highly precise calculations which enable the precise fabrication of form, but not illustrations which might be legible to the casual observer.

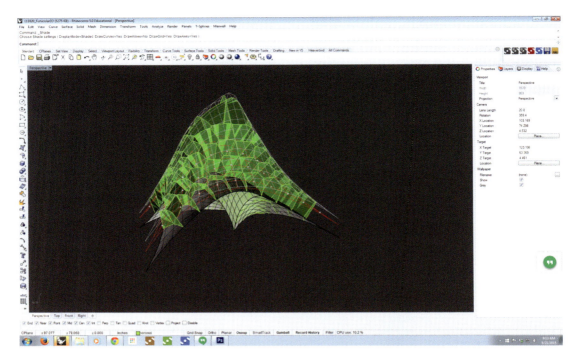

Figure 3.6
By defining an arbitrary shape (gray), not constrained by the efficiency of the structure, the computer generates an additional layer (green) on top of the original to add mass for stability. Matter Design, Thicker Funicular (Cambridge, MA, USA) 2010.
Courtesy of Matter Design.

DESIGN PROCESS

The process of designing forms in the computer is unique from the process of flat conventional drawing. The computer gives feedback in a type of animated drawing process. Unlike the construction of conventional drawings, the environment of the computer allows spontaneous feedback in the form-finding process.

Within the computer, multiple calculations can be seen in sync with one another not only in the form of its geometry but also in the structural behavior of this form. In the digital environment, the design of form is the result of interactions, as the designers interact with the software to explore how much thickness to add to an arbitrary non-structural shape to achieve a structural compression-only system (Figure 3.6).

UNRAVELING FORM FROM EFFICIENCY

It is apparent in these exercises how computation allows for a more interactive negotiation between the demands of structural efficiency and the desires for shapes. In a way, this interaction allows the designer to conceive of designs on the fringe of a structural ideal; never lose sight of the most efficient solution while designing a more elastic version of the same resistance to gravity.

In a way, Clifford and McGee utilize computation to avoid ideality by visualizing the most efficient form and then distorting it, relying on complex thickening to reveal new design opportunities.

Figure 3.7
A freeform thick vault dry-stacked without adhesive, held together by compression forces. Matter Design, Thicker Funicular (Cambridge, MA, USA) 2010.

Courtesy of Matter Design.

Unraveling the relationship of efficiency from structure is not the same as avoiding the reality of structure, in which certain forms are conceived of digitally without concern for structure. On the contrary, these "thicker funicular" forms are derived directly in relation to ideal structural solutions, conscious of their relation to efficient forms, but intentionally transformed into something else (Figure 3.7).

These curious case studies lead to a series of larger inquiries which develop as a result of making these experiments at larger scales and with the particularities of specific sites. Over the course of two large-scale projects, in which these small scale explorations are enlarged to the scale of inhabitation, it is interesting to see how new tensions develop. As these projects are scaled up from small scale prototypes to large scale structures, new realizations about the interactions of structure and form become apparent. These studies present unique insight and feedback to the architects which make the process of physically exploring forms all the more revealing.

LA VOÛTE DE LEFEVRE, COLUMBUS, OH, 2012

In 2012, Brandon Clifford and Wes McGee, completed construction on a large scale inhabitable installation. Like their earlier explorations, the design of this vaulted structure also utilized variable depth and variable volume to add structural stability to an otherwise non-structural form.[13]

For this unique vault, the form was devised specifically to the dimensions and shape of the gallery space where it would be installed. The pre-existing shape of the gallery offered a space to engage with through design, beyond pure structural efficiency, integrating the demands of structure with the existing spatial conditions of the site. By utilizing advanced computational solvers in the process of design, design itself seems to be redefined, as the form is "computed" or "solved" by form finding a compression-only structure from within a structurally non-ideal geometry.[14]

DESIGN DRAWINGS: FROM THIN TO THICK

With the intention of designing a form that produces space and structure, the designers first defined a thin surface by adding thickness and volume where necessary (Figure 3.8).

Often, in the architectural design process, the design sequence begins with a sketch or an unconstrained idea. That sketch may exist as a series of lines or brushstrokes on paper or even as a sketch model.

In this familiar sequence, drawing is instrumental in advancing and developing a design. However, Clifford and McGee do not make drawings, at least not in this typical sequence of development. Beginning in the three-dimensional virtual environment of the computer, the architects define surfaces. They are not drawings of what will be built, but more like definitions of a path along which structure and form will flow. Instead of drawings, they rely on flat screenshots to quickly pass images back and forth. Three screenshots from the process illustrate Clifford and McGee's initial thoughts for transforming a thin surface into thick parts that could be fabricated from known materials.

Figure 3.8 A three-dimensional drawing of the vault-structure and the geometric lines of each individual unit, drawn after construction, as required for publication. Matter Design, La Voûte de LeFevre (Columbus, OH, USA) 2012.
Courtesy of Matter Design.

Beginning with the space of the gallery, a surface is first drawn in space. Then, the singular form is broken into a series of smaller modules. Lastly, an image map of the material is assigned to the modules (Figures 3.9 and 3.10). These sketches within the computer are simply intended to quickly communicate possible outcomes (Figure 3.11). Clifford and McGee do not ordinarily produce renderings. They only produce drawings when publications or competitions require them. But even then, they are a portrait of what will be built, not an instrumental part in the process.

Figure 3.9 Screenshot of initial spatial surfaces, which are input and then computed or solved, through interactions with the computer. Matter Design, La Voûte de LeFevre (Columbus, OH, USA) 2012.
Courtesy of Matter Design.

Figure 3.10 A screenshot illustrating how the vault's form is being broken from a singular massing into a series of smaller but thicker structural modules called voussoirs. Matter Design, La Voûte de LeFevre (Columbus, OH, USA) 2012.
Courtesy of Matter Design.

Figure 3.11 A Screenshot of a sketch rendering where wood is image-mapped onto the model, suggesting a possible material outcome. Matter Design, La Voûte de LeFevre (Columbus, OH, USA) 2012.
Courtesy of Matter Design.

CONSTRUCTION DOCUMENTS: TRANSLATING VIRTUAL TO ACTUAL

The form was conceived of as three columns that merge together into an overhead canopy with one upturned column which reaches up, casting doubt on the stability of the three load-bearing elements below.

Moving from design into fabrication, no real construction documents were produced. Instead, the digital model was processed more like the way film is developed. The virtual model is prepared and ultimately translated into a series of toolpaths for the complex cutting of the individual shapes, translating the virtual into the physical through a digital fabrication process (Figure 3.12).

What would ordinarily be considered as construction documents are just a set of screenshots to document the various pieces of the project. These screenshots are just previews of the steps taken within the computer environment to prepare the parts for the tools which will be used to fabricate them (in this case on a 5-axis Computer Numerically Controlled (CNC) milling machine) (Figure 3.13). Once these images are translated into fabricated objects, it is the physical artifact itself that depicts the material representation of structure and form.

The first mock-up for this project is the process of fabricating the individual units of the vault called *voussoirs*. Voussoirs refer generically to wedge-shaped elements, typically stone, in the construction of an arch or a vault. The process of building involved the fabrication of individual units through the carving of each part from solid blocks of wood. Initially, each voussoir was analyzed in the computer and digitally sliced into layers of three-quarter inch thickness. These individual slices were flat cut from plywood sheets and glued, then stacked into a rough volume from which

The Impossibly Real

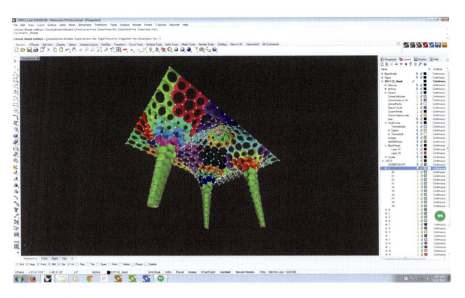

Figure 3.12 A screenshot of the digital model shows the figure, and the various layers of information that go into modeling the structure and form. This has a huge file size as a result of it not merely being an image; rather, it contains embedded information beyond the figure, including the physical reactions of mass and structure. Matter Design, La Voûte de LeFevre (Columbus, OH, USA) 2012.
Courtesy of Matter Design.

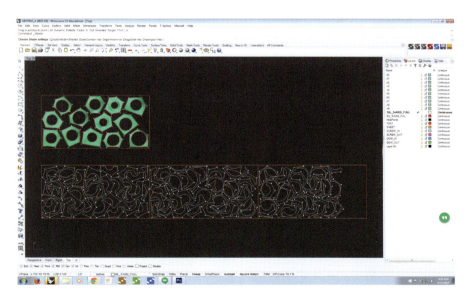

Figure 3.13 Screenshots of the computer model laying out individual units prior to fabricating the structure. Matter Design, La Voûte de LeFevre (Columbus, OH, USA) 2012.
Courtesy of Matter Design.

the final part would be carved. These rough shapes were then arranged on a sheet and prepared for a series of digital carvings, which would remove excess material and leave each as a unique and geometrically precise unit (Figure 3.14).

The Impossibly Real

Figure 3.14 First mock-up illustrating the pieces sitting next to one another flat, with gaps visible between. These gaps close tight once each individual unit is rotated into place and dowels are inserted, locking individual units together. Matter Design, La Voûte de LeFevre (Columbus, OH, USA) 2012.
Courtesy of Matter Design.

The edges of each unit were fabricated to precisely match with the edges of each adjacent unit, allowing assembly by simply aligning individual voussoirs in space. By constructing in this way, no dimensions or measurements were necessary since the pieces snapped together. The first physical mock-up was to verify that the system worked, as each voussoir dry fit with zero gaps, and locked together with dowels inserted through predrilled holes.

The many steps involved from constructing the blanks to carving the multiple passes introduce opportunities for the physical artifact to develop errors. Secondary concerns of this mock-up were to increase the speed of the process to carve these individual parts; instead of carving them from solid blocks, the roughs were precut and stacked to reduce the amount of material which needed to be removed. This step conserved time and reduced wasted material in the fabrication and assembly of the final vault. Once it was clear that the fabricated parts fitted together as anticipated, the process was verified and the remaining voussoirs were fabricated without needing to test each individually.

ASSEMBLING WITH ZERO TOLERANCE

The vaulted structure touches down at three points, and there is a difference in the physical reactions occurring at the contact points. Voussoirs refer generically to wedge-shaped elements in the construction of an arch or vault, typically stone. While each part of a structural stack vault or arch is a voussoir, two units are distinct in the reactions that flow through them|: the keystone and the springer. The keystone is the center unit at the apex of the arch, typically the highest voussoir, while the springer is the lowermost voussoir marking the transition point where the arch springs from the vertical support. While the vault is constructed of the many individual voussoirs, the column is a single unit. Because the physical reactions between the vaulted voussoirs are progressively horizontal, the verticality of the column can resist the vertical load.[15] As a result, the column is carved as a solid piece of wood, with the texture of the upper voussoirs carved into its surface, blurring the apparent transition point (Figure 3.15).

Construction of the vault began by assembling the fabricated parts, beginning with a perimeter rail which was suspended in space at the precise dimensions of the outer perimeter of the vault. The process of fitting the units together to form the vault began at this outer perimeter and progressed inward, toward the center, intended

Figure 3.15 A photo of the monolithic column at the base, with the textural pattern of individual units. Matter Design, La Voûte de LeFevre (Columbus, OH, USA) 2012.
Courtesy of Matter Design.

to make contact with the top of each prepositioned column. Each voussoir must align exactly with its adjacent neighbor, coordinated with pins inserted into precisely pre-drilled holes. This connection detail allowed the assembly team to verify that each unit was in the correct location as the assembly proceeded (Figures 3.16 and 3.17).

Because the actual tolerance of the existing floor is something the computer could never account for, Clifford and McGee were aware they needed to have a strategy for isolating this tolerance.

As they assembled the structure, the voussoir did not fit between the upper vault and the lower column as it showed it would in the digital model. In fact, the difference between the piece and the space was off by several inches.

As the assembly progressed inward from the perimeter rail, the three columns were placed on the ground in their precise location as the vault neared the transition point from vault to column or keystone to springer (Figure 3.17).

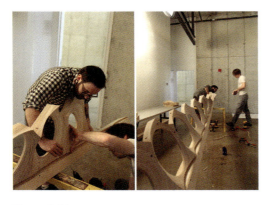

Figure 3.16 Assembly of the vault beginning by mounting the first few voussoirs before lifting the completed perimeter above the gallery floor. Matter Design, La Voûte de LeFevre (Columbus, OH, USA) 2012.
Courtesy of Matter Design.

Figure 3.17 Assembly progressing inward toward three supportive columns. Matter Design, La Voûte de LeFevre (Columbus, OH, USA) 2012.
Courtesy of Matter Design.

The Impossibly Real

Figure 3.18 The moment where the upper canopy makes contact with the lower column support, but the voussoir which connects the top and bottom does not fit as anticipated in the digital model. Matter Design, La Voûte de LeFevre (Columbus, OH, USA) 2012.

Courtesy of Matter Design.

If the thick edges were as precise as they knew them to be, there should not be a discrepancy because the material was not flexible. This discrepancy highlighted a collision of factors not apparent in a mathematically ideal digital model. Using lasers to scan the floor of the gallery, the differences between high and low points in the surface of the floor were surveyed. However, it was measured to be off by less than an inch, while this voussoir misaligned by nearly 6 inches (Figures 3.18 and 3.19).

Clifford and McGee anticipated this conflict between the virtual and actual, and decided to accommodate it by fixing the perimeter condition and letting the columns fly long. This approach would allow them to simply trim the base of the column to accommodate the differences; however, the architects did not expect the discrepancies to be as significant as they were. If they were to cut off the amount required from the bottom, the top would conflict where it was intended to meet.

ACTUAL AND VIRTUAL COLLISIONS

Without fully understanding exactly what was causing the conflict, the decision was made to cut 3 inches from the bottom of the column and 3 inches from the top to get the center and perimeter to meet (Figure 3.20).

Figure 3.19 The voussoir unit which is too big for the space where it is intended to fit with zero tolerance. Matter Design, La Voûte de LeFevre (Columbus, OH, USA) 2012.

Courtesy of Matter Design.

Figure 3.20 The digitally precise joint is manually chiseled to remove material allowing the unit to fit. Matter Design, La Voûte de LeFevre (Columbus, OH, USA) 2012.

Courtesy of Matter Design.

This conflict between the virtual and the actual environment was not something they would have discovered without building the structure physically. While the architects considered the issue of flexibility in the selection of the materials, other factors exist which could produce this misalignment. These factors include temperature and moisture content which can cause the wood to swell, and also the material impossibility of a zero-tolerance edge. These edges could be considered much like shorelines are represented on maps, which are drawn as lines with a fixed position in space, but ultimately are affected by the flux of tides and the ability to infinitely subdivide the ideal line into fractal formations.

Building is precisely about the negotiation between parts, accommodating differences and allowing for conflicts, but because this vault was intended to be dismantled at the end, there was no mortar or glue used between the individual voussoirs. The dry-fitting of these units instead relied on the exact alignment of adjacent faces with a zero-tolerance approach.[16] The accuracy of the computer model was both desired and necessary for aligning the individual parts; however, without mortar between the parts, there was no ability to resolve the conflicts at the joints. As a result, the zero-tolerance approach of the vault-structure conflicted with the site conditions which were not nearly as precise (Figure 3.21).

Ironically, because the fabrication system for the vault was so precise, it created conflicts based on the imprecise realities of the site. This design became an impossibly real representation of something less ideal and subject to the ebbs and flows of materials and tolerance. While not foreseen or desired, the conflicts revealed between the virtual and the actual in this project expanded the focus of the work. In the next project, we see a design which continues to construct the interactions between structure and form, but also to specifically allow within their design the conflicts and distortions that are found in translation (Figure 3.22).

Figure 3.21 After manually carving the column, the top and bottom finally connect and assembly can continue in sequence. Matter Design, La Voûte de LeFevre (Columbus, OH, USA) 2012.
Courtesy of Matter Design.

Figure 3.22 Completion of the plywood vault, which was achieved by manually removing material from the column to allow differences of tolerance between the virtual model and the actual environment. Matter Design, La Voûte de LeFevre (Columbus, OH, USA) 2012.
Courtesy of Matter Design.

ROUND ROOM: REVEALING ZERO TOLERANCE

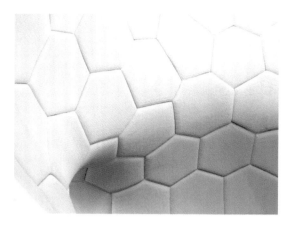

Figure 3.23 The smooth interior side of Round Room with tight-fitting joints. Matter Design, Round Room (Cambridge, MA, USA) 2014.
Courtesy of Matter Design.

REVEALING REALITY

A common practice in construction detailing is to incorporate something called a "reveal." A reveal exists at the joint between two pieces of material, building a gap between edges, which disguises inconsistencies by absorbing misalignments of the edges into a gap of space. This space accomplishes two goals: to hold the edges apart and to absorb physical collisions of inconsistency. The first goal allows for the visual comparison of the inconsistencies in the edges which are more noticeable when joined flush. The second goal of the reveal is to allow the buildup of inconsistency to occur without being visibly noticeable and prevent small collisions from compounding into distortions at a larger scale. If parts are brought together with zero tolerance, then any inconsistencies which build up will shift the overall definition of the whole. In construction, inconsistency is not desired or intended, rather it is accepted as a difference between the precision of what is drawn and the actual conditions of the physical construction.

In a project titled Round Room, Clifford and McGee attempt to renegotiate zero tolerance with the observed inconsistencies encountered in the construction of the plywood during the La Voûte de LeFevre project. This design addresses how to negotiate the virtual precision of the computer with the realities of actual material conditions. Building on the observations of the last project, this design seeks to construct exactly the negotiation of two realities: the zero tolerance of the computer and the unknown tolerances of physical materials and sites (Figure 3.23).

Like the plywood vault-structure, Round Room is also a variable-volume compression-only structure, but it is distinct in two key ways: it is constructed of a different material, a special form of concrete, and it is conscious of the errors that can build up and cause large collisions when constructing without reveals. Having encountered the difficulties of zero tolerance, Clifford and McGee look to the seemingly impossible tight edges of Incan wedge stone construction. How could a centuries-old practice accomplish what they could not, using primitive tools, prior to mechanization (Figure 3.24)?

The answer resides in a clever detail located on the backside of the stone wall and also in an older process of construction. The Incan process involved the complete customization and manual craft of carving each stone to fit precisely into place, a process known as dry-fitting and templating. As each stone is formed to fit as needed, any inconsistency is absorbed live as the piece is being fabricated by hand. In the Incan walls, the design and fabrication of each stone occur simultaneously. Whereas in Clifford and McGee's plywood vault, the parts were entirely prefabricated and then not able to accommodate errors or accumulations of inconsistencies in the field. Clifford and McGee modified their approach to mirror their observations of the Incan's wedge-stone system by designing a wedge-shaped joint on the backside of the voussoirs. This wedge was to be packed with wet mortar allowing for some minor adjustments before solidifying (Figure 3.25).

Figure 3.24 Incan wall construction with seemingly impossible tight joints. Matter Design, Round Room (Cambridge, MA, USA) 2014.
Courtesy of Matter Design.

ROUND ROOM

The design for Round Room consisted of a relatively small inhabitable space, accessible through a low opening. Visitors slid into the space while laying on their backs, gazing up into the space of this complex form. The room, which was constructed in a gallery, was enclosed within a box, which not only hid the messy joinery between

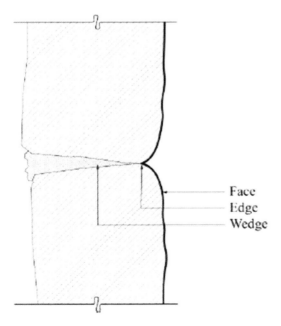

Figure 3.25 A drawn section of an Incan wedge-stone wall joint revealing the wedge on the backside which enables the appearance of zero tolerance on the front, but allows for misalignments on the back. Matter Design, Round Room (Cambridge, MA, USA) 2014.
Courtesy of Matter Design.

parts, but also contrasted with the soft interior of the space. The figure of Round Room is complex, and while the Incans primarily constructed vertical walls by dry-fitting and templating along the way, this space is freeform and prefabricated, intended to be constructed without the aid of templating.[17] The goal was for any errors to aggregate within the tolerance built into the outside of the wedge-shaped joints.

An initial prototype of this structure was fabricated and assembled with three units, each digitally carved from autoclaved aerated concrete and then fit together by packing plaster into the cavity on the back of each joint. This allowed for slight adjustments along the edge during assembly. While this first mock-up fit precisely, light was observed to be visible between the gaps as the material tapered to a zero-thickness edge (Figure 3.26). These sharp edges made positioning the individual blocks difficult, with no surface depth to bear upon it exaggerated the misalignments which became more visible. As a result of this observation, the design of each joint was adjusted by rounding over the edges and adding a small nub to the sidewalls to assist in correctly positioning the blocks in space (Figure 3.27).

A second mock-up was constructed from ten modules, each revised to have rounded edges and side spacers to act as a check, or jig, to better position the blocks in space to build up the overall geometry. In this mock-up, the precision of the interior can be seen in contrast to the sloppiness of the mortar packed into the back joint (Figures 3.28 and 3.29). This mock-up was approved as a final proof of concept seeming to solve the problem of the previous project, by allowing some degree of workability in the assembly of the units while giving the appearance of zero tolerance on the inside surface.

To construct Round Room, Clifford and McGee partnered with Quarra Stone to fabricate the individual units, which were CNC milled from the autoclaved aerated concrete (AAC). Ordinarily, this is something Matter Design would do themselves as they commonly assume the design and fabrication role for each project, as in the previous La Voûte de LeFevre project. However, for the Round Room project,

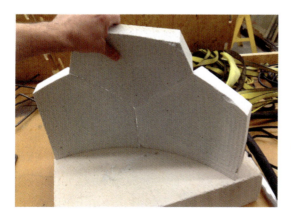

Figure 3.26 The first mock-up constructed by Matter Design, consisting of three machined pieces of autoclaved aerated concrete. Light was visible through the zero-thickness edges. Matter Design, Round Room (Cambridge, MA, USA) 2014.

Courtesy of Matter Design.

Figure 3.27 Individual units with rounded edges and side edge nubs visible. Matter Design, Round Room (Cambridge, MA, USA) 2014.

Courtesy of Matter Design.

Figure 3.28 A second mock-up with rounded edges which align precisely while the backside of the units allow a degree of workability and appear sloppy in comparison. Matter Design, Round Room (Cambridge, MA, USA) 2014.
Courtesy of Matter Design.

Figure 3.29 The backside of the mock-up with plaster packed into the joints. Matter Design, Round Room (Cambridge, MA, USA) 2014.
Courtesy of Matter Design.

instead of fabricating the parts themselves, they only shared the computer files to be used for fabrication. Communication is typically smooth and accurate when it comes to sharing digital files, as there is nothing lost in translation; rather, a set of instructions is extracted directly from the digital model and fed to the machine virtually assuring an accurate fabrication.

Individual blocks were machined from slabs of autoclaved aerated concrete using a tool mounted to a 5-axis CNC robotic arm. AAC is a lightweight cement mixture that is full of pockets of air, and therefore less dense than typical concrete and far more lightweight. As individual units were machined, they were labeled and shipped for assembly in the Keller Gallery in Boston.

Initially, a plywood base was set up as a template for aligning the first course of blocks. This template prepared an accurate base upon which to stack. Instead of plaster, masonry adhesive was used to fill the wedge cavity during construction. As stacking of the individual units progressed, midway through the second course, everything appeared precise, coming together as expected (Figure 3.30). Each unit was labeled prior to assembly and placed based on the corresponding number in the digital model.

At a certain point, the edges began to subtly pull away from each other, not by much, but the expanding gaps defined the extreme end of what is acceptable. See unit C3 (Figure 3.31).

Figure 3.30 The first two courses stacked in place. Matter Design, Round Room (Cambridge, MA, USA) 2014.
Courtesy of Matter Design.

The Impossibly Real

The assembly team could not understand why the gaps were increasing and, as they progressed, the gaps built up, sometimes pulling away from each other, while colliding at others. They began the process of manually shaving the individual units to get them to fit, without fully understanding what was causing the errors.

This is in fact how the Incans assembled their wedge-stone walls; however, Clifford and McGee realized that every time you shave one, you throw off another unit. The misalignments began to propagate as the results of shaving telegraphed problems to the other subsequent courses (Figure 3.32).

Eventually, it was determined to create a void by removing one of the voussoirs, which would create a space to absorb all of the structures compounded conflicts. Later, this void was templated and carved out by hand. A paper template was traced in the void and then the original stone was cut away to match. The difference between the resulting space and the original stone is significant when viewed together (Figure 3.33).

Figure 3.31 The edges of Unit C3 appearing to pull away from the others, with gaps increasing in size. Matter Design, Round Room (Cambridge, MA, USA) 2014.
Courtesy of Matter Design.

Figure 3.32 As the individual units are slightly shaved down to fit, the differences are telegraphed to adjacent edges throwing off the alignments of the other wedge stones. Matter Design, Round Room (Cambridge, MA, USA) 2014.
Courtesy of Matter Design.

Figure 3.33 A template of the void in the structure overlaid with the piece which must fit into it before being manually cut to fit. Matter Design, Round Room (Cambridge, MA, USA) 2014.
Courtesy of Matter Design.

As the voussoirs were progressively stacked, manual modification of each one was required and at a certain point, while the whole system did go together, it failed to verify the intention of the project. That intention was to prove that the Incan wedge-stone system could be adapted to negotiate between a zero-tolerance digital model and the unpredictable interactions of site and material conditions. As the stacking of the blocks neared the top, the accuracy was so off that it was no longer interesting or relevant to the motivations of the project, so the team decided the remainder would be withheld and the top was cut off. If the beginning of this process was like digital assembly, by the end it was like building a sandcastle, lacking precise positions, and becoming loosely piled as each part became generic or in conflict with its neighbor.

One of the more important motivations for mock-ups is to test why things fail, but in this actual mockup a simple unforeseen error threw off the whole experiment, masking the lessons to be learned. It was later discovered in the process of assembling Round Room that a single module had been mislabeled and as a result misplaced in the sequence, throwing off all subsequent pieces. This is a shortcoming of the zero-tolerance assembly sequence; there is no chance for the process to absorb and adapt, the way the Incans dry fit and templated each piece.

Because the Incans shaved each stone as they stacked, they created a process where each unit would not disrupt future pieces by shifting them out of alignment. This enabled the masons to fine-tune each piece by templating the space for each block as they proceeded. That process allowed for the evolution of each piece, with the ability to be fabricated precisely based on a placement that is unknown until it is built. This is a subtle but significant difference from the approach for Round Room, which was ultimately only realized, once again, as a result of building the structure physically (Figure 3.34).

To Clifford and McGee, the distortions are potentially catastrophic as the freeform geometries of stacked structures rely on accurate adjacencies.

Realizing this lack of adaptability, Clifford and McGee are pursuing a new approach they have not yet achieved. This new approach is pursuing the goal of how they could simultaneously template and fabricate in an automated process.

In Round Room, they were employing two processes: carving and assembling. They are currently developing a workflow using three servos which can monitor progress and map spaces as construction progresses, and then fabricate to fit.

This new system is intended to negotiate the overlaps of the zero-tolerance digital model and the conditions of the materials and site simultaneously, utilizing scanners to digitize and verify the position of each piece, working back and forth between the virtual and the real. While designs could be predetermined, by re-measuring at each moment collisions could be absorbed back into the virtual environment.

Incorporating feedback along the way allows design and construction to be negotiated better. Verifying one by means of the other simultaneously. This proposed process fits exactly with the intentions of the mock-up, perhaps more frequently than before. This demonstrates how, even with new technology, the realities of the actual material world could be better embraced and incorporated into the virtual (Figure 3.35).

Figure 3.34 A photo of Round Room, showing the smooth interior and the loose joints of the exterior. Matter Design, Round Room (Cambridge, MA, USA) 2014.
Courtesy of Matter Design.

Figure 3.35 The exterior of Round Room with workability clearly visible in the loose joints which contrasts with the interior smooth surfaces. Matter Design, Round Room (Cambridge, MA, USA) 2014.
Courtesy of Matter Design.

BUILDING TRANSLATIONS

The differences between the terms "prototype," "mock-up," "performative mock-up," and "visual mock-up" are not as important as the distinct motivations for each. What they each have in common is that they need to be physical to be fully understood. The work of Matter Design uniquely illustrates a paradoxical motivation for physically building what is virtually known.

Their projects uniquely address many of the central goals of full-scale mock-ups moving beyond the two-dimensional virtual drawing and seeking deeper interactions of structure and form within actual materials.

This process of revealing the tensions between the virtual and the actual, or the digital and the physical, acknowledge the new territories opened up through advancements in technology. Their work seems to negotiate these differences through a more active agency of structure. Thrust vectors, particle spring systems, and compression-only structures become the subjects in their work. Re-imagined through new fabrications based on the old traditions of stereotomy and Incan wedge-stone construction.

As Clifford and McGee state, "The purpose of this research is not to revert to this antiquated architecture, but rather to re-inform contemporary practice with the knowledge of the past."[18]

Perhaps this work seems most clearly connected to the new definitions of Bernard Cache, as Brett Steele observes in the preface to his collection of essays: "the very thing that many mistakenly assume to be the basis for a contemporary revolution in architecture – the arrival of digital and computational design technologies – instead offers us confirmation of architecture's return to its ancient origins."[19]

The projects of Matter Design operate on the fringe of practice, existing as large scale physical constructions, which are intentionally not buildings. While tempting to describe their work as buildings because they are physically constructed, it is more appropriate to consider these constructions as translations in pursuit of building, a potential definition for mock-ups themselves.

While their work is formally recognizable, it is distinct in key ways. While the recent generational surge in digital production seems to have given new vitality to spatial installations as a new subject of architectural experimentation, I would argue that a majority of contemporary digital fabrications and spatial installations are formal exercises. Digital technologies may have opened new realms of formal imaginations; however, their construction is by any means necessary in service of the formal representation, even when fabricated physically. Even though their work certainly engages the formal territories of architecture, it is the collisions produced within their work between the formal and the physical, and the real and the representational, which enable the pursuits of buildings by other means.

By investing in the relationships between forces and forms, through computation and construction, Clifford and McGee are drawn beyond the flat laminar tendencies of bureaucratic construction.

This work admirably utilizes the observations of the physical material realm, to reconsider the digital, moving back and forth in the pursuit of new forms of old architecture. Counterintuitively, their sophisticated explorations through advanced computational means, allow a reconsideration of the basic details of construction and form, which seem prehistoric. It is notable that advances in technological prowess do not render these ancient considerations obsolete, but reposition them as newly vital and thrilling, albeit by other means. Their work provides new answers to the questions of why physical mock-ups remain vital even in an age of increasing digital existence.

Notes

1. Bernard Cache, *Projectiles* (London: AA Publications, 2011), 27.
2. Bernard Cache, *Projectiles* (London: AA Publications, 2011), 29.
3. Bernard Cache, *Projectiles* (London: AA Publications, 2011), 28.
4. Bernard Cache, *Projectiles* (London: AA Publications, 2011), 20.
5. Bernard Cache, *Projectiles* (London: AA Publications, 2011), 20.
6. Bernard Cache, *Projectiles* (London: AA Publications, 2011), 20.
7. Bernard Cache, *Projectiles* (London: AA Publications, 2011), 28.
8. Brandon Clifford (principal, Matter Design), in discussion with the author, October 28, 2015.

9   Brandon Clifford, *Thicker Funicular: Particle-Spring Systems for Variable-Depth Form-Responding Compression-Only Structures* (Conference: International Conference on Structures and Architecture, At Guimarães, Portugal, Volume: 2, 2013), 5.
10 Brandon Clifford, *Thicker Funicular: Particle-Spring Systems for Variable-Depth Form-Responding Compression-Only Structures* (Conference: International Conference on Structures and Architecture, At Guimarães, Portugal, Volume: 2, 2013), 5.
11 Brandon Clifford, *Thicker Funicular: Particle-Spring Systems for Variable-Depth Form-Responding Compression-Only Structures* (Conference: International Conference on Structures and Architecture, At Guimarães, Portugal, Volume: 2, 2013), 7.
12 Robin Evans, *The Projective Cast* (Cambridge: The MIT Press, 2000), 179.
13 Brandon Clifford, *Thicker Funicular: Particle-Spring Systems for Variable-Depth Form-Responding Compression-Only Structures* (Conference: International Conference on Structures and Architecture, At Guimarães, Portugal, Volume: 2, 2013), 1.
14 Brandon Clifford and Wes Mcgee, "La Voute de Lefevre: A Variable-Volume Compression-Only Vault," In *Fabricate: Negotiating Design & Making*, eds. Fabio Gramazio, Matthias Kohler, Silke Langenberg (Zurich: ETH Zurich, 2014), 148.
15 Brandon Clifford and Wes Mcgee, "La Voute de Lefevre: A Variable-Volume Compression-Only Vault," In *Fabricate: Negotiating Design & Making*, eds. Fabio Gramazio, Matthias Kohler, Silke Langenberg (Zurich: ETH Zurich, 2014), 150.
16 Brandon Clifford and Wes Mcgee, "La Voute de Lefevre: A Variable-Volume Compression-Only Vault," In *Fabricate: Negotiating Design & Making*, eds. Fabio Gramazio, Matthias Kohler, Silke Langenberg (Zurich: ETH Zurich, 2014), 151.
17 Brandon Clifford and Wes Mcgee, *Digital Inca: An Assembly Method for Free-Form Geometries* (Conference: Design Modelling Symposium 2015, At Copenhagen, Denmark, 2015) 10.
18 Brandon Clifford and Wes McGee, "Round Room," *Matter Design Website*, www.matterdesignstudio.com/#/roundroom/.
19 Brett Steele, "Preface," in *Projectiles*, by Bernard Cache (London: AA Publications, 2011), front cover.

4 Unpredictable Petrifications: The Unnatural Forms and Transformations of a Concrete Museum

The Pérez Art Museum Miami, Miami, FL, USA
Herzog & de Meuron, Basel, Switzerland

Figure 4.1 An exquisitely crafted, full-scale mock-up on-site at the Pérez Art Museum in Miami days before its demolition. This built mock-up was never open to the public. Herzog & de Meuron, the Pérez Art Museum Miami (Miami, FL, USA) 2013.
Courtesy of Herzog & de Meuron.

NATURAL TRANSFORMATIONS OF MIAMI

The Pérez Art Museum Miami (PAMM) was designed as the new home for the former Miami Art Museum and completed in 2013. The building was conceived of as a series of floating volumes beneath an overhead trellis, each of which hover above the ground, precariously close to the edge of the sea and the rising tides of Miami's Biscayne Bay (Figure 4.1).

The building draws upon several examples found locally. First, a series of primitive wood buildings built a mile offshore in the 1930s, each of which sit above the ocean on wood and concrete pilings known collectively as "Stiltsville." In addition, it is difficult to miss the reference to Paul Rudolph's Umbrella House built in 1953 in Sarasota, Florida, defined by a house where the roof reaches out to overhang the pool, bathing it in patterns of shade.

While these references are apparent in Herzog & de Meuron's design, more interesting than the building type is the use of ordinary materials to extraordinary effect. The Pérez Art Museum Miami presents something altogether unique to Miami, not only in its re-imagination of local building types, but in its profound reinvention of local materials and qualities.

In Miami, buildings were historically constructed of wood. Dade County Pine is a local and native tree that was harvested to near extinction for the lumber it produced. The wood of this tree was extremely high in resin, and once kiln-dried rivaled concrete in its durability and hardness, becoming impervious to termites and decay, which affected less dense species of wood. While once abundant and used widely in the construction of residential homes in South Florida, the tree is no longer plentiful or commercially available. Additionally, the modern forms of local building codes have since practically mandated concrete for the construction of hurricane-proof buildings in the region.

Wood suggests a local connection to the land, as tree species are specific to particular regions, to the local climate, geological conditions, and environmental factors. Wood is widely regarded as a "natural" building material, in that it is not manmade, but organic and naturally occurring. Concrete, on the other hand, is generic and unnatural because it is manmade, inorganic, and not particular to any region.

In the book *Concrete and Culture*, Adrian Forty observes that despite the fact that concrete does exist in naturally occurring geological formations, such as limestone, Mexican Tepetate, or Italian Tufo, it is primarily regarded as unnatural and artificial. Culturally, concrete is not natural. However, Forty argues that it is this unnatural status of concrete, which is its virtue, by allowing concrete when reinforced with steel to accomplish something that natural materials cannot.[1] He states,

> Concrete is not natural – but that is not to say that it is "unnatural." Its being not natural is both its virtue and its failing. Its virtue in that, as a synthetic material, and especially when reinforced with steel, it can achieve things that would be impossible with any naturally occurring material.[2]

While the PAMM is conceived of as something particular, drawing on local precedent, it also seems intended from a very early stage to possess the qualities of something naturally occurring. These intended qualities were designed to transform the generic concrete of the building's construction, into something seemingly more native and local, like the wood of a tree.

In the tropical environment of Miami, the design team's challenge was to build with concrete, but to evoke the qualities of wood in the constructed forms, by

Figure 4.2 A view of the construction site in 2012 with a late occurring set of mock-ups in the background. Herzog & de Meuron, the Pérez Art Museum Miami (Miami, FL, USA) 2013.

Photo by the author.

embedding this inorganic construction material with the qualities of something natural, almost like a reverse petrification. It is the transformed qualities which are the result of the design team's profound investigation into the natural potentials of concrete. While concrete is well-known and an ancient building material, it still remains rich with mystery and uncertainty.

Concrete is utilitarian, not special; more commonly used in foundations and infrastructure projects like bridges. But to build a culturally significant institutional building with transformational qualities, the application of concrete was to be transformed from something quotidian and utilitarian into something more intimate and rarified. This ambition to transform its qualities began to reveal concrete's many mysteries, as the design team grappled with the particularities of the material and attempted to finely gauge its interactions with the local craftsmanship and the effects of a tropical environment.

In the same title by Adrian Forty, the argument is made that concrete since its inception exists as both modern and non-modern. The fact that it was developed out of speculative research and technologies, and to be marketed, qualifies it as predictable and modern; however, the fact that it is a product of "messy hit-or-miss experiments of tradesman and contractors on the building site" qualifies it as "wholly non-modern."[3] That messy uncertainty fully engaged the architects.

Because concrete is a composite, requiring the skill of multiple material trades, its production is inherently collaborative, and as a result by definition embodies a process of dialog. In the essay, "Concrete: Dead or Alive?," Sanford Kwinter highlights the fact that concrete is a material which embodies transformation, like living tissue, it is "dependent on the mysteries of electrical bonds, organic chemistry, and nested gradients of order and disorder."[4]

Through the use of many full-scale mock-ups, the design team repeatedly found themselves grappling with the material behavior of concrete, and with the tension between what it naturally does and what they wanted it to do (Figure 4.2).

In some ways, these mysteries and uncertainties became an opportunity for the design team to produce a localized vision of concrete, no longer generic to place. Their transformational approach not only created a dialog between wood and concrete, but also a dialog between a young city coming of age: itself becoming solidified with the addition of this new building.

For the PAMM, in the transition from design to construction, the usual sequences are transformed through the use of mock-ups, as the design team continually explored new ways to build. There seems to be a conscious effort to embrace the consequences of this site's unique qualities. While, of course, they go into this project demanding certain standards and qualities generally, they remain flexible enough to see how things actually turned out on site. At all phases, this flexibility is acknowledged through such pervasive use of mock-ups over the course of the project.

Perhaps no other architect could better execute a building constructed out of concrete than Herzog & de Meuron, and yet the concrete behaved in unexpected ways. The form system itself was composed of large panels of Finnish Birch with a resin phenolic surface film, which had such a high quality of formwork that when released it gave the concrete a nearly polished surface appearance. Despite this high-quality formwork, it was the interaction of the weather and the concrete itself which caused unexpected results. None of the unexpected occurrences were catastrophic, and indeed many of these issues might not even be considered problematic to architects less concerned with the particularities of the materials itself. But for Herzog & de Meuron, the degree of investment in this material was more than mere command over matter. Their process is best described by their discoveries along the way, and by their eagerness to embrace these discoveries in an active exchange.

Viewed from a distance, the PAMM appears to have been constructed as any other concrete building, albeit with an unusual massing, but upon closer inspection the details reveal a depth of design investigation unique to this building. The design team's inventive approach not only allows new forms and expressions of concrete, but paradoxically creates new mysteries of material: mysteries which need to be solved through construction in the field, not through the flat media of drawing.

Perhaps it is more instructive to understand this building by examining the uniquely extensive set of mock-ups utilized in its design and construction than the actual building itself. There exist at least three sets of mock-ups that occurred at different moments in the design process: very early during the concept design, later as the design was transitioning into construction, and then very late as the construction process was nearing its end. This is unusual in practice. We might expect mock-ups to occur at a certain point to inform decisions, but here mock-ups pose new questions that cause additional considerations, which then also need to be mocked up (Figure 4.3).

In fact, I would argue that the building itself is simply the most recent version of the many mock-ups constructed along the way. These mock-ups demonstrate

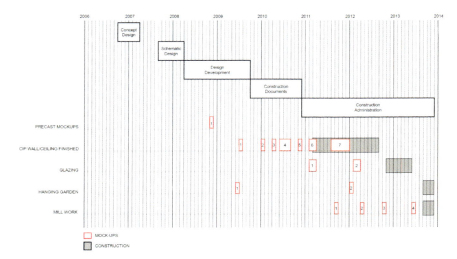

Figure 4.3 When viewed in relation to the project schedule, mock-ups can be seen in red, occurring throughout the entire project, instead of in a discreet phase before construction begins, illustrating their importance. Herzog & de Meuron, the Pérez Art Museum Miami (Miami, FL, USA) 2013.
Diagram redrawn by the author.

that the ambition to embody this building not as something concrete and fixed but as something fluid and dynamic is a negotiated moment in a constant state of transformation.

DETAILS, MOCKED UP

The design for the PAMM was developed in collaboration with Handel Architects LLP, an architect licensed in the state of Florida acting as the "Architect of Record." Herzog & de Meuron are not licensed to practice in the state of Florida, and throughout this text will sometimes be referred to collectively along with Handel Architects as the design team.[5]

PRECAST FROM AFAR

Out of a vast sequence of mock-ups to occur in service of the design of the PAMM, the first was an enormous mock-up of a conceptual building element, constructed in Basel, Switzerland. Within this early mock-up, the initial attempts to transform concrete by infusing it with the organic textures and qualities of wood are visible. This mock-up occurred particularly early, during the Conceptual Design Phase of the project, when initial design ideas included constructing the building's volumes out of precast concrete elements shipped to Miami (Figure 4.4).

In what could potentially be termed a "concept-mock-up," immensely long planks were uniquely cast: planks the length of the vertical section of the building. These planks were engineered and reinforced with steel and cast before being hung on a temporary scaffolding to parse their impact.

To execute this mock-up Herzog & de Meuron first digitally machined a form liner which abstracted a wood-grain pattern at an immense scale. These textures lined the molds for the precast planks, and once cast the textures of wood grain could be seen in the shadows of its surfaces when hung vertically on temporary scaffolding (Figures 4.5 and 4.6).

Figure 4.4 An early presentation model of the Pérez Art Museum Miami, showing vertical precast concrete planks to be utilized in the construction of the buildings' facades. Herzog & de Meuron, the Pérez Art Museum Miami (Miami, FL, USA) 2013.
Courtesy of Herzog & de Meuron.

Early images and renderings of the building reflect the serious consideration of this idea, and highlight the early considerations of construction and constructability. For a variety of reasons, including cost and construction detailing, the precast façade system was ultimately abandoned in favor of a cast in place, something which would create a more local application of concrete on-site in a less controlled environment.

Figures 4.5 and 4.6 A mock-up of massive precast vertical planks hung on scaffolding, constructed in Basel, Switzerland. Form liners were machined with the textures of wood grains to transform the material qualities of concrete into something organic and naturally occurring despite their artificial concrete composition. Herzog & de Meuron, the Pérez Art Museum Miami (Miami, FL, USA) 2013.
Courtesy of Herzog & de Meuron.

COMPETITIVE MOCK-UP: CONCRETE TOMBSTONES

Having decided to construct the building out of cast in place concrete, the design team made the decision to use concrete in a similar application to one of their earlier projects, the Schaulager, Laurenz Foundation building in Basel, completed in 2003. For the Schaulager, Herzog & de Meuron wanted to express the heaviness of the building, as something both durable and solid. One method to accomplish this was to scrape or scratch the surface of the concrete while it was still in the process of curing. This allowed the pebbles which were first excavated from the site and then cast into the concrete mix to be exposed, and so giving texture to the concrete walls from within the depth of the wall and site. The exposed layers of the materials express the structure as something heavy and massive, not thin and immaterial. Having previously researched and executed this approach, Herzog & de Meuron decided in lieu of the precast wood textures to attempt something less literal and more organic in the construction of the new PAMM building.

To select the contractor who would ultimately construct the building, with reference to the concrete scratch texture from the Schaulager, the design team issued written instructions to a shortlist of bidding contractors. The instructions asked for the construction of several wall fragments, referred to as "tombstones," each with a different texture, some raked or scratched, some out of form, and others polished smooth. While the process for the Schaulager was known, the design team was also interested in something rooted locally; thus, they opened up that process to the influence of the local trades. When inspecting these competitive mock-ups, they evaluated both the quality of craft and the innovation of each approach.

Figure 4.7 Architects and contractors inspecting the variety of concrete "tombstones" constructed as part of a competitive mock-up process to select the contractor. Herzog & de Meuron, the Pérez Art Museum Miami (Miami, FL, USA) 2013.
Courtesy of Herzog & de Meuron.

Figure 4.8 The architects documented the quality of the textures executed with detailed photos indicating the scale of the effect with their hands in the image in addition to the precise tool utilized. Here a rough organic texture was produced by hand utilizing a rock-hammer. Herzog & de Meuron, the Pérez Art Museum Miami (Miami, FL, USA) 2013.
Courtesy of Herzog & de Meuron.

Figure 4.9 A smooth polished surface texture utilizing a mechanical grinding disc. Herzog & de Meuron, the Pérez Art Museum Miami (Miami, FL, USA) 2013.
Courtesy of Herzog & de Meuron.

Figure 4.10 A rough-textured surface produced with a powered jackhammer. Herzog & de Meuron, the Pérez Art Museum Miami (Miami, FL, USA) 2013.
Courtesy of Herzog & de Meuron.

Apparent in the tombstone, the mock-ups were a variety of qualities and conflicts. Some were impressive in their quality of finish; however, some were constructed in an unworkable process. For example, one set of mock-ups had very high-quality surface textures, but had been cast flat, and then tilted up. While the quality was satisfactory, the approach would not work as the building was to be cast in place (Figure 4.7).

CAST GLAZING

The textures animated the concrete walls of the building, establishing them as something within a set of many possible permutations. These permutations shifted concrete from something predetermined to something potentially more reactive to its environment, something less artificial and more naturally occurring. These textures opened up new interactions in the applications of concrete in the PAMM, and another such unique application was in the substitution of concrete for building elements that were typically constructed of wood. This creative transformation of materiality resembles a type of natural petrification, one seen in several details of the building, particularly the glazing system which is cast Figures 4.8, 4.9 and 4.10).

For the glazing system which encloses the spaces between the museum's concrete volumes, the design team decided to structure the large panels of glass with structural elements that are themselves cast of concrete. What is typically a metal structural element for supporting glass, a mullion, here becomes cast concrete. The vertical cast mullions become deeper, a full 12 inches deep, because while steel is ordinarily used for its slenderness to maintain transparency this additional depth is due to the material specificities of concrete, a necessary permutation of form in service of this transformation. This distinct use of concrete highlights this other approach to the transformation of the PAMM's material qualities (Figure 4.11).

This additional depth is significant but only subtly perceived in space, as a new texture to what is typically a shallow surface. The strange proportions of this

Unpredictable Petrifications

element intrude into the spaces around it, pressing the dimensional realities of this detail into the environment of the museum. On the upper floor, the cast mullions are turned in, pressing into the gallery spaces and providing a flush exterior glass surface. On the lower floors, the cast mullions are turned out, presenting themselves as artifacts to the public promenade level which surrounds the museum.

The process of achieving this transformation was mocked up in detail at least three separate times. The first mock-ups were constructed in a millwork shop, with substitute members first fabricated from wood. A millwork shop produced three unique mullion profiles constructed at full scale before one was selected to be fabricated from concrete. The profiles vary in thickness at their leading-edge; a thicker example was rejected for its bulkiness, and the thinnest was deemed too slender. The middle thickness was selected, one whose leading-edge tapered down to just over 2 and a half inches wide.

Within this mock-up, the joint lines of the exterior pavers are machined into the flooring. The design team used photographs of the mock-up to collage different finishes and colors in an attempt to imagine even more details in relation to these cast mullion profiles. On the interior of the glazing is a wooden glazing cap, masking the joint between the glass panels. These caps are left with a raw wood finish, while the exterior mullions are painted gray to mimic the color of the concrete from which they will be constructed. This transition explicitly demonstrates how wooden material is transformed into concrete for the purposes of being exposed to the weather on the exterior of the building (Figure 4.12).

Figure 4.11 A mock-up of the precast structural glazing elements constructed of wood and painted gray to resemble the color of concrete. The vertical cast elements of this mock-up have subtly unique profiles from which one was selected. Herzog & de Meuron, the Pérez Art Museum Miami (Miami, FL, USA) 2013.

Courtesy of Herzog & de Meuron.

Figure 4.12 The exterior out-turned cast mullions cast from concrete transform into wood compositions on the interior of the glass. Herzog & de Meuron, the Pérez Art Museum Miami (Miami, FL, USA) 2013.

Courtesy of Herzog & de Meuron.

Once the final sizes and proportions of the cast mullion profiles were decided in this mock-up, they were prototyped and tested for NOA, or Notice of Acceptance, per the Florida Building Code.

Because this glazing system was custom, it lacked the necessary product approval and therefore needed to go through a process of testing which simulates the effects of a hurricane's impact. The specific tests are known as Large Missile Impact Tests and Small Missile Impact Tests.

Large Missile Impact Tests (ASTM E 1886-05) fire a piece of dimensional lumber at the glazing system, and then cycles positive and negative air pressure to see if moisture can infiltrate the cracks caused by the impact. The Small Missile Impact Test fires a 2-gram ball bearing at the glass and then tests with the same cyclic pressure procedures as with the Large Missile Impact Tests. The purpose of these tests is to empirically test if the system is resilient enough to resist the impact of such windborne debris in the event of an actual hurricane.

SURFACE FINISH

A final mock-up for the cast mullion glazing system involved the surface finish of the glazing members, which were to be precast off-site, before being brought to the site for installation. Because these elements would be made differently than the cast in place concrete surfaces of the building, the design team wanted to coordinate their integration into the overall construction. The design team requested three distinct samples from the fabricator, each with a unique surface finish.

The first finish specified was termed "out-of-form," meaning the raw surface finish once the formwork is removed without any additional treatment. Where the surface generally exhibits some inconsistent surface coloration. The second sample specified the finish as "acid-etched," in which an acidic solution is applied to the surface of the cast mullion. This process provides a more uniform surface finish and appearance. The third sample specified that the finish should be "Dry-sanded," in which the surface is buffed with an abrasive pad.

The design team found that the acid-etched surface became too "hairy," because as the outer layer was etched away, the embedded fiber reinforcing from within was now visible on the surface (Figure 4.13). Likewise, the out-of-form finish was inconsistent with too much variety and surface staining. Dry-sanding each member better smoothed out inconsistencies and the design team found that light hand sanding was better than the chemical polish. Precisely because it could be selectively applied and it did not expose the internal fibers on the surface.

The mechanical dry-sanding had a tendency to darken the tone of the cast mullions. This darkened tone was almost unnoticeable until viewed in relation to the cast in place concrete of the actual building. Here, the colors of the two unique processes are noticeable when viewed together. In addition to this darker tone, the dry-sanded precast glazing elements were actually too consistent, lacking the organic quality of the cast in place concrete, which had bug-holes and other unpredictable signatures of concrete (Figures 4.14 and 4.15).

 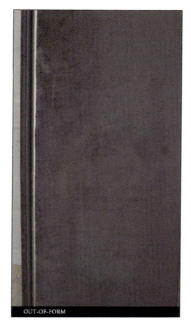 

Figures 4.13, 4.14, and 4.15 Detailed study of the various options for surface treatment finishes for individual precast mullions. Herzog & de Meuron, the Pérez Art Museum Miami (Miami, FL, USA) 2013.
Courtesy of Herzog & de Meuron.

AN INTEGRATIVE VISUAL MOCK-UP

In a more comprehensive and integrative mock-up, a variety of different trades came together, practicing their work, by constructing typical details. The work of these individual trades would not exist in isolation. The goal was to illustrate how the various trades could reduce constructive conflict. The finishes needed to independently exhibit high standards, but also needed to retain those standards once placed in relation to the other trades. This mock-up is surprisingly thorough, highlighting the integration of details on the exterior and interior.

Beginning with exterior construction methods and systems, the mock-up is then finished on the interior, testing a variety of products and finishes. Finally, the mock-up is studied for how it will become visible in-depth, as shallow surface details are considered against the backdrop of the constructed space. This mock-up is like a building, with a coherent interior and exterior, and an enclosed space where these two complementary futures come together.

CAST IN PLACE SHELL

The integrative mock-up was constructed in stages, in a sequence determined both by construction logic and by what needed to be studied at any given time. The roof and trellis structures were actually installed much later than the glazing, even after the lighting studies. Construction began by first casting the concrete shell of the building, consisting of the walls and the roof slab. The underside of the roof slab had cast grooves or voids called "rebates" for integrating lighting systems, HVAC, security, and sprinklers. These rebates were designed into the underside of the slab, because there was no dropped ceiling to conceal cables and fixtures; rather, the underside of the slab was exposed as the finished surface for the gallery ceilings. The back side of the mock-up was left open, with the vertical concrete walls extending past where the flush glazing will sit, and turned-in mullion representing the upper-level recesses in the massing between gallery volumes. The front side of the mock-up has an overhang, under which the glazing system was later installed with out-turned mullions representing the lower plaza level of the final building. In this way, the design of this mock-up is a seamless collage of conditions sampled from various regions of the final building.

INTEGRATED TEXTURES: SCRATCHING AND CHIPPING THE SURFACE

Upon completion of the shell, the design team and contractors began transforming its exterior. On one side of the mock-up, a variety of rough-textured finishes were executed, while on the other side a variety of smooth ones (Figure 4.16).

On the smooth side of the mock-up, the elevation was divided into thirds. The central portion of the concrete elevation was left in its original state, displaying a surface quality directly from the forming process. On either side of this central portion, two smooth finishes were tested, utilizing different depths of grind during a mechanical polishing process.

On the rough side of the mock-up, the design team attempted to evolve from the "scratched-concrete" finish of the Schaulager project. In order to reproduce this texture, Herzog & de Meuron specified a form retarder, which is applied to the inside of the concrete formwork before the concrete is poured into the mold. The retarder prevents the concrete from curing on the surface for several days, and after the mold is released the surface is easily chipped. In the case of the Schaulager, it is scratched with a rake to remove a shallow layer of material.

The elevation of the mock-up to display the rough textures was also divided into three sections. The central region of the concrete was left in its out-of-form state for reference. To either side, the concrete was scraped with different techniques, exploring procedural options for the intended finish. The scratched finishes displayed on this elevation of the

Figure 4.16 The rough side of the mock-up divided into three regions, with the resulting out-of-form surface in the middle and two regions of the rough textured concrete on either side. Herzog & de Meuron, the Pérez Art Museum Miami (Miami, FL, USA) 2013.

Courtesy of Herzog & de Meuron.

Figure 4.17
Detailed photograph showing the organic scratched texture of the mock-up, utilizing form retarders to keep the surface soft in order to be raked or scratched. Herzog & de Meuron, the Pérez Art Museum Miami (Miami, FL, USA) 2013.
Courtesy of Herzog & de Meuron.

integrative mock-up were accepted and approved for use in the construction of the final museum building. The design team was able to see first-hand the consequences of the Schaulager surface specification. They ultimately accepted this iteration and approved its use for construction. This scratched finish gave an organic quality to the resulting surface, one which does not obviously reveal the tool utilized to remove the outer layer of material disguising evidence of its artificiality, creating the quality of something natural (Figure 4.17).

QUESTIONS OF SEQUENCE

While the integrative mock-up is intended to animate the individual trades in relation to one another by constructing their interactions, this mock-up also clarifies the consequences of the process and construction sequencing. Because this mock-up is a neatly cropped sample of the final building, some interactions will always remain unaccounted for.

This mock-up was constructed on grade instead of the structure on which it would actually sit, isolating it from the other portions of the building. The sequencing of the mock-up differed from the actual construction process based on how mock-ups are designed. The mock-up was constructed quickly, as independent layers based on what the design team wanted to study at particular moments during design. In this case, first the concrete, then the glazing, then the other elements and finishes, each installed independently with significant gaps in the schedule.

For a variety of reasons, it was later discovered that the approved scratched-concrete finish from this mock-up was not possible in the construction of the final building. While structural concrete takes a full 28 days to fully cure to structural strength, the formwork can typically be removed after only a day or two. Even though the concrete is not yet fully cured, it is typically solid enough to retain its shape as it continues to harden through its own internal chemical reactions.

The form retarder utilized in the construction of the full-scale mock-up delays surface hardening of the concrete by several days, leaving it soft and easily textured by scratching and raking. However, this form retardant is effective only temporarily. If it extends beyond the duration it allows for the concrete to remain soft; the surface will set and complete the curing process, hardening to a durable state. The duration that the concrete remains soft enough for the texture to be scratched is crucial for the approved finish in the mock-up. Because the mock-ups were constructed quickly over the course of only a few days, the retarder was effective and the concrete was easily textured by scraping it. If the walls of the museum were not scratched within a week of releasing the forms, the concrete would cure to the point where the approved finish was no longer possible.

Figure 4.18 A construction photograph shortly before the precast trellis elements were be installed, showing the complex stacking of cast in place structural elements and volumes. Herzog & de Meuron, the Pérez Art Museum Miami (Miami, FL, USA) 2013.
Courtesy of Iwaan Baan.

In reality, the museum's lower floors must be partially hung from the top. There are many beams concealed within the top of the second-floor volumes that extend out and hang the roof of the volumes below. The entire structure is not truly self-supporting until the entire building is topped out (Figure 4.18).

As a result of this structural reality, the temporary shoring used to support the concrete formwork throughout the building could not be removed for a period of 90 days. Because the formwork needed to remain in place for the full 90 days, far beyond the effectiveness of the form retarder, the outer layer of concrete could no longer be simply scraped.

This unforeseen reality, which was not anticipated in the mock-up, required a new surface finish and procedure to be designed. To address this unanticipated reality, the design team and contractor constructed three additional mock-ups on site later in the project. The design team used these mock-ups to test several new methods for texturing the hardened concrete, primarily by manually chipping it with a variety of hand tools.

While the original scratch texture was organic, these new chipping processes created legible patterns as a result of repetitive action, a reading Herzog & de Meuron hoped to avoid. The concrete used in the PAMM was combined with an additive, blast-furnace-slag, which is used in highly structural applications for concrete, such as bridge construction.

The slag not only increased the strength of the concrete but also made it less permeable to the corrosive saltwater surrounding the site. An ultra-high-strength concrete resulted from the mix, which needed to be manually chipped by hand high above the ground. In softer forms of concrete, if the surface was struck, the concrete might flake off beyond the point of impact, but because this concrete was ultra-hardened the fractures did not extend much beyond the tool's point of impact.

An additional mock-up was constructed and divided into areas of focus to test various procedures for achieving the desired texture (Figure 4.19). Different tools were tested, including a small automated jackhammer and hand tools, chisels, and

Unpredictable Petrifications

Figure 4.19 A new mock-up wall divided into regions for fine-tuning the revised process of chipping the surface after it had hardened, utilizing hand tools to do this. Herzog & de Meuron, the Pérez Art Museum Miami (Miami, FL, USA) 2013.

Courtesy of Daniel Azoulay.

rock hammers. While certain regions of the mock-up were preferred over others for the rough texture based on different tools, the emergence of undesirable visible patterns from repetitive strikes became visible. This visible repetition undermined the natural qualities desired in these transformational textures, so combinations of tools were used to attempt to camouflage this visibility. Together with the craftsmen, the design team developed a process which first required *spalling* the concrete, a process of removing shallow wider surface flakes by striking it with tools at oblique angles followed by further chipping the underlying surface. This layering of steps created a preferred pattern which was more ambiguous, disguising evidence of its own process.

Herzog & de Meuron focused enormous energy to perfect the exact procedure that would achieve the final surface texture they wanted. This seemingly low-tech and low-skill process was surprisingly complex to specify with precision. The design team had to collaboratively create the method and ultimately train the craftsmen to use the best practice.

Because this change of plan occurred late in the process, the design team was limited by the amount of time available to come up with a new strategy. Over the course of a month, they experimented and fine-tuned this new process, training a single worker to execute the desired chipping pattern.

Seemingly at odds, while the building is huge, the design team hoped to prevent a variation in texture between different areas of the building, limiting the number of workers performing this work. Instead of a generic artificial pattern which could be specified with tight measured tolerances, this finish was intended to be organic and non-repetitive, and therefore highly subjective. They determined it would be better to keep it to fewer workers despite the immense surface area of the building, because the bigger the team the more potential was created for variety of appearance. Their work was executed slowly but deliberately, over the course of many weeks and months, high up on scaffolding manually chipping the exterior of the building by hand (Figure 4.20).

Figure 4.20 Craftsmen slowly chipping the hardened face of the building by hand. The legibility of the tie holes, form joints, and cold joints are still legible but absorbed into a larger organic texture. Herzog & de Meuron, the Pérez Art Museum Miami (Miami, FL, USA) 2013.

Courtesy of Daniel Azoulay.

MOCKING WHILE BUILDING: A LATE SEQUENCE OF MOCK-UPS

Figure 4.21 shows four mock-ups sitting side by side as the museum building is nearing completion.

MOCK-UP A: INTEGRATIVE VISUAL MOCK-UP

The largest mock-up on the north end of the site, on the right side of the image, is the early integrative visual mock-up. Three other concrete-mock-ups were built much later during the construction administration phase of the project. Those three mock-ups were constructed by a different sub-contractor than the one who built the original mock-up on the right.

MOCK-UP B

The tallest mock-up on the left of the image demonstrated a range of possible textures and finishes for the final building. The vertical supporting wall can be seen divided into regions, each now finished with the new manual chipping process.

MOCK-UP C

A shorter mock-up was constructed which sits lower than the others. In this shorter mock-up, steel reinforcing is left exposed, extending upwards beyond the slab. This mock-up was constructed specifically to test the slab forming method, not the walls, and as a result the older tombstone mock-ups, which were still sitting on-site, were recycled and used as the vertical supports. The mock-up is shorter than the others, with a lower ceiling than in the spaces of the actual galleries because the existing tombstones were of an arbitrary height. The shorter supports allowed the slab to be closer to the ground and easier to be seen up close.

MOCK-UP D

The fourth, subsequent full-scale mock-up proved that the smooth forms would be satisfactory. These smooth walls were cast with focus, not only on the quality of their smooth finish, but also the cold joints between pours, the treatment of tie holes, patching, and the smooth grind and polished finishes themselves. This mock-up served as the final approved smooth finish mock-up.

Unpredictable Petrifications

Figure 4.21 Four mock-ups on site of the PAMM labeled A, B, C, and D. Herzog & de Meuron, the Pérez Art Museum Miami (Miami, FL, USA) 2013.
Courtesy of Daniel Azoulay.

PRECAST BOARD FORMS

The shell which has been cast sits directly on the ground in this mock-up, but in reality, these volumes will sit above the ground. A raised floor is constructed in front to mimic the exterior plaza level, constructed of a cast structural grid with members that are spanned across with precast concrete planks resembling the proportions of wooden planks (Figure 4.22).

Next to be tested were the overhead precast trellis elements that consist of precast columns and beams. Below the main structural beams, another set of precast "T-beams" (customized versions of typical double tees used in parking structures) are

Figure 4.22 Photo of the coordinated precast concrete planks and columns resembling wood decking construction. Herzog & de Meuron, the Pérez Art Museum Miami (Miami, FL, USA) 2013.
Courtesy of Herzog & de Meuron.

131

suspended from above. These precast T-beams are spaced at regular intervals, bracing the system. They have coordinated voids that allow a thinner system of wooden slats to be inserted, marking another integration of wood and concrete (Figures 4.23, 4.24 and 4.25).

Figure 4.23 Photo of the precast trellis elements installed on top of the cast in place shell. Herzog & de Meuron, the Pérez Art Museum Miami (Miami, FL, USA) 2013.
Courtesy of Daniel Azoulay.

Figure 4.24 Photo of the precast concrete trellis elements being installed in the final building. Herzog & de Meuron, the Pérez Art Museum Miami (Miami, FL, USA) 2013.
Courtesy of Iwaan Baan.

Figure 4.25 The T-shaped, precast trellis elements being hung below the precast structural elements. These elements provided the bracing to lock the entire structure together. Herzog & de Meuron, the Pérez Art Museum Miami (Miami, FL, USA) 2013.
Courtesy of Daniel Azoulay.

CAST GLAZING SYSTEM INSTALLED

The cast glazing system was installed in the shell of the building by first bolting the dry-sanded cast mullions onto the sill of the concrete opening, then by installing three different widths of glass. This process served as a final test run for the glazing system before attempting this action in the final building.

Each façade of the mock-up was installed with one of the two different orientations of the glazing system from the building. On the south side of the mock-up, which simulated the exterior plaza level, the cast mullions were out-turned, projecting 12 inches into the plaza where the public would come in contact with these artifacts on the outside of the building.

On the north side of the mock-up, the glazing was installed turned inward, presenting the cast mullions on the interior of the building; matching the flush smooth finish of the concrete on the exterior cuts of the upper galleries (Figure 4.26).

PRINTING AND TAPING ON MOCK-UPS: GLASS FRITTING TESTS

On the exterior of the glazing, unique fritting finishes were specified for each of the glazing units. The architects' goal for these different frit patterns was to hide the areas behind the glass where various technical connections existed. One idea was to mask these conditions with a mirrored frit pattern on the outside of the glass. Another was to use black, and the third was a light gray to match the concrete. After ordering the glass panels for the mock-up, each was specified with one of these three different frit patterns; the design team was still not yet convinced by any of the three. The mirrored finish actually highlighted the area they were trying to hide, while the black was too dark, and the gray frit was too light.

It is challenging to observe the effects of small scale decisions out of context, and so the design team first had hand samples, like swatches, that they would hold up next to the concrete

Figure 4.26 On the other side of the mock-up the glazing is installed flush with the mullions turned-in representing the upper story condition of the flush glass in the recessed volumes between galleries. Herzog & de Meuron, the Pérez Art Museum Miami (Miami, FL, USA) 2013.
Courtesy of Herzog & de Meuron.

before the glass was produced. Based on this first step, the design team then made selections for the big mock-ups and ordered the glass with these specified frit patterns printed directly on the glass to see it in context. Herzog & de Meuron judged the visual appearance of the specified finishes in the context of the mock-up and selected new colors, further fine-tuning the optics in the process. Because it is both expensive and time-consuming to order new full-scale glass panels with custom frit patterns, the design team themselves began printing options on paper that they then pasted on the mock-up.

One of the new patterns they developed had a mirrored frit pattern with transparent dots, which the design team liked but which ultimately proved too costly. Instead, they narrowed it down to two dark gray colors. Finally, the design team chose a dark gray tone, one which was much darker than the concrete itself, because when the glass is viewed in context with shadows the background it is to blend in with appears much darker.

In the construction photos, one can see how the dark gray fritting blends into the dark reflections of the glass, something not immediately apparent without observing this phenomenon (Figure 4.27). If the design team had simply selected a color swatch without integrating it through multiple iterations of the mock-ups, there would be no guarantee of this optical integration. The final specification for the fritting was made quite late in the process, and was only possible because of the extensive use of on-site mock-ups.

Figure 4.27 The actual configuration of the glazing in the final building. Below the overhanging galleries the cast mullion systems are out-turned, and above they are turned-in reflecting the smooth finish of the concrete in the recesses between gallery volumes. Herzog & de Meuron, the Pérez Art Museum Miami (Miami, FL, USA) 2013.
Courtesy of Herzog & de Meuron.

INDETERMINACY IN THE FIELD

Unpredictable Transformations

Having extensively studied so many detailed and integrated considerations of concrete in mock-ups as constructed experiments, it is somewhat surprising that anything unpredictable could still occur later in the process. Yet concrete's internal transformations are not simply formal. They are the result of the internal chemistries of matter and their interaction with external environmental factors. At a certain resolution, these transformations will always remain subtly unpredictable, particularly when constructed outside of a controlled environment. Of any environment, Miami's is as uncontrollable as they come. As Sanford Kwinter again observes:

> The fact that concrete owes everything to its fluid, or rather its rheological phase, and especially to water as its necessary vehicle and substrate, alerts us to the fact that for at least one phase of its life it may be just that: a protolife of sorts, like our own living tissues, dependent on the mysteries of electrical bonds, organic chemistry, and nested gradients of order and disorder.[6]

SLAG STAINING

Because constructing with concrete incorporates its own internal transformations, the complex relationships between internal and external factors can become unpredictable and sometimes mysterious. As earlier noted, the concrete of the PAMM was embedded with the additive, blast-furnace-slag, to improve its permeability and hardness. This additive usually improves the concrete's internal performance invisibly. However, upon releasing the concrete formwork, many areas of the exposed concrete exhibited a dark-bluish stain (Figure 4.28).

These strange bluish regions were not anticipated and the causes were not immediately apparent. It was determined after much investigation and consultation with outside concrete experts that there were two likely causes. The first was believed to be due to the fact that the formwork remained in place for such an extended period of time because of the unique structural configuration of the building. This prolonged placement of formwork ultimately starved the slag-concrete of oxygen, causing a mysterious type of chemical bloom. The second suspicion believed to contribute to this staining was the fact that these walls were cast during the wet rainy

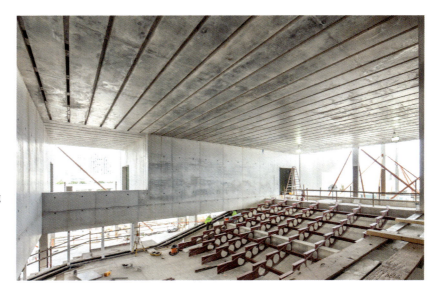

Figure 4.28 Slag staining visible on a south-facing interior wall. Herzog & de Meuron, the Pérez Art Museum Miami (Miami, FL, USA) 2013.
Courtesy of Daniel Azoulay.

months, causing some work delays and drenching the site with combinations of fresh and saltwater. The combination of these conditions led to an episodic dark-blueish staining effect.

Although constructed with extremely high-quality formwork and careful coordination between trades, the chemistry of the concrete and the weather itself created problems in the field. The concrete consultant indicated that the slag staining would burn off over time with exposure to UV light, but because some of the interior walls were not exposed to light, they placed large fans in the galleries to increase oxygen flow over the surfaces for months. With exposure to sunlight, the dark blue staining eventually burned away over time on the exterior. Because the mock-ups were constructed faster, and the formwork was released sooner, during a dryer time of the year this phenomenon was not seen or expected before being observed in the construction of the final building.

REBAR SHADOWING

In addition to the unanticipated and unseen staining, another unexpected phenomenon occurred on the interior of the building. Mysteriously, the interior walls facing north and south exhibited rebar shadowing, in which the steel reinforcing within the wall creates a darkened visible pattern on the surface of the walls.

The interior double wythe gallery walls are only 5 to 6 inches thick, but have significant amounts of embedded steel reinforcing. Because of the density of steel cages inside the formwork, it was a challenge to get the 3-inch hose down into the bottom of the forms when pouring the walls. To better accomplish this, the steel reinforcing was pushed toward the interior finish side of the wall to make space for the hose and to prevent cracking on the exposed surface of the galleries.

When the interior formwork was released, this condition was visible on certain surfaces, and some walls appeared uniform while the others displayed dark horizontal banding. The concrete specialists concluded that this phenomenon most likely occurred because the concrete was being poured during the day, in the hotter seasons of the tropics. The rebar facing north and south would heat up during the day and create microclimates around it causing the concrete immediately adjacent to it to set differently (Figure 4.29).

Two treatments were developed to reduce these shadow markings on the interior walls. The first step was to mechanically polish the vertical surfaces with a light diamond grit polish, removing the first layer. Applying this light polish exposed the small air bubbles below the surface, reinforcing the mineral qualities of the walls and blurring the differences in tone diffusing the legibility of the shadow pattern.

A second process was developed in which restoration artists would selectively apply a thin layer of living mineral paint, consisting of pulverized concrete and

Figure 4.29 Rebar shadowing visible as patterns of dark horizontal banding. Herzog & de Meuron, the Pérez Art Museum Miami (Miami, FL, USA) 2013.
Courtesy of Daniel Azoulay.

cement. This finishing touch would fuse with the wall behind, creating a more uniform surface appearance. Initial attempts were rejected as the finishing layer was applied with too much thickness, appearing too much like paint. In subsequent applications, the finishers attempted to surgically apply this mineral layer to the areas identified by the presence of rebar shadowing. This selective application ultimately allowed the walls to retain the tectonic evidence of their construction without appearing uniform or artificial.

Observed in the final building itself, it seems strange that these unpredictable phenomena were not first witnessed within the extensive series of mock-ups. I would argue this fact situates the building itself as a final mock-up, bigger and more integrative than the rest, not completely in control, and even in this final phase it is still in the process of revealing concrete's hidden interactions.

The fact that Herzog & de Meuron had to revise their premeditated approach later on in the project only highlights the degree to which they've opened up concrete. Concrete here is not used passively as something predetermined and unchanging. It is instead subtly but actively opened through manipulation, creating a less static condition, one which is influenced by its adjacencies.

MOCKING NATURAL TRANSFORMATIONS

There is evolving tension within the design of the PAMM, between the reluctance to surrender control and an enthusiasm to embrace change by transforming concrete's solid-state. It is this creative tension that exists both conceptually and physically. While the design team first began thinking about this building from afar, they engaged precast concrete as a system that would afford a greater degree of control and avoid the unpredictable effects of this exotic environment. This approach not only allowed increased control of construction qualities, but also attempted to precast new textures and qualities.

The design team abandoned this precast approach, I would argue for the better, in favor of a cast in place technique previously utilized in their earlier project, the Schaulager. By establishing this new tectonic relationship, the Schaulager building is conceptually transformed into a new but distant proto-mock-up for the PAMM.

This new approach intended to translate this distant example into a different context by introducing new local interactions into the process of construction, something not possible with the previous precast system. Herzog & de Meuron admirably opened this process to local craft, hosting a competitive mock-up that allowed room for improvisation within an overall framework.

Figure 4.30 A worker polishing the concrete surfaces of the upper gallery floor. Herzog & de Meuron, the Pérez Art Museum Miami (Miami, FL, USA) 2013.
Courtesy of Daniel Azoulay.

PETRIFIED TRANSFORMATIONS

The building for the PAMM is best understood, not by its forms, but by its transformations. At its core, it is constructed of concrete, a material that embodies transformation, beginning as a fluid full of potentials, and solidifying into something stable and unchanging. As Sanford Kwinter again observes about concrete's definitive transformations:

"It exhibits the strength and obduracy of stone and the flexibility and robustness of steel, yet it begins its life as a liquid, a river-slurry that is flowed into form and place."[7]

But the transformations of the PAMM are not typical, they are subtly unique, more like a building constructed out of wood that is petrified than out of concrete. Petrified wood is a puzzling form of matter, naturally occurring yet seemingly artificial as a result of its unexpected material composition of form.

By preserving its original form, petrified wood sustains a connection to a previous state, one which serves to evoke, not a previous form, but a previous set of qualities. This hybrid form represents, not a form, but the embodiment of transformation itself. Of something becoming something.

Like petrified wood, the PAMM is a kind of physical paradox: at once as solid as any structure can be; hardened and impermeable to an encroaching harsh environment, yet exhibiting evidence of its own plasticity and processes of solidification (Figure 4.30).

UNPETRIFYING THE MUSEUM

While this change of state from fluid to fixed is consistent, it is the smaller-scale details of this material transformation which are themselves often unpredictable and the subject of so much consideration in the form of mock-ups. Herzog & de Meuron are searching for something through the use of these mock-ups beyond the ability to construct the building. Their pervasive use of mock-ups in the design process provides a new framework, which locates a narrow but deep form of creativity. Particularly within this project, that creativity is embedded in concrete, expanding its definition from something material into a unique process of transformation. It is once again through the compelling evidence of premeditation we see in their many mock-ups, that a deeper conceptual understanding of the subtle material transformations within this building are made possible.

While concrete knowingly transforms from a liquid to a solid, and petrified wood transforms from organic into something inorganic, in the Pérez Art Museum in Miami the architects Herzog & de Meuron reverse these processes. Through deliberate strategies they un-petrify the concrete of the museum's construction, suggesting a previous state flush with the organic qualities of naturally occurring wood. Through these fictional transformations, the building takes on a new material definition, transforming the unnatural into something organic, like a reverse petrification, suggesting new experiences to the city around it. This transformation not only gives a new identity to the building, through its multiple layering of organic and mineral elements, but also gives new definition to a young city, establishing itself on a constantly shifting ground. Reflecting on concrete's natural capacities, Adrian Forty observes:

> It has the capacity to resist nature (gravity, the sea, weather) and so gives us power over nature to a greater degree than most other materials. Its failing, though, is in its perceived lack of qualities found in so-called "natural" materials, while it is often seen as cutting people off from nature, or obliterating nature.[8]

Through the use of mock-ups, this museum embodies the perceived definitions of solidity into something more malleable. And indeed the museum itself becomes a test for the city, pressing on its stabilities, and infusing it with suggestions for new transformations.

Notes

1 Adrian Forty, *Concrete and Culture: A Material History* (London: Reaktion Books; 2nd edition, 2016), 43.
2 Adrian Forty, *Concrete and Culture: A Material History* (London: Reaktion Books; 2nd edition, 2016), 43.
3 Adrian Forty, *Concrete and Culture: A Material History* (London: Reaktion Books; 2nd edition, 2016), 43.
4 Sanford Kwinter, "Concrete: Dead or Alive?" in *Solid States: Concrete in Transition*, eds. Michael Bell and Craig Buckley (New York: Princeton Architectural Press, 2010), 39.

5　Herzog & de Meuron Website, "306 Pérez Art Museum Miami/FACTS," www.herzogdemeuron.com/index/projects/complete-works/301-325/306-perez-art-museum-miami.html
6　Sanford Kwinter, "Concrete: Dead or Alive?" in *Solid States: Concrete in Transition*, eds. Michael Bell and Craig Buckley (New York: Princeton Architectural Press, 2010), 39.
7　Sanford Kwinter, "Concrete: Dead or Alive?" in *Solid States: Concrete in Transition*, eds. Michael Bell and Craig Buckley (New York: Princeton Architectural Press, 2010), 39.
8　Adrian Forty, *Concrete and Culture: A Material History* (London: Reaktion Books; 2nd edition, 2016), 43.

Massive Impressions: The Materials of Representation

The Cité de L'Océan et du Surf Museum, Biarritz, France
Steven Holl Architects

Figure 5.1 The architect Steven Holl writing notes on a mock-up constructed of Portuguese stone pavers and planted with vegetation for the plaza of the forthcoming Cité de L'Océan et du Surf Museum in Biarritz France. Steven Holl Architects, the Cité de L'Océan et du Surf Museum (Biarritz, France) 2011.

Courtesy of Steven Holl Architects.

MASSIVE IMPRESSIONS

In 2005, Steven Holl Architects won the international design competition to design and build the new Cité de L'Océan et du Surf Museum in Biarritz, France. Biarritz is a city renowned as the surf capital of Europe, and for a building intended to celebrate the cultural relationship of the city to the ocean Steven Holl Architects designed a building consisting of a double-sided horizon. On the top side is a warped roof plaza, open to the sky and shaped like a shallow canyon. Below this surface is a space in which the impression of the overhead roof plaza pushes down from above, imposing its shape on the space beneath as a low slung ceiling. From inside, the individual is constantly aware of the presence of the plaza above but not quite conscious of it, only feeling its pressures, giving the interior of the building the suggestion of being below something massive and imposing; something like the space beneath the ocean's rolling swells.

This warped surface informs the spaces above and below, and despite it being constructed of concrete it suggests something which is dynamic and still in the process of formation, implicating the spaces around it in its transformations. In this building, the spaces below push up at the edges of the roof plaza above, while the plaza presses down as both produce impressions of the other forming a pressurized boundary.

The scale of the warped roof surface is massive, extending beyond the interior spaces of the entire building. Its simple shape transforms a typically passive and utilitarian flat roof that is generic into a roof-space which is suggestive, informed by the masses below that seem to swell up around it. The massive scale of this swelling form is not the only place where mass is observed in the building.

MASSIVE REPRESENTATIONS

In physics, mass defines a seemingly paradoxical state. It is not the weight of an object but the property of a physical body that determines how much it will be affected by gravity, thus determining its weight. While weight is a force, mass is a property that determines the impact of that force. An object with low mass will weigh less, and in effect it will remain passive to the forces of gravity.

It is not exactly understood what it is that determines the mass of a physical body. Mass is independent of size and scale. With regards to massiveness, the certainty of physical objects leads to uncertainty about what is acting upon it, transforming the physical from something literal and actual into evidence of something else like a physical representation.

In the Biarritz Museum, and throughout the work of Steven Holl Architects, the physical bodies of architecture are embedded with massive properties, transforming the absoluteness of what is constructed into subtle questions and implications about the world acting on what we see. These properties are inherently physical, emerging out of experiments rooted in construction and material interactions with space, charged by subtle fine tunings of interactions between form and material. These interactions break down the certainty of physical bodies into the details and forces acting upon them, exaggerating and making apparent the qualities of light and shadow and the textures and formations of space, which often go unnoticed. It is these qualities that are difficult to represent through drawing, only able to be revealed through the construction of many full-scale mock-ups.

SKETCHING WITH MATERIALS

Throughout the work of Steven Holl Architects, there exists a unique set of material interactions from the early stages of imagination through to the final phases of construction. Ordinarily, the translation of the virtual and representational forms of drawing are translated into the actual built forms of architecture at the end of the design process. But in Steven Holl's unique approach, these interactions are present in the design process from the very first sketches. It is in these early sketches where forms are already influenced by unique massive interactions.

Steven Holl begins sketching using not only lines but also an overlay of watercolor paint. Typically a sketch is drawn with lines, which, despite being crisp markings, are less absolute in search of the figure they are trying to articulate. A watercolor sketch is less stable in its detailed marks since the paint and paper exert influence on one another and the forms emerge subtly altered as a result of these interactions. Instead of imposing a sketch on the paper, the sketch emerges out of the feedback of the watercolor and the page.

From his insightful essay, which summarizes Steven Holl's process and influences, Sanford Kwinter beautifully details the components and forces present within the watercolor itself, which, when considered further, highlight the lack of interactions found in sketching with pencil and paper.

> In the watercolor the originary page is not blank and the depths are not homogenous. The carrier or medium is in fact rife with traction; it pushes back, distributes with its own pre-existing capillary action; it carries pigment along and away, flocculates, deposits grain, imposes osmotic constraints; it "plows" pigment up along boundary areas, introduces backruns – "blooms" or "blossoms," especially when working with wet on wet.[1]

In addition to the mechanics of these interactions, there is another significant difference between the line drawings and the watercolor: the distinct representational capacities of each to communicate information. The line generally notates edges, joints, outlines, and boundary conditions, while the brushstrokes of watercolor can communicate more. They are able to communicate light, texture, material affects, and form.

The feedback present in the watercolor sketches of Steven Holl is privileged throughout the design process, not only in the initial imaginations, but also notably in the construction phase. Representing these interactions is not a matter of picturing their forms, but of provoking them the way the materiality of the watercolor interacts with the deep structure of the paper. It is later in the design process when a more nuanced convention of representation allows for more elaborate designed interactions of form and material to be tested through mock-ups. The mock-ups are perhaps the equivalent versions of the original watercolor and its ability to produce experimental interactions during the construction phase.

As a teacher, Steven Holl begins his design studios by asking his students to sketch using materials; first, constructing a physical cube which serves as a spatial sketch, not drawn but built. Out of these experimental constructions emerge interactions of light, space, transparency, texture, and tactility (all qualities difficult to represent in drawing particularly early on in the process).

The designs of Steven Holl do not produce certainty, and they use the physical nature of materials to destabilize the concrete presence of building, breaking down what is familiar into a series of unfamiliar and interactive parts that are difficult to represent. According to Holl, this phenomenon is something that cannot be photographed or simulated; it must be interacted with and experienced personally.

> You have to go visit architecture, you cannot look at magazines, or videos or films … you must go there with your own two feet and walk through it, look at it and make your own opinion … what is it really like inside, make your own opinion … then you can say something about a building … but you cannot just look at images of the outside.[2]

These buildings confront us with the representation of interactions, between the certainty of the material world and the mysterious dynamics of the forces acting on it. These representations reveal evidence of what causes the architecture we observe, instead of simply establishing what it is constructed of. The forms of buildings alone remain static, but it is their physical interactions with light and space that are dynamic and everchanging. These elements continuously pull on one another in a state of constant flux.

Holl carefully constructs this tension by explicitly allowing the qualities of the materials to show through in his buildings, but then confounds its material reading by leaving each element incomplete, requiring us to consider why. According to Holl, the material is there to suggest new interactions. Of these interactions, he states, "Let's focus on the idea instead of the material, and the implication instead of the actuality. More important than what we are is what we suggest."[3]

MATERIAL TENDENCIES

The many mock-ups documented in the design of the Biarritz Museum are not unique within the larger body of work from Steven Holl Architects. In fact, throughout his work, Steven Holl has always exhibited a consistent embrace of materials and their conceptual capacities to reinforce spatial ideas. This consistency is present from the very beginning of his practice, focusing more on the pursuit of a deep material representation of ideas rather than the technical issues of construction.

> So I started with materials, always worked with materials … my father always made things, had a shop at home, it wasn't something that I decided to move into, just gradually moved into it, thinking materiality is integral to the concept of whatever it is you're doing as an architect …[4]

Early in his career, before his architecture was commissioned by clients, Steven Holl imagined architecture by working on models that came as close to the actual imagined ideas as possible. For one of his first projects, the Bridge of Houses project from 1979, he constructed a small scale model of his design out of the actual materials which were analogous with what the building was intended to be.

The model was built of a welded steel frame, like the steel structure of the old railroad bridge of what is today the highline. On top of this welded steel frame were four individual houses, each modeled from a different alloy of brass and copper, with unique acid etches that turned them different colors. These unique combinations of materials and properties represented the uniqueness of each house that occupied the bridge at a time before Steven Holl had actually built anything.

This model was like a scaled-down version of a building, never substituting representational model making materials for the materials of the actual building.

Growing up, Steven Holl worked in his father's sheet metal shop, cutting thicker materials, and bending and folding the thinner gauges of steel into complex shapes. It is in this early interaction with the behavior and capacities of materials where Holl recognized a conceptual relationship between materials and forms. This is the relationship that is present in the early Bridge of Houses model. Holl states the use of real materials in the construction of the model was, "trying to come as close to the material that you're considering … the conceptual strategy that you're considering …"[5]

ILLUMINATED INTERACTIONS

Materials of construction actively contribute to the interactions of space throughout the buildings of Steven Holl's Architects. Most importantly, it is light itself that plays the most active role. Light is a strange material, famously existing both as a particle and a wavelength. It is visible but not tangible, only able to be influenced by the way mass influences physical bodies in space. It is hard to draw light and represent it on paper; perhaps this is why Holl uses actual materials in his models to reveal the interactions that will occur.

Figure 5.2 A view inside the half-scale mock-up of the gallery spaces for the Kiasma Museum of Contemporary Art with a 3-foot tall cutout of Bela Bartok as scale figure. Steven Holl Architects, Kiasma Museum of Contemporary Art (Helsinki, Finland) 1993.
Courtesy of Steven Holl Architects.

It is in the interactions between light and the materiality of form where Holl moves beyond flat representations into the realm of material depth. These complex and unpredictable interactions are difficult to represent in drawings, and as a result, rely on the construction of the strange material models that are typical of Steven Holl's architecture. These material models exist at many scales, and only when they are scaled up do they become more formally recognizable as mock-ups.

You don't have to build a building, you can just make models or mock-ups and see these phenomena and realize they're going to happen at a larger scale, and you can't do that with the computer …[6]

FIRST MOCK-UP

Perhaps the first recognizable form of a mock-up occurred in 1993 for the Kiasma Museum of Contemporary Art in Helsinki. The design of the building is composed of two intertwining volumes, creating complex intersections of space. Once designed, the architects had to demonstrate that the building could be built within a fixed budget or the project would be canceled. To do this, Steven Holl directed the building of a half-scale mock-up on-site, capturing a portion of the gallery space with skylights and interior and exterior finishes. While the cost of the structure was a known quantity, it was in the finishes of the space where the most uncertainty existed. Because the mock-up was built, all the bidders could understand the roughness of the floor and the plaster. They could even touch and feel the nature of the Rheinzinc exterior.

The mock-up was instrumental because it proved that the building could be constructed under budget and that the poetry of light could be animated and reinforced through the rough nature of materials. Most notably, the walls are hand-troweled plaster in which the motion of the hands and the texture of the tools are visible in the textures of the finish. Steven Holl was present on the site during the construction of the mock-up and actively involved by directing the motions of the finishers. He instructed the workers to trowel three times in one direction and then three times in the other, forming a basket-weave pattern, and then to leave this textured scratch-coat exposed without a finish coat.

This exposed scratch-coat transforms the troweled plaster wall into a textured trace of the interaction of its materials and its workmanship. On-site, Steven Holl explained to the workers, "these are your marks on the wall … you're inscribing the wall with your energy … with your hand."[7] The concrete floor and walls of the museum are similarly stained uneven black, existing in a rougher state. The uneven surface of the floors and scratch-coat texture of the walls were not only more affordable as a result of eliminating the more high-skill labor, but the resulting textures interacted with the daylight, animating it into woven fibers of alternating refractions (Figure 5.3).

Figure 5.3 A view inside the gallery of the Kiasma Museum of Contemporary Art, illustrating the interactions of the scratch-coat texture of the walls with natural light of the gallery, animating otherwise uniform surfaces with evidence of the process of construction. Steven Holl Architects, Kiasma Museum of Contemporary Art (Helsinki, Finland) 1998.

Courtesy of Paul Warchol, photo Paul Warchol.

The mock-up was constructed at half scale, but because the floor to ceiling heights of the galleries were so tall it could be half-size and you could still walk around in it on your knees and sense the entire building. A half-scale cutout of Bela Bartok, the Hungarian composer, was placed in the mock-up as a scale figure to give reference when photographed (Figure 5.2).

Also, since it was so rough, labor was removed, saving the cost and improving the acoustical value of the space. Of the four bidders, three came in under budget as a result of these constructed representations.

DESIGN THROUGH CONSTRUCTION: MATERIAL ORCHESTRATION IN FOUR MOCK-UPS

While Kiasma is defined through the interactions of two intertwining forms, the museum in Biarritz is defined by the pressures that the occupiable roof exerts on the two spaces of the building. Pressing down on what is below and swelling up around what is above. With some consistency to Kiasma, the horizontal surfaces of Biarritz are likewise animated by the textures of smaller elements that form patterns and transform the scale of the larger forms into arrays of detail. Through the textures of the parts, the effects of this swelling form are transformed in the plaza level which is paved in many thousands of square Portuguese paving stones. These pavers register the distortions of this massive up-swelling of space, seeming to be swept up in the swells of an aqueous plane.

Figure 5.4 A note handwritten on the Portuguese pavers of a full-scale mock-up indicating the ideal spacing. Steven Holl Architects, the Cité de L'Océan et du Surf Museum (Biarritz, France) 2011.

Courtesy of Steven Holl Architects.

MOCK-UP 01: PORTUGUESE STONE PLAZA MOCK-UP

The top side of the Biarritz Museum is not simply a passive roof surface. Instead, the roof is an undulating space that serves an inhabitable plaza whose edges seem to swell up from below forming a shallow valley. The surface of this plaza was designed from something commonly found in public plazas throughout history: square Portuguese pavers. Like the scratch-coat of Kiasma, the placement pattern of these pavers became the subject of much experimentation on-site through mock-ups.

Several samples were prepared by filling small square frames with ideal configurations of pavers. These frames served to specify the typical arrangements of stones to be repeated at the immense scale of the plaza (Figure 5.5). While these initial mock-ups were taken out of context, they illuminated a number of additional factors to be considered. How would the plants thrive in the interstitial space between pavers? How much spacing would be necessary for the plants? How much spacing was required for the blocks to be stable on an uneven surface? Which patterns would work best with the distorted geometry of the plaza, and what effects would these interactions reveal? As a result of these questions, it was determined that a larger mock-up was necessary to study the larger scale configurations of pavers.

A base for the next mock-up was prepared by mounding up soil to simulate the slope of the plaza's edge. The pavers were initially placed with a random pattern, with each block slightly rotated towards one another, with generally consistent spacing in between (Figure 5.6). Where the slope of the plaza inclined, the blocks were packed tighter to prevent them from sliding downhill. Upon inspection of the mock-up, Steven Holl asked for a few more rows of pavers to be installed in uniform rows to compare the random with the repetitive coursing. Several more rows of pavers were added to the mock-up and the differences produced by these patterning exercises were explored visually and physically.

Figure 5.5 A frame representing a sample of the intended pattern of the pavers, which are oriented at right angles but with irregular dimensions, typically referred to as random ashlar in masonry construction. Steven Holl Architects, the Cité de L'Océan et du Surf Museum (Biarritz, France) 2011.
Courtesy of Steven Holl Architects.

Surveyors' strings were stretched to align the pavers into rows. What was initially a random placement of pavers was reconfigured into uniform alignments, which the architect thought were too repetitive once compared side by side. So reverting back to a random alignment, more pavers were installed in the mock-up (Figure 5.7). Studies were then conducted into the amount of spacing between blocks, which would ultimately affect the amount of vegetation growing in the joints of the plaza. At the far

Figure 5.6 A mound of earth approximates the curvature of the plaza's form, which will be suspended above the galleries below, with varying paver patterns installed side by side for consideration. Present in the photo are the builders and design team including Steven Holl. Steven Holl Architects, the Cité de L'Océan et du Surf Museum (Biarritz, France) 2011.

Courtesy of Steven Holl Architects.

Figure 5.7 A view of the paver mock-up with the various patterns of coursed and random alignment visible in distinct zones. Steven Holl Architects, the Cité de L'Océan et du Surf Museum (Biarritz, France) 2011.

Courtesy of Steven Holl Architects.

end of the mock-up, the pavers were spaced out considerably, testing greater amounts of soil between the stones (Figure 5.8).

What became clear as a result of this spacing was that these blocks would not stay positioned on the sloped portions of the site. Because of the slope, they needed to be packed tightly. The larger-scale form required the tight packing of stones on the inclines and then more random patterns of misalignment on the subtly sloped areas of the plaza. As a result of the mock-up, they determined that the pavers on the slopes required mortar between the blocks to be stabilized and kept from sliding.

Figure 5.8 As the installation of the mock-up progressed, the pavers were spaced farther apart to allow for vegetation to grow in the interstitial spaces. This potential was observed in the mock-up over time. Steven Holl Architects, the Cité de L'Océan et du Surf Museum (Biarritz, France) 2011. Courtesy of Steven Holl Architects.

Only then, could soil be utilized where there was less of a slope. The mock-up was planted and allowed to weather for several weeks and then revisited to see how the plants had grown in between the variety of stone spacings. These observations were factored into the final arrangements (Figure 5.9).

Figure 5.9 One can see the various coursing and tests of alignments in the completed state of the paving mock-up as a sequence of tests and decisions made in the built form. Steven Holl Architects, the Cité de L'Océan et du Surf Museum (Biarritz, France) 2011. Courtesy of Steven Holl Architects.

MOCK-UP 02: WHITE CONCRETE WALL FORMS

This elaborate arrangement of pavers was fine-tuned at full scale in order to test the interactions of details with the immense horizontal roof surface of the building. Vertically, the exposed finishes of the concrete walls became the focus of an equally compelling investigation.

The walls of the museum are cast in place concrete. The contractor was in fact quite good at concrete construction and could deliver a very smooth clean finish, a typical indicator of quality. However, the concrete provides an opportunity to engage the material in its variety of unique formations to provide new and unexpected interactions with space, light, small-scale details, and large-scale form.

The architects ordered the construction of several mock-ups as freestanding concrete wall sections. These wall fragments incorporated a variety of conditions to be tested: the use of several types of plywood board form, the working joints between pours, and how to handle the voids left in the wall from the form ties (Figure 5.10).

The construction material was to be white concrete, using a local white stone as an aggregate from this region of France. White Taavo Portland cement or white Ordinary Portland cement (WOPC) is similar to the more commonly used gray Portland cement in all respects except for its high degree of whiteness.

The unusual whiteness of this concrete enables the highlighting of the subtle textures of the walls' construction the way a rough canvas sometimes telegraphs through the paint. This use of white allows the typical application of white paint to become embedded color, opening the walls toward the integration of other built-in conditions. Through this approach, the concrete is not simply utilized for its strength and structure but also for its ability to be interacted with.

Figure 5.10
A series of white concrete wall fragments, constructed on-site testing a variety of surface finishes and textures. Steven Holl Architects, the Cité de L'Océan et du Surf Museum (Biarritz, France) 2011.
Courtesy of Steven Holl Architects.

These free-standing concrete wall mock-ups were each constructed using a different type of wooden formwork, resulting in unique patterns of cast textures: smooth, the grain figure of standard birch ply, and oriented-strand board (OSB), a reconstituted plywood made from the scraps of wood (Figure 5.11).

Typically, OSB is used within the wall section for its economy and performance, making a good substrate on which to apply other finish materials, but rarely exposed as a finish itself. Placing the texture of this material on the exterior of the surface suggests a flipping of the wall sections sequence, as if we are seeing it from within, as the hidden layers are revealed and brought to the front.

Figure 5.11 A photo of one of the wall fragments cast from a formwork lined with oriented-strand board. Steven Holl Architects, the Cité de L'Océan et du Surf Museum (Biarritz, France) 2011.
Courtesy of Steven Holl Architects.

Utilizing OSB produces a pattern which calls attention to the smaller scale details of the board. Instead of seeing a wall constituted of the nominal dimensions of the plywood sheet, we instead see a field of finer grain strands shifting the scale of interaction between detail and form. There is a compounding effect beginning with the wooden shavings, which are layered up to make a board. These are the impressions of process and translation, and while the smooth finishes were executed with sufficient quality, they lacked in their capacities to animate the atmosphere of the project on-site, something needing to be viewed under the sun to be understood (Figure 5.12).

The texture was further emphasized in the selection of hole-plugs for the tie-holes, which remained after the removal of the temporary formwork. Initial solutions to manually fill the voids by hand were rejected, based on the differences of texture between the pattern of the OSB form liner and the hand-troweled infill

Figure 5.12 The architect Steven Holl inspecting the surfaces of the mock-up with the note "OK" and the date written on the side. Steven Holl Architects, the Cité de L'Océan et du Surf Museum (Biarritz, France) 2011.
Courtesy of Steven Holl Architects.

Figure 5.13
A photograph of the mock-up with a hand for scale showing the detailed uniform texture on the surfaces of the plug-holes, which were cast separately and later inserted into the voids left by the form ties. Steven Holl Architects, the Cité de L'Océan et du Surf Museum (Biarritz, France) 2011.
Courtesy of Steven Holl Architects.

which created a noticeable difference in finish. This small detail only evolved after a closer inspection of the full-scale mock-ups, something most likely passed over in drawings.

Once the texture of the form liner was chosen to be OSB, custom molds of cone-shaped plugs were fabricated like ice cube trays to be filled with white cement and stamped with the impression of OSB. These small precast plugs were mortared and inserted into the voids, giving the uniform impression of a material interaction across scales (Figure 5.13).

Like in the Kiasma museum, where the workers inscribed the walls with their own improvisational scratch-coat, the concrete walls of Biarritz are inscribed with the results of much consideration. In many projects of Steven Holl Architects, the materials used are brought to the fore, and thus allowed to inform space through their own subtle impressions. Walls are not simply the basic element of space; they are constructed canvasses, which receive and transmit light through smaller-scale interactions with material aggregates and textures.

WRINKLED AND CRUMPLED

A few projects reveal the diversity and creative approach through which Steven Holl treats and inscribes the surfaces of walls, breaking what we would consider to be a uniform set of elements into unique permutations.

For the Herning Museum of Contemporary Art, built in Herning, Denmark, the architects chose to inscribe the surfaces of the concrete walls with the influences of the buildings' past. The existing building on site was a former shirt factory in the shape of a shirt collar. The new museum building was to house many significant artworks by the artist Piero Manzoni, who worked in the original shirt-maker's factory in Herning using the cloth and textiles from this exact place.

Steven Holl wanted the building to reflect the artist's origin in this shirt-maker's factory. He conceived of a material strategy to construct the museum of white concrete and line the formwork with wrinkled fabric so the cast walls would exhibit a fabric texture as a reference back to Manzoni. The spaces of the building were simple rectangular frames with ceilings that resembled large shirt-sleeve elements draping overhead, forming sleeves of light. The architects actually used large tarps and drove over them with trucks to wrinkle the fabric. The references to the textiles are echoed in the spaces and in the texture of these elements (Figures 5.14 and 5.15).

Figure 5.14 A mock-up showing the wrinkled concrete vertical walls, and shirt-sleeve ceiling overhead. Steven Holl Architects, Herning Museum of Contemporary Art (Herning, Denmark) 2009.
Courtesy of Steven Holl Architects.

Figure 5.15 Inside the final building constructed of white concrete walls, using wrinkled fabric formwork. Steven Holl Architects, Herning Museum of Contemporary Art (Herning, Denmark) 2009.
Courtesy of Iwan Baan.

For the new expansion to the JFK Center for the Performing Arts in Washington, DC, Steven Holl Architects again proposed a system of cast in place concrete with another unique texture. While many of the previous textures are intended to capture light and inform the space through optical influence, at the Kennedy Center the random crinkle-textures are intended to influence the acoustics of the room. Inside the practice rooms of the building, there were acoustic demands which seemed to require the application of acoustical tiles. Instead of pushing the walls to the background thus concealing the structural element behind a superficial layer of tiles, the architects began to experiment with the textures of the form liner in order to achieve the required acoustic softening.

The original mock-up for this idea was constructed by hand in the New York office of the architects. Initially, a large piece of thin gauge aluminum

Figure 5.16 A mock-up of the crinkled cast in place concrete walls for the Kennedy Center practice rooms. Steven Holl Architects, The Reach, The Kennedy Center for the Performing Arts (Washington, DC, USA) 2016.
Photo Garrick Ambrose, Courtesy of Steven Holl Architects.

Figure 5.17 A mock-up of the crinkled cast in place concrete walls for the Kennedy Center practice rooms. Steven Holl Architects, The Reach, The Kennedy Center for the Performing Arts (Washington, DC, USA) 2016.
Photo Garrick Ambrose, courtesy of Steven Holl Architects.

was simply crumpled by hand over a wooden frame. The crinkled metal was then filled with expanded foam on the back side to stabilize it and from this a form liner fabricator produced rubber molds to be cast with concrete. The initial mold was a simple 2-foot by 2-foot square which was rotated and repeated in a simple running bond pattern to avoid repetition and suggest a larger scale of texture (Figure 5.16).

The acousticians wanted the walls to be live and absorptive. A random texture was desired to break up the noise, and the hand crumpled formwork accommodated this without adding additional layers on top of the concrete. This process extracted the acoustical performance out of an existing process, transforming the nature of a typical condition without having to rely on the addition of another material (Figure 5.17).

GEOLOGIC IMPRESSIONS

In another project built high on the bank of a picturesque river, the architects photographed the craggy cliffs visible from the site when looking across the water. The photographs of the geological formations were digitally translated into a contour map by assigning heights to the range of values between light and dark. What were once shadows cast by the mineral outcroppings on the cliffs were transferred to the contours

Figure 5.18 The subtle contours of the geologic formations from across the river, cast shadows at certain times of the day. Steven Holl Architects, Wrinkled Planar Villa (USA) 2017.
Courtesy of Steven Holl Architects.

of a digitally translated wrinkled surface. This surface was machined from layers of plywood and used to line the formwork of the new cast in place concrete walls constructed for this process. The geological forms of the site were now embedded in the surface of the cast concrete walls, echoing what is already present within its own surface formations.

The height of this geological texture was the subject of much investigation. Deepening its folds would make the texture more apparent. However, after several studies, a very shallow depth of field was established. This shallow relief of pattern allowed for the surfaces to animate over time. At times receding into a uniform field appearing smooth while at other times emerging into view. When the sun is in a certain position, the shallow formations of the artificial geological concrete become animated with its protrusions casting subtle shadows across its surfaces. The final depth of form was only determined after observing it built and on-site as a full-scale mock-up (Figure 5.18).

These experiments are sketches that define an idea. While sketching typically occurs on paper long before construction commences, these sketches occur on the construction site. However, not all of the mock-ups executed on-site are accepted. For the new Hunters Point Community Library in Queens, a full-scale mock-up was constructed on-site in which the concrete forms were lined with standard bubble-wrap packaging. When the concrete was poured into the forms, the concrete would sometimes pop the individual bubbles. Other times it would preserve the pocket of air, casting a void into the concrete surface. The walls would contain these pockets of solid and void, and were intended to then be painted reflective silver, lending a transformative appearance to the surface of the concrete. While this mock-up was successfully constructed on-site, for a variety of reasons it was excluded from the project, perhaps to be revisited in a future building, demonstrating the experimental nature of these full-scale tests (Figure 5.19).

Figure 5.19 Steven Holl reviewing a concrete wall mock-up of bubble-wrap formed concrete on the site of the Hunters Point Community Library in Queens, NY. Steven Holl Architects, Hunters Point Community Library (Queens, NY, USA) 2016.

Courtesy of Steven Holl Architects.

MASSIVE IMPRESSION: POOL FORM AND FORMWORK

In the Biarritz project, the building establishes the site as something malleable, pressing into it and drawing it up into a series of surface swells. At large scale this occurs through constructed surfaces. At small scale this occurs as the building materials produce detailed impressions of texture. While typical building materials such as plywood formwork and pavers animate larger elements such as walls and floors, a third element seems to exist between scales.

While the various finishes and material formations of the project are expressive of the thematic ideas of small scale impressions, a very large pool-like indentation provides a contrast in scale. Within the vast form of the swelling roof, we find a small organic shaped space that is pressed down, like a crater, marking the evidence of some foreign artifact which was once there.

Instead of a familiar building material producing tensions in a recognizable element through strange detailing, an unfamiliar space is encountered, which seems newly uncertain in two distinct ways. First, there is very little evidence of its construction. Second, the space suggests a void carved into the ground. The form of the space resembles an empty pool and seems as if it has been pressed into something malleable, distorting the form of the roof deck the way the smaller scale aggregates of material distort the surface.

The formwork for this pool is not evident in its seamless construction. While every other surface seems to have finer grain textures of material, this void space is void of surface texture as well. Like the grains of materials from the OSB marking impressions in the surface of the concrete walls, this element is scaled and produces a void of texture the size of an inhabitable space. It presses down into the space below and interrupts the otherwise continuous plaza above.

POOL FORM

When constructing with concrete, a building is actually constructed twice. Throughout the Biarritz Museum, the constructed elements reveal evidence of the materials used to construct them; but in the pool space, the scale, form, and smooth texture conceal the evidence. This space is the result of something that is not found but imagined.

In the case of the organic pool-shaped impression on the plaza at the Cité de L'Océan et du Surf Museum, the temporary wooden formwork used in the construction of this space is an elaborate orchestration of geometry, construction, and immense scale. Below the roof deck on the ground floor, the porch is the only area of the project with exposed concrete overhead. As a result of a desired seamless surface finish combined with the strange and complex geometry of the pool form, the large scale fabrication constructed a mysterious element that will never be seen. It will only be suspected as a result of its impression (Figures 5.20 and 5.22).

In another type of inversion, Steven Holl did not design this constructed element, but designed the void space into which it was to fit. It was the contractors who went to great length to establish the artifact, similar to the way the scratch-coat textures at Kiasma reveal the process of the workers in the exposed surfaces of the building.

The contractors asked for a detailed computer model and asked for the model to be sliced into flat sections every 24 inches. This translation of complex three-dimensional space into flat two-dimensional sections allowed them to construct individual sections of wood framing and join them together using traditional wooden shipbuilding techniques.

Two full-scale components needed to be fabricated. First, the underside of the pool form which was constructed of ribs and tightly spaced flexible wooden

Figure 5.20 The large impression pressed into the floor of the museum's plaza, resembling the form of an empty pool. Steven Holl Architects, the Cité de L'Océan et du Surf Museum (Biarritz, France) 2011.
Courtesy of Steven Holl Architects.

planks, and second a top positive figure to place into the void to assure a uniform thickness and finish. These two components when assembled, one convex and one concave, would leave a uniform cavity for the concrete to flow (Figure 5.21).

The scale of these components is large enough that they required large scale manufacturing similar to the way ships hulls are constructed with individual ribs

Figure 5.21 A photo of the massive formwork to be used in the construction of the concrete plaza surface forming a very large and single void. Steven Holl Architects, the Cité de L'Océan et du Surf Museum (Biarritz, France) 2011.

Courtesy of Steven Holl Architects.

Figure 5.22 The view from below the plaza, as this single pool form pushes down suggesting its buoyancy as it seems to float above. Steven Holl Architects, the Cité de L'Océan et du Surf Museum (Biarritz, France) 2011.

Courtesy of Steven Holl Architects.

Figure 5.23 The construction of the formwork for the smooth underside of the pool form. Steven Holl Architects, the Cité de L'Océan et du Surf Museum (Biarritz, France) 2011.

Courtesy of Steven Holl Architects.

constructed as flat profiles and then spanned across with wooden planks, bridging the ribs to form a surface. In the case of this void, all of the surfaces were coated and finished smooth to hide construction joints and leave the impression of a different scale artifact (Figure 5.23).

The construction sequencing had the wooden formwork for the underside of the porch roof installed on temporary supports. This surface was assembled in several large sections and joined together in exactly the place it was to be cast. Joints were filled and smoothed and painted to a pristine smoothness, as this surface would define the exposed underside of the slab. Large scale fabrication utilized ribs and individually bent planks which were cut at the seams then painted and gap filled to provide a blemish-free surface texture to the concrete which creates the ceiling in the Porch-space of the building (Figure 5.24).

Figure 5.24 The installation of the formwork for the underside of the concrete plaza deck on-site, prior to casting. Steven Holl Architects, the Cité de L'Océan et du Surf Museum (Biarritz, France) 2011.

Courtesy of Steven Holl Architects.

Figure 5.25 The large pool form placed in the void, and held in place with concrete blocks before concrete is pumped into the formed cavity. Steven Holl Architects, the Cité de L'Océan et du Surf Museum (Biarritz, France) 2011.
Courtesy of Steven Holl Architects.

On top of this formwork, steel reinforcing was formed and laid on top of which projected concrete or shotcrete was sprayed on to lock all the reinforcing together. On top of this base layer, additional reinforcing was spread across the entire deck, with the positive figure of the pool placed and weighted down while the concrete was pumped into the uniform cavity between the two layers. The positive formwork was assembled in five sections and craned into place, then joined and patched and ultimately cast (Figure 5.25).

This pool form is not recognizable as a conventional mock-up, but again marks an exchange between what is drawn and what is built, relying on the construction process to reciprocate. Much as the full-scale mock-up of the museum leaves its impressions on the building, these unusual scale formworks literally do make impressions in the plaza and ceiling and are noteworthy for their scale and the construction of an otherwise imaginary space. The large scale formwork was removed and discarded in the landscape to be later demolished (Figure 5.26).

Figure 5.26 The discarded formwork placed to the side of the construction site, after being stripped revealing the pool form impression. Steven Holl Architects, the Cité de L'Océan et du Surf Museum (Biarritz, France) 2011.
Courtesy of Steven Holl Architects.

DRAWING ON BUILDINGS: INTEGRATIVE MOCK-UP

A final mock-up was constructed to test the integration of many of the individual components of the building. Instead of experimenting individually with the elements, this mock-up tested the impressions that each would leave on the other.

In March of 2009, Steven Holl Architects issued a written brief with a set of detailed drawings for the contractor. These drawings described the construction of this final full-scale mock-up with the following dimensions: a square of 5m x 5m, with a roof supported by two concrete cast in place walls (Figure 5.27).

The brief which accompanied the drawings described five separate sets of details within the mock-up to be constructed in greater detail. Not only did each of these five need to be resolved individually but each needed to be resolved in relation to the other, negotiating the different geometric issues as well as the boundary conditions between each. The brief described the first element as a full height (foundation through roof) L-shaped white concrete wall to be cast in place; the second set of details described a full-height glass curtain wall corner; the third described a roof; the fourth the interior space; and finally the fifth described the outside stair mock-up, marking the boundary between metal and stone pavers.

The details requested in the brief for this final building mock-up were not so much to test if they were technically feasible, but rather to zoom in and focus on how each would encounter the others. By constructing these adjacent details side by side, the various materials and surfaces, which were individually predictable, could be observed to either complement one another or to produce conflicts.

Although this mock-up was a practice run for the contractor to be sure that they would execute to the tolerances expected by the architect, these temporary constructions allowed the architect to extend their craft, engaging the contractor as craftsmen, extending the design into the field through this mock-up as a framework for collaboration.

Figure 5.27 A view of the final integrative mock-up built on site, which was designed to capture the various materials and details testing how they would meet at their boundaries. Steven Holl Architects, the Cité de L'Océan et du Surf Museum (Biarritz, France) 2011.
Courtesy of Steven Holl Architects.

MOCK BOUNDARIES: DRAWING ON BUILDINGS

In this final mock-up we can see the various five regions of the document merging together and meeting at the joints. Walking around the outside of the mock-up we would see exterior material conditions abutting one another: glass, concrete,

Massive Impressions

Figure 5.28 A view of detail 1F as described in the mock-up brief, marking the boundary between the plaza landscape and the glass walls, with an accessible stainless steel gutter. Steven Holl Architects, the Cité de L'Océan et du Surf Museum (Biarritz, France) 2011.
Courtesy of Steven Holl Architects.

Figure 5.29 The mock-up being constructed with a particularly sharp piece of glass being installed in the framing, while concrete is simultaneously being pumped through the hose in the background, indicating the speed of construction in the mock-up. Steven Holl Architects, the Cité de L'Océan et du Surf Museum (Biarritz, France) 2011.
Courtesy of Steven Holl Architects.

the paved landscape, and ultimately the joints between vertical and horizontal surfaces (Figure 5.28).

In an interesting image of this integrative mock-up under the final phase of construction, we can see glass being craned into place with concrete being poured through a hose in the background, illustrating the rapid assembly of this temporary construction (Figure 5.29).

GLASS

The glass was constructed of a central insulating core sandwiched between two layers of glass. The insulation is a product called Okalux, which significantly whitens the appearance of glass, an innovation of detailing utilized in earlier Steven Holl projects such as the Nelson Atkins Museum in Kansas City. We can see very precise adjustments made to the manufacturing of these panels based on a familiarity with the product. In one image, a note can be seen drawn on the glass unit stating, "Problem with Okalux gap" (Figure 5.30).

Typically, one must coordinate how hard conditions that are not easily modified in the field will be accommodated as tolerances build up, usually with the interface of a soft material such as gaskets or softer materials such as wood which can be scribed in the field to absorb imperfections. In many of the notes drawn on the full-scale mock-up we can see comments which address concerns with how these hard materials and layers are going to come together for the first time (Figures 5.31 and 5.32).

Figure 5.30 A handwritten note by Steven Holl on the exterior of the mock-up indicating a problem area with a void between the edge and the Okalux insulation between the glass panels. Steven Holl Architects, the Cité De L'Océan et du Surf Museum (Biarritz, France) 2011.
Courtesy of Steven Holl Architects.

Figure 5.31 A handwritten note by Steven Holl on the exterior of the mock-up indicating a problem area with a void between the edge and the Okalux insulation between the glass panels. Steven Holl Architects, the Cité de L'Océan et du Surf Museum (Biarritz, France) 2011.
Courtesy of Steven Holl Architects.

Figure 5.32 Interior photo of the translucent insulated glazing units forming an unusual geometric transition anticipated in the buildings final form. Steven Holl Architects, the Cité de L'Océan et du Surf Museum (Biarritz, France) 2011.
Courtesy of Steven Holl Architects.

STRUCTURE

The shape of the Cité de L'Océan et du Surf Museum is a warped U shaped roof plaza which tapers with the street grid of its site and tilts in elevation, resulting in a subtly strange geometry. Instead of squaring off the building and floating it within the irregular boundaries, Steven Holl absorbs the irregularities of the site, allowing it to exert pressure on the spaces and construction of the building. In this way, the site indeed pushes back on the building's form, seeming to extend the interactions of his watercolors with its paper to the urban scale of the building and its site configuration.

In order to construct the building, the contractor relied on a contemporary method of sectioning more similar to boat building construction. A virtual model was sliced into a series of two-dimensional sections.

From these sections, the builder cast custom concrete structural ribs of each section and lifted these into place on site. Each individual concrete beam was then bridged with decking to form the surface of the warped roof and low hanging ceiling. The contractors utilized an adjustable formwork that could be tightened up or loosened to define the various unique profiles in the section. Individual shapes of plywood were cut at full scale based on the sliced section model and the adjustable formwork was tightened around each before being filled with reinforced concrete (Figure 5.33).

Figure 5.33 A view of the adjustable formwork being cast with the structural ribs of the roof. Steven Holl Architects, The Cite de L'Ocean du Surf Museum (Biarritz, France) 2011.

Courtesy of Steven Holl Architects.

Figure 5.34 The warping roof structure is added to the mock-up by using earth to fill in the approximate shape of the plaza above, with a profiled side wall in the shape of the section. Layers of insulation are added on top of the earth, followed by reinforcing and finally Portuguese pavers as the finished surface. Steven Holl Architects, The Cite de L'Ocean du Surf Museum (Biarritz, France) 2011.
Courtesy of Steven Holl Architects.

After the beams had been individually lifted into place, precast panels were placed between them on the flat areas of the plaza and high-density plastic panels were shaped to fit between individual beams. On top of these steel reinforcing was overlaid and shotcrete was sprayed onto the curved upturn areas of the plaza and built up slowly to a uniform thickness at the edges.

In this final mock-up, the curvature of the landscape is actually estimated by again mounding up dirt instead of the actual structural members in the building. This mounded dirt acts as a false substrate on top of which paving details will be tested, indicating that the surfaces and its detailing are the subject of this mock-up, not the structure itself (Figure 5.34).

On the interior of the mock-up we see a dropped plaster ceiling, initially planned to be the exposed finish of concrete. This finish represents a softer solution that would allow the concrete construction of the free form beams to be rougher in finish. From the concrete structure, lightweight metal hangers would drop and attach to

Figure 5.35 The interior of the mock-up testing the installation of gypsum board and insulation to form the ceiling finishes of the museums' interior gallery spaces. Steven Holl Architects, the Cité de L'Océan et du Surf Museum (Biarritz, France) 2011.
Courtesy of Steven Holl Architects.

the preformed bent metal framing, onto which layers of gypsum and then plaster was applied, mirroring the shape of the structure above (Figure 5.35).

After this mock-up, research was done into another ceiling product that had been used in other Steven Holl buildings which could be applied directly to the suspended framing and then sprayed with acoustical plaster and troweled without requiring the extra layer of gypsum board as a substrate. This product eliminated the extra layer of gypsum across the entire ceiling of the project, representing significant reductions in cost and labor.

ORCHESTRATING RANDOMNESS

Having exhaustively explored the arrangements of the Portuguese paving patterns for the top deck in the previous sequence of mock-ups, the determination had been made to arrange the stones in a random array. As the final building mock-up was constructed, the pavers were installed along the warped roof surface in a random orientation, often seeming to radiate into offsetting concentric bends.

The strategy for randomly misaligning the paving stones had been to allow the pattern to absorb inconsistencies in the field and in the quality of labor. Because the placement of blocks was specified as random, individual areas of randomness would begin to clash with other areas of randomness, forming unwanted boundaries between regions. This could be seen in the mock-up as the horizontal surface began to warp into a vertical orientation (Figure 5.36).

As a result of the random orientation, it was difficult to specify why some areas were acceptable and others not. This was ultimately a function of scale, as the dimensions

Figure 5.36
Installation of the Portuguese pavers in the final mock-up. Steven Holl Architects, the Cité de L'Océan et du Surf Museum (Biarritz, France) 2011.

Courtesy of Steven Holl Architects.

of the plaza were so immense that the randomness which looked so promising within a cropped frame ultimately lacked repeatability and metrics for quality assurance over such large dimensions.

As a result, a final revision was made to arrange the pavers into aligned rows, in order to provide a reference of tolerances for acceptable workmanship within the installation. The prescribed randomness of the small scale frame became unmanageable at the scale of the entire plaza, marking an interesting boundary condition in the work of Steven Holl Architects. While the often unpredictable vicissitudes of process and material introduce an aspect of chance into the textures and forms of Steven Holl's buildings, there is a line beyond which randomness is unacceptable and no longer interesting. The chance operations must operate within a consistent framework.

In the final mock-up, half of the pavers can be seen being removed and subsequently reinstalled into aligned courses. Steven Holl revisited the site and approved the new arrangement of pavers with repetitive courses, which would assure a consistent degree of quality (Figure 5.37). After

Figure 5.37 A photo of the mock-up, showing a final revision and change of the paver patterns as a section is removed and replaced with aligned paver coursing. Steven Holl Architects, the Cité de L'Océan et du Surf Museum (Biarritz, France) 2011.
Courtesy of Steven Holl Architects.

Figure 5.38 The final mock-up being inspected after some time, with grass visibly grown in between the pavers, and glass handrail details installed. Steven Holl Architects, the Cité de L'Océan et du Surf Museum (Biarritz, France) 2011.
Courtesy of Steven Holl Architects.

exhaustive effort and experimentation, this simple alignment of blocks was decided upon, but only after first seeing it built, allowing the construction at various scales to influence its final form (Figures 5.4 and 5.38).

BUILDING UNCERTAINTY

A unique tension occurs in the building between the tangibility of material forms and the tensions of the detailed impressions. The contractors for the Biarritz Museum were valued for their experience in high-quality concrete work. Yet, the architect resisted a sterile oversimplification of the project, embedding randomness and uncertainty into the built configuration of form.

By engaging the building through a finer grain scale, the tensions of the details were slowly coaxed out collaboratively through mock-ups. Throughout the process of translating drawings into material building, certain typical decisions were accepted, while others were subtly transformed. What we see in this sequence of mock-ups is perhaps a more general approach to design, representing a strategy for mocking-up and engaging the material with an ambition for the small scale details to provoke larger scale tensions.

Steven Holl's buildings do not just make statements, they ask questions; they do this by extending the boundaries of the design phase into the construction phase, increasing the overlaps ultimately between drawing and building.

As is stated in Steven Holl's strange meditation on the implication of the material instead of the actuality, there is as a persistent focus in his work on the role of the material, which is beyond the technical. This statement no doubt seems contradictory, but what we see in the progression of the projects presented here is a consistent reliance on the physical feedback of materials. From the watercolor sketch itself to the use of actual materials and patinas in his representational approach. What can be seen is a strange tension of certainty, seemingly concrete and tangible because the representational palette is not virtual nor speculative, but actual and physical.

In the case of Biarritz, we can see a thematic rejection of oversimplification and adherence to the fluid roles of randomness in process, no doubt in support of the project's relationship to the water.

The examples highlighted here combine to paint a picture of the Cité de L'Océan et du Surf Museum as a peculiar case of attempting to negotiate several scales of resolution in relation to one another. What is most interesting about the project is not simply the shape of the concave rooftop, but of the destabilizing pressures that this large scale gesture places on the finer scale orchestration of detailing.

While the larger scale configurations of space are singular in their legibility from the urban scale, the various micro-configurations of material study and detail coalesce to not only support the larger geometric narrative but also conspire to produce various readings of space; defining a zone between certainties, standing on what is simultaneously the roof and ground, and seemingly both firm and fluid.

There is something intuitive about examining the design as a final building, but there is perhaps something more revealing about examining the process of arrival.

For Steven Holl Architects, mock-ups seem to provide the opportunity to operate between the statement and the question.

This duality represents the impression of randomness, from the random arrangements of the OSB wood fragments in the concrete form liners to uncertain geometries of space. These swells reveal the interaction of scales, just as Steven Holl uses material textures to reveal something unexpected about the behavior of light and space.

It is logical that for someone who sketches differently, not with crisp lines but with the preferred interactions of pigment, water, and paper, that other more dynamic forms of representation would be considered. Holl breaks down what was presumed singular into new subdivisions, only to recombine these platonic parts into elucidated interactions. It is these massive interactions which rethink old approaches by mocking the divide between drawing and building, providing an architecture based on the mysteries of mass through mock-ups and the materials of representation.

Notes

1. Sanford Kwinter, "PLENUM," in *Steven Holl – Color Light Time*, eds. Steven Holl and Lars Muller, (Zurich: Lars Muller Publishers, 2012), 66.
2. Steven Holl (architect, Steven Holl Architects), in discussion with the author, December 13, 2016.
3. Steven Holl, "Notes on Weight and Weightlessness," In *Solid States: Concrete in Transition*, ed. Michael Bell and Craig Buckley (New York: Princeton Architectural Press, 2010), 86.
4. Steven Holl (architect, Steven Holl Architects), in discussion with the author, December 13, 2016.
5. Steven Holl (architect, Steven Holl Architects), in discussion with the author, December 13, 2016.
6. Steven Holl (architect, Steven Holl Architects), in discussion with the author, December 13, 2016.
7. Steven Holl (architect, Steven Holl Architects), in discussion with the author, December 13, 2016.

6 Acclimated Transformations: The Surprising Materialities of the Harvard Art Museums and its Surroundings

Renzo Piano Building Workshop, Genoa, Italy
Harvard Art Museums Renovation and Expansion, Cambridge, MA, USA

Figure 6.1 The diverse material massing of the new Harvard Art Museums renovation and expansion, brick, glass, and wood, complementing the concrete of the Carpenter Center in the foreground. RPBW, the Harvard Art Museums renovation and expansion (Cambridge, MA, USA) 2014.
Courtesy of RPBW, photo Nic Lehoux.

HARVARD ART MUSEUMS RENOVATION AND EXPANSION

The recent renovation of Harvard University's three art museums, the Fogg, the Busch-Reisinger, and the Arthur M. Sackler, combined three separate museums into a new cohesive whole. The new building design by the Renzo Piano Building Workshop consolidated the three existing museums under one roof, now named the Harvard Art Museums. The design included a combination of demolition and restoration of the existing 1920s Georgian revival building. The existing building houses the Fogg, with the construction of a new extension along the east side of the site fronting Prescott Street. This new hovering extension which sits adjacent to the restored building is connected above by an inhabitable sloping glazed roof, which houses a conservation lab and a study center.

Through a dynamic combination of the previously separate buildings into a new singular volume, an unusual building is defined, one composed of three distinct regions of material.

When viewed together, the restored brick masonry building of the Fogg seems to be sliced off at one end where it joins a curious wood-clad volume that sits lower. Despite the combination of new and old, there is a noticeable lack of effort to align the rooflines of both volumes, leaving a recognizable change in volumetric reading. It is on top of this misalignment where the third volume is stacked: an asymmetric glass pyramid that stitches the two volumes back together by negotiating solar angles and geometric differences between the new and the old.

The massing of this building can be distilled into three material parts: brick masonry, wood, and glass, and instead of static boundaries between the three volumes, they exist dynamically in relation to one another. These three materials distinguish the three institutions merged within the volumes of the building. They also reference a fourth institution and its defining materiality across the street: Le Corbusier's iconic Carpenter Center for the Visual Arts, singularly constructed of concrete (Figure 6.1).

Piano's new addition acknowledges these identities of new and old by establishing new material definitions. First, the brickwork of the existing building was restored. Second, glass was used in the conservation lab, which allows light to permeate from above. And third, the new extension was cladded with wood, presenting a softer front to the street.

This selection of wood articulates a clear organizational strategy for the museums, dramatically differentiating the exterior of the new addition from both the existing brick building as well as the cast in place Carpenter Center across the street. These differences of material constitution form a repetitive pattern, suggesting new connections. This pattern of difference casts the disparate material parts into more certain relationships, which seem to bridge across the street, suggesting the volumes of the Harvard Art Museums as consistent varieties that must be considered in relation to the physically disconnected Carpenter Center.

This use of wood not only differentiates the new addition from the past, but also addresses the vernacular of the surrounding residential building fabric, which utilizes wooden clapboard siding as an exterior treatment. This organic exterior is unusual for an institutional building, but serves to negotiate a softer relationship between the impermeable hard boundaries of the institutions and the more temporary improvisational stature of residential buildings. While the original entrance to the museums is accessed through the university campus, this wooden extension provides a new entrance, opening the museum to the local community across the street and acknowledging this connection by presenting a peculiar surface which both absorbs and distinguishes itself from its surroundings.

The design of the Museum's wooden façade required a design more ambitious than the typical clapboard siding of residential construction. A variety of wood species, lumber sizes, and sectional profiles were explored to serve as the exterior cladding. Because wood is subject to more active distortions than other inorganic materials such as brick and concrete, many full-scale mock-ups were conducted to evaluate the design of various lapping profile shapes and the consequences of their forms in relationship to the behavior of wood itself. Using a less naturally durable material like wood seems counterintuitive for a museum intended to last much longer than most modern residential construction.

It seems that this decision would not be possible if made later in the design process, rather this idea must be established and integrated into the design early on and with the capacity to deepen the conceptual relationships of the project.

Very early in the design process, RPBW made the decision to use wood for the construction of this new addition. Consistently throughout their work, their approach to any given project involves generating design concepts that simultaneously consider the project from a variety of scales. Instead of only considering issues of site, massing, context, and program at the macro scale, from a very early stage of design, they connect with an idea about material and detail at the micro-scale. This combination of micro and macro within their approach prevents the large scale thinking of planning and program from becoming disconnected from the smaller scale considerations of detail and experimentation with materials.

Decisions are made quite early in the project, and while the larger-scale massing of the project is defined, so is the smaller scale design of details. These early design decisions made at opposite scales are resolved later, but they produce tensions that inform the evolution of the design.

For the design of the Harvard Art Museums building, RPBW considered wooden construction materials at the earliest stages. RPBW has a woodshop and a courtyard in their offices in Genoa, Italy, where they build representational models of their buildings in unique ways. The models they build in their woodshop are not only small scale presentation models but also small pieces of the building at a 1:1 scale. These full-scale design studies exist in between models and mock-ups, constructed of the actual materials being considered, jumpstarting considerations of materials detailed interactions with form.

In order to achieve a building with such unusual depth of materiality, the architects forged deep relationships with wood and its behavior initially through empirical research by physically mocking up their designs at full scale, and later through the consultation of outside experts. These deep considerations with materials began early in the career of Renzo Piano, and mark a consistent engagement with materials in practice which would continue throughout. Using wood for the construction of a museum is unusual, but it is not for Renzo Piano. He has already executed this surprising detail in his career in 1981, in the design of The Menil Collection building in Houston.

THE MENIL COLLECTION (1981–1986)

Much like the new building for the Harvard Art Museums renovation, The Menil Collection building in Houston, Texas, was similarly wrapped in planks of cypress wood and illuminated from above through a skylight roof. The exterior of The Menil Collection building was detailed with a wooden clapboard exterior. While the interior

Figure 6.2
Exterior of The Menil Collection building in Houston wrapped in wooden clapboard siding. RPBW, The Menil Collection (Houston, TX, USA) 1987.
Courtesy of Fondazione Renzo Piano, photo Hickey & Robertson Photography.

gallery spaces of the Menil were naturally illuminated and open uninterrupted spaces, the exterior of the building itself sat among many smaller residential-scale buildings. The Menil Foundation already owned several adjacent bungalow buildings, and Piano conceptualized the building as a type of "Village Museum," connected to its context.[1] Through the unique material treatment on its exterior, the perception of a building disconnected from its surroundings because of its size was transformed into something more consistent and connected to its context through its material (Figure 6.2).

But even beyond the surprising use of wood for the exterior of The Menil Collection building, there exists a deep integration of surprising materiality throughout the design. This deep consideration of new materials and forms emerges from a process of research into the subtle differences of material tendencies and performance, which is not always visibly apparent. In the gallery space, the skylight-canopy system is composed of two parts: a three-dimensional, ductile iron spaceframe, and a system of ferro-cement light diffusing leaves. The story of the research into the use of these unusual and surprising materials began prior to the museum's construction in 1980 when Renzo Piano was working on an industrial design project for Fiat.

Ductile Iron

The Fiat VSS project was an experimental lightweight car prototype built with a load-bearing frame onto which more lightweight panels were attached.[2] For the VSS project, a material called ductile iron was explored for the structural chassis of the car. The material could be cast into sculptural forms, but unlike cast iron it possessed considerably higher tensile strength.

Figure 6.3
Ductile iron members being tested for fit. RPBW, The Menil Collection (Houston, TX, USA) 1987.

Courtesy of Fondazione Renzo Piano, copyright © Gianni Berengo Gardin.

Because one of the central programmatic requirements of The Menil Collection was for the art to be displayed in natural light, Piano developed a glazed spaceframe roof truss system using this same material.

The truss was designed as a series of bolted members, each individually cast. This way they could be uniquely designed to possess characteristics specific to their fabrication, such as complex sculptural features instead of the rational extrusions of steel. The individual triangular elements were bolted together to produce a spanning element more closely resembling something natural and organic, like bone, which resulted from this unique combination of material and manufacturing process (Figures 6.4 and 6.3).

Figure 6.4
Ductile iron members assembled to form a three-dimensional truss without a bottom chord. RPBW, The Menil Collection (Houston, TX, USA) 1987.

Courtesy of Fondazione Renzo Piano, photo Shunji Ishida.

Like in the VSS project in which lighter weight panels were mounted to a structural frame light, diffusing "leaves" were designed to be mounted to the ductile iron spaceframe truss for the Menil Collection skylight. Renzo Piano collaborated with the engineer Peter Rice, and together shared the ambition to eliminate redundancy by designing the light diffusing leaves as an integral part of the structural roof truss system.[3]

Ferro-Cement

Piano and Rice were both admirers of Pier Luigi Nervi, who advanced the applications of a material called ferro-cement, a very compact practically flexible composite of steel and cement. Piano had recently designed and built for himself a yacht utilizing this material.

These leaves were constructed at a factory in Britain that typically manufactured boat hulls from this material. The leaves were manufactured by plastering into a mold, with the top and back sides of the leaves taking their finish from the mold itself, while the front and bottom of each leaf were trowel finished by hand (Figure 6.5).[4] After the cast leaves were removed from the molds, the ductile iron spaceframe elements were tested for accuracy and fit (Figures 6.6 and 6.7).

Figure 6.5
Ferro-cement leaf still in its mold being trowel finished by hand. RPBW, The Menil Collection (Houston, TX, USA) 1987.

Courtesy of Fondazione Renzo Piano, © Gianni Berengo Gardin.

Figure 6.6
Ferro-cement leaf prototype in a shipbuilding facility whose typical products are the ferro-cement boat hulls visible in the background. RPBW, The Menil Collection (Houston, TX, USA) 1987.

Courtesy of Fondazione Renzo Piano, photo Shunji Ishida.

Figure 6.7 Hoisted mock-up demonstrating the spanning ability of the ferro-cement leaf acting as the bottom chord for the ductile iron three-dimensional space frame. RPBW, The Menil Collection (Houston, TX, USA) 1987.

Courtesy of Fondazione Renzo Piano.

In the boat building factory, the ductile iron elements were attached to a test leaf and hoisted above to demonstrate the structural ability of the leaf itself, acting as the bottom chord of the upper space frame truss. These separate elements function cohesively to interact with light while retaining their inherently structural integrity.

Original design concepts for the leaf were far thinner, serving primarily as diagonal bracing for the truss. However, after much testing and development, utilizing models for solar and structural analysis, Piano increased both the leaves' size, and thickness. This increase allowed more precise levels of natural light to permeate into the exhibition spaces below, but also required more complexity to accommodate the structural response to the design evolution.[5]

Many study models and mock-up prototypes were constructed in order to predict the precise interaction of the ferro-cement leaf with Houston's particular solar environment. These many studies evolved the form of the leaf over time, in search of an even light that reflected the natural lighting outside the building. The design of the leaf element reflected some light with a horizontal cap, limiting the amount of indirect light to permeate through to the gallery spaces below.

Many study models were constructed and observed on-site through a variety of weather conditions. This was done to measure the amount of light that would permeate into the gallery spaces over time. Study models of the skylight of leaves were built on top of an interactive solar jig to simulate the various lighting conditions specific to Houston. Various positions of the jig displayed the range of lighting conditions that would occur, allowing the form of the leaves to be fine-tuned to respond to these various conditions (Figure 6.8).

Through the development of forms in relationship to their particular materiality, we see these unique design elements in the construction of The Menil Collection. Additionally, it seems the interactions between the forms and their materials are allowed the appropriate time to adapt to the unique conditions on-site in Houston.

Figure 6.8 A solar study model constructed of an interactive solar jig that orients a study model to various solar exposures, demonstrating at small scale the real amounts of light to permeate the spaces. RPBW, The Menil Collection (Houston, TX, USA) 1987.
Courtesy of Fondazione Renzo Piano, photo Shunji Ishida.

These adaptations occur both in terms of structural forms and performance, as well as the particular light and context of the project in relation to the unusual particularity of the material selections. The design decisions made early in the project allowed the necessary time for the elements and forms to acclimate, shrinking and swelling to the various influences of the project more generally

DESIGNING WITH MOCK-UPS

RPBW consistently develops unique sets of design details on a small scale, which correspond to larger conceptual ideas for the project. Building with wood presents a unique set of concerns. Because wood is an organic material, it is subject to bio-deterioration once it is harvested. Wood is the preserved tissue from a living organism, and each species of tree produces a tissue that uniquely responds to various environments based on its chemical constituents. All materials will degrade: steel oxidizes, concrete spalls and develops stress cracks, but wood presents the unique challenge of mitigating the environmental factors that act to physically transform it through shrinking and swelling, geometric distortions, and ultimately decomposing. This decomposition is not internal, but imposed from the outside, only occurring if the wood is attacked by fungi or insects. In addition to structural durability, appearance is also less predictable, as wood not only distorts, deteriorates and develops, warps, and checks, but also discolors and patinas over time. This patina is a function of the wood and its exposure to precipitation, ultra-violet light, and wind-blown debris. Wood is like a canvas that attracts and receives the hidden micro-processes of the environment, displaying evidence of their impact through its more noticeable and significant reactions.

Acclimated Transformations

Figure 6.9 First wooden mock-up built in the courtyard of RPBW office in Genoa, showing spacing of wooden boards and the roughness of the provisional lumber initially used before specifying a particular species of wood. RPBW, the Harvard Art Museums renovation and expansion (Cambridge, MA, USA) 2014.
Courtesy of RPBW, photo Stefano Goldberg – Publifoto.

Ordinarily, museums and institutions are built from steel and stone, the type of materiality associated with memorials and cemeteries, suggesting permanence and eternity. Wood is predictably unpredictable. It is known to distort and change from the state of its initial milling. Predictability is highly contingent on the species of tree and the way in which the wood is processed. These anticipated transformations are considerations that must be designed. To use wood on the exterior of the Harvard Art Museums presented unique challenges specific to the typical behavior of wood. Challenges that the architects anticipated and tested through the execution of many full-scale material mock-ups.

First Mock-Ups: Sketching with Full Scale Components

In the courtyard of their workshop, the team constructed the first detail mock-ups that were built using a species of wood that was available to them in Genoa, Italy. Not much attention was paid to the quality of the wood initially. These first mock-ups were used to quickly visualize the scale, material quality of details, and confirm initial design decisions (Figures 6.9 and 6.10). In these first mock-ups the wood appeared faded and split. However, the team was not concerned because this early form of mock-up was really a rough sketch (Figure 6.10).

The first two mock-ups were constructed in-house, not for presentation to the client, but for the design team to make decisions about schematic design. Much of this design thinking emerges from the lessons from the Tjibaou Cultural

179

Center building in New Caledonia, in which RPBW designed a wooden, louvered rain screen, which created natural heating and cooling through natural airflow dictated by the spacing of the wood slats. These three original mock-ups can be seen as articulating a simple mitered corner condition and variations in vertical spacing. The design of these mock-ups was generic but productive, materializing simple ideas from past projects and evaluating them for a new context. Certain problems became apparent, particularly the mitered corner condition, because as the wood moved, the tight consistency of the corner gap between boards would begin to vary and misalign over time (Figure 6.9). The initial observations of this detail were recorded in this first mock-up and resolved over the course of subsequent mock-ups.

Dynamic Board Mock-Up

A second sequence of mock-ups captures new qualities of the design through a different framework. This sequence builds upon the first mock-up's continuous drip edge, developing the detail of the profile into a more dynamic transformation. Unlike typical siding or cladding constructed of ship-lapped flat board, on one end of these new profiles, the boards are stacked with a square profile which transforms into a thinner diagonal at the other end that overlaps the board below. Not only do the profiles transform, but Piano departs from the thin, mitered corner condition of the first mock-up. Here, he constructs a new detail where the boards transform into square profiles at their ends, held back from each other revealing a more massive and dimensionally stable corner.

Figure 6.10 Early wooden mock-up built in the RPBW office in Genoa, showing a tight mitered corner condition. RPBW, the Harvard Art Museums renovation and expansion (Cambridge, MA, USA) 2014.
Courtesy of RPBW, photo David Lewis.

This corner detail acknowledges that the thinner diagonal mitered joint would be less stable both as a result of cutting the wood on a bias as well as thinning it to a point. The square ends are anticipated to better maintain position, but Piano also reintroduces the drip edge sloping profile at the other end, where the wood flares out and overlapped above the board below.

By introducing a transformation into each board, two conditions are merged into one profile, providing stability at the corners while articulating thinness and texture at the other end. The profile of each member appears to twist along its length, transforming from a flush stack of square profile at the corners, to a jagged lapped arrangement at the opposite ends. This transformation animates each piece of wood and creates a sense of motion. By twisting, Piano's design seems to anticipate and co-opt the ways wood will naturally warp, neutralizing that disturbance by suggesting it from the beginning.

The corner of the mock-up illustrates how the square ends stack flush and as they transform away from that corner flare out into a system of overlaps. What is apparent from the corner view is that the individual pieces are not physically interlocking, as each piece of wood remains detached from the others. From an engineering standpoint, the wood profiles are considered "*boundary-free*,"[6] meaning they are free from contact with the others and as a result un-restricted in movement, which could otherwise cause their individual distortions to compound and build up along the height of the building. This boundary-free configuration maintains the position of each piece, and additionally allows for airflow on all surfaces of the board, thereby enhancing drying when the wood becomes wet.

Subtly, they are only attached to the supporting frame behind with screws, punched through extruded aluminum. This gap between wooden members allows each piece to behave independently without disturbing its neighbor. The lack of contact creates a tectonic tension in this detail, between permanence and instability via both the material choice and the free-floating end condition.

The timing of this mock-up is noteworthy, occurring between the first set of internal material sketches, and a third set of presentation mock-ups. This corner profile mock-up was constructed in January, well in advance of the first presentation to the client scheduled for September of that year. While the initial mock-up studies were constructed internally, these subsequent mock-ups were fabricated with help from outside the office to achieve the more complex geometric profiles via a computer numerical controlled (CNC) milling process (Figures 6.11 and 6.12).

The configuration of this design is surprisingly close to the final outcome of the cladding in the final constructed building. This mock-up is constructed of Douglas-fir, which is a typical selection for wood, chosen before more extensive species research.

Figure 6.11
Transformations along the length of each board from a square end to a drip edge profile, RPBW, the Harvard Art Museums renovation and expansion (Cambridge, MA, USA) 2014.

Courtesy of RPBW, photo Stefano Goldberg – Publifoto.

Figure 6.12
Transformations along the length of each board and the square profiled corner reveal. A single board can be seen missing from the center of the stack, revealing the transformed void between boards. RPBW, the Harvard Art Museums renovation and expansion (Cambridge, MA, USA) 2014.
Courtesy of RPBW, photo Stefano Goldberg – Pubufoto.

Presentation Mock-Ups

A third series of mock-ups were constructed based on these isolated and conceptual material details. These subsequent mock-ups further explored the material details by integrating them with the design development of the project. This new set of mock-ups experimented with alternate arrangements of the wooden cladding by varying the spacing, dimensions of the boards, and other pattern details to visualize physically and present to the client. These mock-ups included the typical and basic integration of handrails and glass, exhibiting a delicate balance between revealing enough to provide convincing proof of concept for the unique material selection without showing too much of the building. Taken out of context, the mock-ups are difficult to understand as they would exist in their final configuration because they are physically full of potential but not yet finalized. These mock-ups function as a kind of compelling evidence, revealing essential details without negatively constraining the ability to acclimate and influence the design itself.

In total, six separate mock-ups were constructed during the design development phase. Each of these design development mock-ups was constructed with higher qualities of materials and finish. While constructed as presentation mock-ups to the client, they were also intended to be observed for their tendencies to slowly acclimate over time (Figure 6.13 and 6.14).

The initial mock-up in this series was constructed as a simple ladder configuration, with rectangular profiled boards stacked vertically and flush, revealing a larger vertical spacing between the more massive boards. Through observation of this initial study, the team became concerned about water sitting on the deeper horizontal tops

Figure 6.13
A series of presentation mock-ups in the courtyard of the RPBW office in Genoa, Italy. RPBW, the Harvard Art Museums renovation and expansion (Cambridge, MA, USA) 2014.

Courtesy of RPBW, photo Stefano Goldberg – Pubufoto.

of each member. The adjacent mock-up was constructed with a sloped profile and an outward-facing drip edge for contrast (Figure 6.14). In this alternate arrangement, the sectional profiles become thinner and lap over one another. The overlapping is more complex than is typical and the profiles can be seen notched to receive the stacked member below, with a drip edge that seems malleable as it folds down shielding the gap from rain and allowing it to drain away.

The unique sectional profile, which not only laps over the lower cladding member, is also notched out and stacked behind, preventing water infiltration through the cladding. What appears to be flat wooden slats when viewed in elevation are revealed to be much more integrative from the edge.

Figure 6.14
Inspecting the thin overlapping drip edge profile with more robust rectangular sections behind. RPBW, the Harvard Art Museums renovation and expansion (Cambridge, MA, USA) 2014.

Courtesy of RPBW, photo Stefano Goldberg – Pubufoto.

The first three mock-ups in this series share a useful simplicity ideal to demonstrate the concerns of each profile independently. They are simply stacked, revealing a static repetitive condition resulting from different types of uniform boards. In the fourth wooden mock-up of this series, the individual cladding members are transformed, combining the conditions of the three previous mock-ups into one, blurring identities into a single hybrid.

Perhaps not incidentally, this small scale arrangement

Figure 6.15 One of the mock-ups constructed above the ground to simulate the angle of view when constructed on-site. RPBW, the Harvard Art Museums renovation and expansion (Cambridge, MA, USA) 2014.
Courtesy of RPBW, photo Stefano Goldberg – Pubufoto.

of details reflects the bridging transition between the Fogg, the Busch-Reisinger, and the Arthur M. Sackler at a larger scale.

Viewed as a set of mock-ups, the variety of conditions can be seen as a collective sequence; initially a flush stacked cladding, followed by the jagged, thinner lapped cladding, followed then by a third and again by a fourth which combines the independent qualities of all three previous mock-ups.

This fourth mock-up is built elevated above the ground and with slightly larger proportions. The design captures a corner condition and presents a new possible configuration of elements unique from what we had previously seen. The individual cladding members can be seen to warp from the jagged lapped edge profiles at the far ends to square profiles, which are finger-jointed together at the corners in an alternating sequence of stacking. Each layer of wood alternates as one board extends past the end of the other, exposing only one end profile at a time, like a typical interlocking finger joint. This fourth mock-up elevates the cladding to replicate the perspective from street level, at the same upward angle from which the addition to the Harvard Art Museums building will be viewed, above Prescott Street (Figure 6.15).

In later developments of these details, the interlocking finger joints are removed, as well as the mitered corner condition of the lapped edge, in favor of the revealed square profile corners, which are more dimensionally stable.

Acclimated Transformations

Figure 6.16 Renzo Piano presents the mock-ups in sequence, as a progression of design ideas constructed of their intended material, wood. RPBW, the Harvard Art Museums renovation and expansion (Cambridge, MA, USA) 2014.
Courtesy of RPBW, photo Stefano Goldberg – Pubufoto.

Integrative Mock-Up

The design team built a final visual mock-up in the courtyard at the office of the Renzo Piano Building Workshop in Genoa. This final mock-up defined the final forms and dimensions sizes of the various parts, including for the various cladding members. The forms of the members were defined in three-dimensions and digitally fabricated utilizing a computer numerical controlled milling machine (6.17).

The design utilized steel members on the surface of the building to support a cantilevered portion of the building, called the Winter Garden. As the design of the building neared its final stage and the rest of the building was defined, this final mock-up studied how the wood cladding would be attached and detailed around the large steel members (Figure 6.16). All of the prior mock-ups had been constructed in isolation, but in this mock-up the small scale thinking can be seen to interact with the type of detailing which structures the larger scale massing of the building. Here is where we see RPBW's simultaneous considerations of micro and macro coming together for the first time.

Natural Reconsiderations for Wood

Out of experience from past projects, including The Menil Collection and the Tjibaou Cultural Center, Renzo Piano was familiar enough with wood to know that deeper

Figure 6.17 Integration of complex wooden boards with steel structural elements, RPBW, the Harvard Art Museums renovation and expansion (Cambridge, MA, USA) 2014.

Courtesy of RPBW.

considerations were necessary to plan for its long-term use. The architects hired a wood scientist as a consultant to the project to help navigate and predict the unexpected behaviors of wood beyond the formal shapes they had designed.

Ron Anthony's expertise with wood developed from his extensive experience in historic preservation and forensic analysis of wood structures as a scientist. In a subtle twist, while typically Anthony's experience examining historic wooden buildings requires him to look back in time forensically, here he is asked to look into the future. Many of the buildings he has examined are centuries old, and while some have endured remarkably well, some have not; based on what he has seen, he is in a unique position to advise on how to best avoid long-term problems.

Anthony guides conversations about wood focused on the short term and long-term tendencies about the intended design of the wood, and how different wood species will perform over time. As with most materials, the goal is for the wood to require as little maintenance as possible. Because the client and the architect have seen wood that warps and deteriorates in many normal applications, their initial questions to Anthony typically center on how to avoid such issues without requiring excess maintenance.

The introduction of wood into the design not only creates certain formal and material identities, but also provokes a unique conceptual approach. In conversations with the architects and the clients, Anthony continually emphasizes the fact that wood is a natural material, and no matter how careful you are in specifying, fabricating, and installing, wood will always exhibit some of that natural behavior.

Instead of focusing on preventing the wood from misbehaving, an alternate conceptual approach to the material is required, which creates a new awareness to change expectations. Anthony continually emphasizes that the material will not appear the way it does when it is installed on day one, and depending on the species of tree it can change

Acclimated Transformations

characteristics completely. Wood is a snapshot in time of a material in a constant state of change, and its changing qualities must be expected and negotiated from the beginning.

To address these expectations, a new set of questions about the design and role of the material are more subtly considered, questions that provide material feedback, animating static lines with material tendencies. Anthony approaches projects by asking for reconsiderations of absoluteness. "Why don't you want it to do this?" "If it does warp, how much can it move?" "Can it move one-sixteenth, one-eighth of an inch, or one-quarter of an inch?"[7] The answers to these types of questions guide the species selection and also revisions of the architectural details before finally leading to the design of mock-ups to test these relationships.

Performative Material Mock-Up: Wood Species Test

On-site, in Cambridge, Massachusetts, the team built a full-scale mock-up, clad and finished in the intended size and shape of wood, and left exposed to the elements to observe how the wood weathered on-site over time. This process helped the architects and wood consultant to determine how to most effectively seal and finish the wood in order to produce long-term durability. It also helped them to anticipate problems and make any last-minute adjustments to the design of the wood members. Various species of wood were considered and evaluated for their most appropriate response to the combination of Boston's climate and the specific forms of the cladding system developed by the architect (Figure 6.18).

Figure 6.18 Site mock-ups constructed near the site of the building, to observe that influence of the local environment on the wood. RPBW, the Harvard Art Museums renovation and expansion (Cambridge, MA, USA) 2014. Courtesy of RPBW.

This mock-up allowed the team to observe the tendencies for the wood cladding to weather over the course of a year. Observations revealed how it would develop checks or splits. "Checking" is a separation between the fibers that develop on the surface of the wood, while "splitting" is a separation parallel to the fibers completely through the thickness of the board. These observations guided the specification process for treating the wood, and included coating the ends to avoid splitting once installed.

Movement

Wood warps in a variety of movements, including twisting, cupping, crooking, and bowing. In order to observe the movement of the individual boards in the mock-ups, the architects placed targets on the wood and then photographed the targets over time to observe how the wood was changing shape or position relative to the adjacent boards.

Over time, the spacing between horizontal members was becoming inconsistent. When first installed, the horizontal members were exactly one-quarter of an inch, but after some time, some spaces increased to 9/16ths of an inch. These observations allowed the team to consider the causes of the movements which were monitored and from this, the team established a protocol to measure changes. This protocol led to essential new information, information that was invaluable to a further nuanced façade design (Figure 6.19).

The mock-up provided the opportunity to limit the potential for the cladding to develop gaps, while also helping the contractor to avoid errors once installing the cladding on the actual building.

While observing this mock-up for weathering, the team noticed that a steel beam above the cladding allowed water to drain down the face of the wood, discoloring the wood with iron-stained water. This observation led the design team to modify the position of the beam at the edge, recessing it several inches at the top.

Building this last, fully realized mock-up helped the design team to better understand the assembly process and the interaction between different areas of assembly. Visible within this mock-up is a range of tolerances that better define what is acceptable to the architects, and also what realistic expectations for the material are.

Figure 6.19 The mock-up saturated with rainwater, and the gaps between boards beginning to visibly shift. RPBW, the Harvard Art Museums renovation and expansion (Cambridge, MA, USA) 2014.
Courtesy of RPBW.

SLOWLY ACCLIMATED

Wood is a hygroscopic material, meaning that like a sponge, it is constantly taking in and releasing moisture, primarily as humidity. Living trees and fresh-cut lumber may contain enough water to account for more than 100% of the weight of the wood fibers. This moisture results in changes in the dimensions of the wood. As moisture is released, wood shrinks, and as moisture is absorbed, wood swells. When these actions occur at different rates, they can cause a variety of significant warping and distortions.

To begin to compensate for some of these effects, the team ordered the Alaskan Yellow Cedar used for the Harvard Art Museums a full two years in advance of construction. The wood was harvested in British Columbia, kiln-dried to remove much of the free water from the fresh-cut lumber, monitored for defects, and only then shipped to the wood fabricators in Massachusetts.

The fabricators stored the rough-cut pieces of lumber, each of which was about 3 and a half inches by 5 and a half inches in section. These individual pieces of Alaskan Yellow Cedar were stacked in the shop with wooden spacers called "stickers" to allow air circulation around each piece of wood in the stack.

Exposed to the relative humidity of the same environment as the building site, this stack of boards slowly dried, allowing it to acclimate to its new environment for over a year. After a year, the boards were rough milled using a saw to begin to give each piece its approximate final shape. These rough sawn pieces were then individually milled, and then re-stickered and allowed to acclimate for several more months, before ultimately being CNC milled into their final forms.

The individual pieces were then re-stickered a third time and allowed to further acclimate before being shipped to the site. The idea was that if a piece made it through all these steps but then began to twist or check after this final step, they could cull that outlier.

Each subsequent step of milling introduced new opportunities for the wood to distort. As the deeper cuts penetrate into the core of the wood, the deeper pockets of moisture can rapidly escape from the wood, potentially causing twisting or other distortions. This procedure was specified in the quality control measures provided by the wood consultant. At each step, the wood was verified for moisture content to be sure it was neither too wet nor too dry.

Equilibrium Moisture Content

The goal was to install the wood with the closest moisture content to the environmental conditions on-site as possible, a term called Equilibrium Moisture Content. Over the course of the two years of handling and acclimating the wood, the moisture content was monitored to be sure it was never too far off from where the wood "wanted to be" once installed on the site. This required measuring the amount of moisture in the wood with a hygrometer, which was inserted into the back face of each piece of lumber to a specified depth. The team was interested in what was happening in the core of the wood, because that is what determines the long-term behavior of the wood.

The quality control specifications included measuring moisture at a given depth below the surface, and from at least 12 inches from the ends, to get something truly representative of the moisture content of the pieces.

Sacrificial Coatings: Approximating Future States

While the early mock-ups built in Genoa provided a material visualization of the design, considerations of durability and specific materiality were delayed until later in the project. To help decide how to finish and preserve the wood, three separate areas of the newly constructed site mock-up were treated in unique ways. One portion was treated with a very light coat of wood stain, with another receiving a heavy coat of stain, followed by a portion of the mock-up treated with multiple layers of stain, which each dried before reapplying. Each treatment option provided different degrees of protection, but also different visual consequences, as the lighter stains allowed the texture of the grain to show through the coating, while the heavier treatments masked the figure of the wood grain like paint. The lightly stained wood gradually changed colors and the design team became concerned that if each piece changed colors independently, then the final overall appearance would be unpredictable. Piano's primary concern was that the building would appear bright and new when first built, but then appear faded and weathered.

When the initial site mock-ups were constructed in Cambridge, the actual wood had not yet been decided upon; in fact, only as a result of observing the weathering effects of this placeholder species was it possible to make a more suitable selection, one better able to resist the types of weathering observed in the mock-up. The final species of wood selected was Alaskan Yellow Cedar, which, when fresh cut, as the name implies, has a type of warm yellowish tone. After observing the weathering of the wood over time, the design team selected a light stain which when applied gave the wood a light gray color. This color matched the tone that they observed in the wood as it naturally weathered over time.

This was a strategic decision, with the coating intended to be a sacrificial stain, so that when the stain wears off the wood will naturally weather to a very similar color and appear unchanged. By pre-staining the wood and "graying" it from the beginning, the material would maintain a consistent appearance, while undergoing substantial transformation over the course of many years. This demonstrates an alternate approach toward the material, one which embraces wood's natural characteristics, and acknowledges its unavoidable transformation in appearance. These considerations are greatly informed by the use of mock-ups.

Figure 6.20
A view out of the building, showing the harsh winter conditions of Cambridge and the gray-stained cladding of Alaskan Yellow Cedar, which appears to be weathered beyond its early natural state. RPBW, the Harvard Art Museums renovation and expansion (Cambridge, MA, USA) 2014.
Courtesy of RPBW © Michel Denancé.

Accelerated Weathering

Upon the final selection of Alaskan Yellow Cedar and in combination with the site mock-up, which was constructed to observe the weathering responses to the specific climate of the site, a sequence of accelerated weather tests were commissioned to observe the effects of the climate on the wood over an even longer term. These accelerated weather tests were able to demonstrate the effects of years of exposure not able to be observed in the site mock-up. The information from this mock-up allowed the design team to specify the best coating option for long-term durability.

Types of Weathering

There exist two different types of weathering tests. One is known as a "natural weathering test," where material samples are set up outdoors on racks and observed over a specified period of time while exposed to the elements. A more expedient, and in some ways more traditional method for conducting accelerated weathering tests is in a machine in a lab called a weatherometer. In a weatherometer, samples are placed within and exposed to UV light, and moisture and temperature fluctuations, which are pre-programmed to reproduce natural conditions. This method is highly controllable and consistent, but does not give you the same exposure you would have from precipitation and natural UV light, and the temperature differences that accompany these conditions.

In the daily cycle of weather conditions, there are generally three periods of transition. Before the sun comes up, the least amount of UV light exists along with the most relative humidity and the coolest temperature. As the sun comes up, there is more UV light, the temperature warms up, and things start to dry out as humidity gets lower. By mid-afternoon, the temperature peaks, the relative humidity drops to its lowest, and UV light begins to diminish before the sun goes down and begins the cycle again. The precise dynamics of this cycle are difficult to mimic, and that is the goal of accelerated testing.

Stressed Stains: Weather Testing

Alaskan Yellow Cedar was selected as the wood species to use for the construction of the cladding system. This particular tree grows extensively in Alaska and British Columbia. You do not see much of it in the United States because regionally Western Red Cedar is only used in the western United States. This tree is primarily used for cladding and heavy timber construction where natural durability is needed. It is also commonly utilized in boat building because the wood is so dimensionally stable and durable. While the wood was tested for a variety of factors, one quality in requiring additional evaluation was the coating to be used on the wood. Utilizing accelerated natural weather testing, the design team sent many samples of stained wood to South Florida to observe the impacts of various coatings based on climate factors.

Figure 6.21
EMMAQUA system for accelerated weather testing the wood. RPBW, the Harvard Art Museums renovation and expansion (Cambridge, MA, USA) 2014.
Courtesy of Ron Anthony.

In addition to this natural accelerated testing in Florida, the wood was also stressed at a facility in Arizona. The wood was placed on racks with solar reflectors to subject the material to even harsher conditions. Several samples of wood were placed on racks in the Arizona desert, including raw wood, wood with water repellent, and wood with stains applied. Pieces of Alaskan Yellow Cedar were placed in the center of solar reflector arrays, which multiplied the amount of light exposure that the wood was expected to receive over the course of many years.

EMMAQUA is a trademark name and acronym for "Equatorial Mount with Mirrors for Acceleration with Water," and a widely used method for outdoor accelerated weather testing. In these racks, mirrors are angled to focus the sun's rays on the sample, and the entire machine rotates to track the movement of the sun. This allows the UV light to be concentrated on the sample bed, approximately ten times the amount of natural UV light from the sun.

For the Harvard Art Museums, samples of the Alaskan Yellow Cedar were subjected to UV, freezing, and water exposure to simulate what happens to the samples when they are exposed for extended periods of time. The samples represent different exposures, and the longer the material is exposed, the darker gray it becomes. The chemical constituents of the wood are actually changing in response to UV light and moisture, as it is exposed over time.

Under normal circumstances, the east elevation of a building gets moderate UV exposure in the morning and by

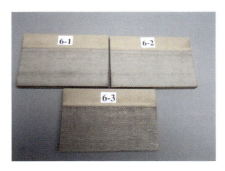

Figure 6.22 The effects of the equivalent of 12 months of exposure on wood coated with three different finishes. Visible upon inspecting the samples, is a fresh looking strip at the top of each of the three samples, where the clamp held the material in place, masking the material from exposure, vs. the faded areas which were subjected to different durations of stress. RPBW, the Harvard Art Museums renovation and expansion (Cambridge, MA, USA) 2014.
Courtesy of Ron Anthony.

Figure 6.23
Testing facility with a large array of solar reflectors for accelerating the intensity of exposure. RPBW, the Harvard Art Museums renovation and expansion (Cambridge, MA, USA) 2014.

Courtesy of Ron Anthony.

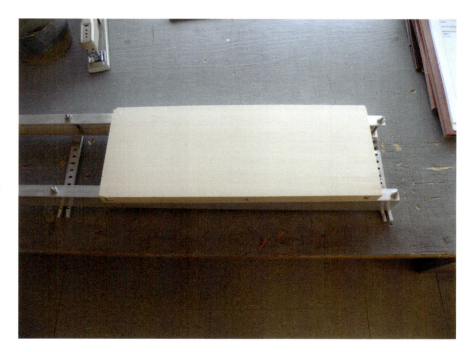

Figure 6.24
A piece of fresh Alaskan Yellow Cedar being placed on a rack prior to being exposed to accelerated UV exposure. RPBW, the Harvard Art Museums renovation and expansion (Cambridge, MA, USA) 2014.

Courtesy of Ron Anthony.

midday it is typically in the shade. If you factor that in to find the exposure that is most concerning, this testing can be customized to reveal much quicker weathering of the material than you would observe naturally, like traveling in time and observing the building 10–20 years in the future.

DEEPER CONCEPTUALIZATIONS

Interestingly, some have criticized the final appearance of the Harvard Art Museums, because the exterior wood cladding looks as if it may have been constructed from some material other than wood. We see in this ambiguity a shift in the way wood is approached, beyond simply displaying its familiar appearance. Instead, this ambiguity reveals its deeper material qualities, which are brought into alignment and allowed to acclimate with the project's many complex relationships.

The design team and the clients had to change the way they thought about wood, which was later presented with a new approach. By utilizing a less stable material like wood, instead of the more intuitive choices for an institutional building intended to endure, the architects subtly unravel our intuitions about the building and the material itself.

This choice was never intended to exhibit the superficial qualities of wood, but rather to establish it as a counterpoint, provoking our attention to the fact that this building will exhibit consistency for a long period of time. By selecting something which is intuitively less permanent, the architects must re-engage the material for its behaviors, beyond its initial appearance. The design starts almost by chance with a superficial embrace of wood for its fresh-cut organic qualities, but ends somewhere else as a future state, only arrived at through deeper investigation of the material itself. That is the goal of any mock-up.

> I love the idea that you go from the general to the detail and then from the detail to the general. It's a double process. You cannot think about the presence of the building in the city without thinking about materiality. And when you think about materiality, you start to think about detail.[8]
>
> Renzo Piano

The Harvard Art Museums renovation and expansion building is far more complex than the simple cladding system of Alaskan Yellow Cedar on its exterior. But it is this compelling surface treatment that gives us insight into the unique design approach of the Renzo Piano Building Workshop. This approach is expanded from the beginning, introducing materials into the design from the earliest moments of conceptualization. There is an almost unnoticed but surprising role of materials in the buildings of the RPBW, a role that is deliberate but perhaps seldom seen or considered for its ability to guide larger formal decisions (Figure 6.26).

We see a tendency toward materiality in both The Menil Collection building from early in Piano's career, to this later substantial investment into a surprising application of timber of the exterior of the Harvard Art Museums project. These material decisions must be made early on in the project, and allowed to slowly acclimate in the context of many other considerations. These slow acclimations inform that

Figure 6.25 Final installation of wooden boards stained gray. RPBW, the Harvard Art Museums renovation and expansion (Cambridge, MA, USA) 2014.
Courtesy of RPBW, photo Justin Lee.

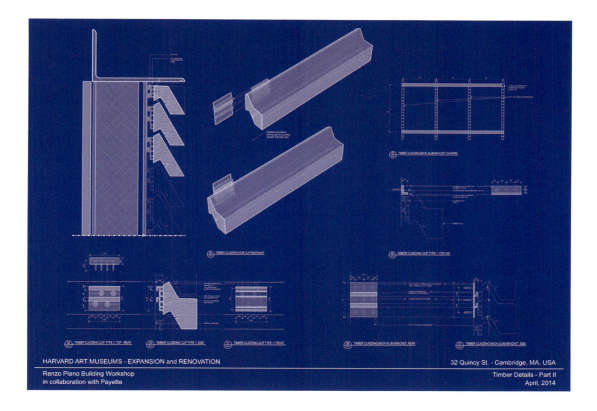

Figure 6.26
Timber detail drawings showing the mounting details. RPBW, the Harvard Art Museums renovation and expansion (Cambridge, MA, USA) 2014.
Courtesy of RPBW.

adjacent design decisions must be made by exerting pressures on them, and offering a new perspective by which to view them.

As Ron Anthony has pointed out, the embrace of natural materials, such as wood, requires a reconceptualization of approach in pursuit of answers to a new set of questions. This is unique from the more typical process in which forms are first determined and then subservient materials are selected for their ability to conform to these ideal states.

Instead, what we see consistently throughout the work of the RPBW is the introduction of a specific material very early in the process of design, which reverses the typical sequence. This reversal collapses two traditionally separate sets of concerns, allowing material to become less subservient, and instead newly positioning it. It is from this privileged position that the particular and unique characteristics of materials themselves now directly exert influence on the development of forms. This subtle but structural shift in the approach to design is as creative and compelling as the novel forms of the buildings, and an approach which is truly unique to the Renzo Piano Building Workshop.

Notes

1   Peter Buchanan, *Renzo Piano Building Workshop: Complete Works (Volume one)* (London and New York: Phaidon Press, 1993), 143.
2   Peter Buchanan, *Renzo Piano Building Workshop: Complete Works (Volume one)* (London and New York: Phaidon Press, 1993), 144.

3. Peter Buchanan, *Renzo Piano Building Workshop: Complete Works (Volume one)* (London and New York: Phaidon Press, 1993), 144.
4. Peter Buchanan, *Renzo Piano Building Workshop: Complete Works (Volume one)* (London and New York: Phaidon Press, 1993), 147.
5. Peter Buchanan, *Renzo Piano Building Workshop: Complete Works (Volume one)* (London and New York: Phaidon Press, 1993), 150.
6. Ron Anthony (wood scientist), in discussion with the author, February 24, 2016.
7. Ron Anthony (wood scientist), in discussion with the author, February 24, 2016.
8. Liz Martin, "Renzo Piano," *Archinect*, https://archinect.com/features/article/31565/renzo-piano

7 Mocked-Illuminations: The Transformed Environments Refracted in the Complex Surfaces of 7 World Trade Center

7 World Trade Center, New York City, USA

Skidmore, Owings & Merrill and James Carpenter Design Associates

Figure 7.1
A photo of the linear lapped glass and spandrel daylight reflector panel design details, constructed as part of a full-scale performance mock-up for 7 World Trade Center. Skidmore, Owings & Merrill and James Carpenter Design Associates, 7 World Trade Center (New York City, USA) 2007.

Image courtesy of JCDA, ©JCDA.

THICKER INTERACTIONS: VOLUMETRIC REFRACTIONS

A curtain wall is thin. It is both thin in its construction and shallow in its contributions, because as its name implies it is hung from some other system of supports without which it could not hold its form. Curtain walls are selfish; they are forms without sufficient structure, drawing on the contributions of others, rarely giving back.

Designed by Skidmore, Owings & Merrill, with the collaboration of James Carpenter Design Associates, 7 World Trade Center was the first building to be rebuilt at the site of The World Trade Center's destruction in Manhattan's financial district. Because of the unique conditions surrounding the project, including the patriotic significance, the economic environment of the time, and a highly specialized and collaborative team, 7 World Trade Center was designed and built under extraordinary circumstances.

Through the compelling use of full-scale mock-ups, a subtle yet special approach was employed in the design of 7 World Trade Center, one which included an unusual amount of creative depth in the design of the curtain wall.

While typical curtain walls are inward-looking, only supportive of themselves, at 7 World Trade Center this simple arrangement becomes more complex. Through a deliberate and clever perceptual thickening of the typically flat curtain wall, these re-imagined boundaries activate new interactions between the building and the atmosphere of the city that surrounds it. This thickened curtain wall uniquely captures light within its depths, transforming an ordinary surface into an expanded dynamic zone between the interior of the building and the public space of the city, one which is also more connective.

The capacity for the curtain walls to capture light and reveal its depth was in fact the result of an extraordinary approach to design through extensive empirical testing with mock-ups. These mock-ups physically explored the interactions of materials, not only between the typical materials of construction, but also between tangible forms of matter, and the more fleeting behavior of light.

The very presence of so many mock-ups in this project is unusual for what amounts to be an otherwise typically mundane program for a commercial office building. But through these compelling physical studies, the design of this unusual office tower is transformed from a shallow ensemble of glass and steel envelopes into an architecture of remarkable depth.

There is a difference between the outward-facing surfaces of 7 World Trade Center and more typical curtain wall façades which appear static, no matter how dynamically composed they are. Instead, the curtain wall façades of 7 World Trade Center are carefully constructed blank canvases. Ones upon which the environmental surroundings of lower Manhattan are dynamically painted as a series of ever-changing refracted interactions.

Instead of putting a face on a large-scale symbolic icon, the unique membranes of this project destabilize the presence of the tower by constructing detailed voids where we would typically anticipate mass. While the scale of the building is massive, these voids occur at the scale of the detail, working in concert to produce a field of implied depth, one which must be filled and activated by a transformed context and the dynamics of its surroundings (Figure 7.1).

COLLABORATION THROUGH MOCK-UPS: ACROSS SCALES

The unique depths of 7 World Trade Center's surfaces are no doubt the result of a deeper design process, one enabled by a special collaboration between Skidmore, Owings & Merrill and James Carpenter Design Associates (JCDA). What is unique about the collaboration is the convergence of two scales of conceptual approach. Typically, concepts are considered large scale outside the small scale technical details of design, but as a result of this unique collaboration, both large-scale concepts and small scale conceptual details are present. The final form of the building is only understood when examined through the tensions produced by the convergence of these two scales of conceptual development.

SOM is a firm with vast experience, having constructed several of New York City's seminal modern office towers throughout modern history, including the 1951 landmark, Lever House. The Lever House tower in particular transformed the way that modern office buildings would be built in New York City. In fact, the Lever House was built using what was at the time the most innovative use of glazing and stainless steel, just as in 7 World Trade Center.

Early in the design process, architect David Childs of SOM asked JCDA to join the design team for 7 World Trade Center, having frequently collaborated on many other projects.[1] At the time SOM had established a large-scale conceptual scheme, which extended the street grid through the site, creating a parallelogram plan for the tower. Light became a focus in the early design concepts for the project, with the design team proposing to conceptually lock the base and the tower with a third interior volume of light, called a "locking block."[2]

By utilizing light to connect and merge the two large-scale volumes of the building at the urban scale, the ambition for the project to incorporate light was established and eventually emerged at multiple scales. JCDA is a cross-disciplinary design firm operating with expertise in architecture, art, design, and engineering. The firm is led by James Carpenter, a renowned artist and designer, who is recognized for his conceptual approach to design through his distinctive use of glass and light. These innovative applications of glass reveal through their interactions with glass and light. Carpenter's unique approach to glass places it in particular relationships with light, revealing through new interactions an expanded set of properties often overlooked.

From the large-scale conceptual ideas of SOM, JCDA developed a complementary set of light-driven design details for the project. As Carpenter notes, "From that point on, we worked on the principle of a volume of light, where the glass curtain would act as a reflector and a subtle reimaging device for its surroundings."[3]

The design of these details was founded on embodying and reciprocating New York City's unique qualities of light influenced by its coastal, island geography, and climate. While the large-scale organizational concepts of the project were applied at the urban scale, these conceptually driven details fit into two zones equaling the depth of the building skins: the glass curtain wall a mere 8 inches thick and a double layer steel podium wall with only 10 inches between. Within these shallow surfaces, JCDA developed the details for a "volumetric light" concept through every phase of the project, and as we will see, it is these details, which were only enabled through extensive engagement with full-scale mock-ups.[4]

BEYOND REFLECTIVITY

The primary design features of 7 World Trade Center do not repose in the static presence of form itself, but rather in the more effervescent interactions that exist between physical forms and the behaviors of light. It is these interactions that give unique definition to this project.

In particular, what we see in this project is an expanded framework through which new applications of glass are engaged. Glass is not only integrated as a physical object, but also as a medium for embodying and revealing the unique information contained in light. The precise, yet mysterious interactions between glass and light, has pre-occupied James Carpenter throughout his career. According to Kenneth Frampton, Carpenter's formation as a designer is most influenced by his early engagement with glass as a consultant to the Corning Glass Works.[5] It was during this time where he participated in the development and evolution of new forms of vitreous materials, including photo responsive glass and other experimental vitreous ceramics.

But beyond static new formulas, it was the dynamic interactions between glass and light that captivated Carpenter. As he states, early in his career, he "came to understand the cinematic potential of glass itself, as it interacts with light in the environment."[6]

It is from this early realization that Carpenter's work has focused on the interactions of glass with light in art and architecture. Often, these realizations have emerged out of fine-tuning details and careful observations of physically constructed artifacts. By working directly with glass, Carpenter engages one material as an interface instrument for revealing the unique forms of another, light.

As Carpenter states, "By balancing its properties of transparency, reflectivity, and translucency, glass can be designed to function simultaneously as a window or weather-membrane and as a medium for revealing light."[7] It is through this consistent trajectory of investigation in their work that JCDA directed the development of two light-driven design details for 7 World Trade Center. The questions which guided their pursuits were how to create a volumetric reading of the skins while transcending the thinness of the surface.

FORMS AND DETAILS

The disposition of the building is itself unique because of the project's site. The primary program of the building is a 42-floor office building, which is not unusual, except for the fact that this chunk of program sits atop a Con-Edison transformer vault, 82-feet high. This vault had many specific requirements the design team had to design for, such as natural ventilation and other protections to ensure successful functioning of this large piece of energy infrastructure. Perhaps the most challenging predicament was the fact that the transformer is not a public space, yet sits on the sidewalk and defines the street level engagement with a substantial building footprint where it first meets the ground.

Because this programmatic piece is an opaque, shadowy bunker at street level, the design team made the decision to illuminate it, activating its surface with a double layer stainless steel podium wall, which captured natural light, refracting it within its double layers.

Above this steel podium, the 42 floors of office space sit detached physically from the street, remaining visually engaged. An essential detail that facilitated this visual engagement was the design team's attention to the spandrel zone, where the edge of the horizontal floor slab meets perpendicular with the vertical glass surface. A primary concern was to address the shadow line produced by the mass of the slab behind the glass curtain wall, thus reinforcing the abstracted reading of a continuous vertical surface, maintaining its continuous reflections. This concern is addressed in the design of the spandrel panels, which like the floor to floor glass panels are also glass. However, instead of transparent glass, they are typically reflective and as a result don't allow the looming presence of the floor to transmit through to the exterior.

At 7 World Trade Center, the design team utilize depth and layering instead of shallow coatings, to devise a detail that offsets the presence of shadows, by absorbing light, drawing it in, illuminating a shallow but voluminous zone.

DETAILED FORMS

Two thematic details define the atmospheric interactions of 7 World Trade Center: glass and steel.

In glass, JCDA and the design team developed a linear lap glazing detail consisting of a double layer zone in which the vision glass of the upper story slips past the floor's edge below. Behind this slippage, the floor's edge, which is normally capped

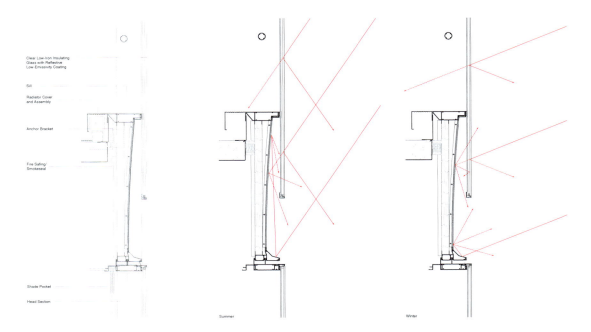

Figure 7.2
A detail drawing of the different interactions between rays of light and their resulting refractions as a result of the shiplapped spandrel zone between floors. Skidmore, Owings & Merrill and James Carpenter Design Associates, 7 World Trade Center (New York City, USA) 2007.
Image courtesy of JCDA, ©JCDA.

with a flush spandrel panel, is pushed back and recessed, creating a cove-like volume of space between the outer layer of the glass and the recessed edge of the floor plate. The edge of the floor plate is faced with a textured stainless steel panel, formed to capture natural daylight within this cove. The cavity between these layers is sculpted and activated with a titanium coated, blue stainless steel sill cover which reflects the light of the sky onto the curved reflector spandrel panel, scattering and refracting this reflected light in this detailed space via a pressed specular texture.[8]

This spandrel cavity is in effect a light cove, which is sculpted by its interactions with light, creating a continually shifting interaction with the sky, merging at times and visible from the street below. This cove brings the sky into the depth of the curtain wall, while the reflective sill bounces a flat image onto the sculpted depth of this detail, scattering it in the process of transforming the sky into a liminal space between building and city (Figure 7.2).

In steel, the design team developed a double layer podium wall concealing the Con-Edison transformer vault behind that activated the boundary between street and vault with a light-filled cavity a mere 8 inches deep. Each layer was constructed of small triangular prismatic wires vertically oriented and rotated at specific angles before being welded in place to capture and conceal light before refracting it back to the street. The podium walls are screens of layered reflectivity, which during the day scatter uniform daylight into various specular directions as a result of the rotations of each triangular wire. At night, concealed LED lighting illuminates the interior cavity between the two layers of screen. This light bounces around inside the cavity of the podium, illuminating the shallow zone, and creates an intriguing sense of depth. Both day and night are transformed through the presence of these screens, suggesting atmospheric boundaries between the building and the street, softened through the activation of light (Figure 7.3).

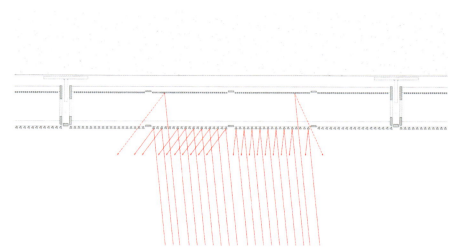

Figure 7.3 A drawing of the double layer podium wall demonstrating how daylighting rays will both reflect from the exterior surface, while also passing through striking the back layer. Skidmore, Owings & Merrill and James Carpenter Design Associates, 7 World Trade Center (New York City, USA) 2007.
Image courtesy of JCDA, ©JCDA.

BUILT-IN LIGHT: REFLECTIONS AND REFRACTIONS

It is micro-scale details such as surface texture and even thicker molecular arrangements of matter that affect how a given material will exhibit a particular reaction upon exposure to light.

Passive strategies for addressing the consequences of daylight include blocking it out, sighting buildings in a way that prevents light from entering the interior, or utilizing reflective coatings to bounce light away. 7 World Trade Center is unique in that it does not distinguish itself from light, rather it merges with light by transforming it, fusing its interactions with the atmospheres of its site. 7 World Trade Center represents a shift from reflective to refractive engagements, drawing light in, bending it, and scattering it within its coves before sending it back out, transformed as a result of its material interactions.

While this high-rise building is constructed primarily of glass and steel, JCDA and the design team's focus on the textural details of surfaces to create unique refractive qualities privileges the light itself as a third construction material which must be engaged. In all three parts of the massing, the light is vital and is further explored through the finer grain scales of detail.

The building is transformed from a static and passive state into a more active and dynamic range of states because light is not a static element. These states interact with the shifting conditions of its site by absorbing light into its coves, transforming it, and sending it back out, transmitting an altered atmosphere to its surroundings.

OUT OF SEQUENCE MOCK-UPS

In its final state, the project is both elegant and refined. However, hidden within its refined tectonics is the influence of a progressive sequence of small models and mock-ups which selectively articulate and pursue a line of thinking and observation.

Both of the detailed light concepts designed by JCDA were developed beyond simply drawing their shapes and forms. In fact, because both details were intended to interact with the light of the surrounding environment, the designs could not simply be represented by traditional convention. By focusing on these reactive outcomes, the material details were selected for the interactions they would produce instead of the appearance of their static non-reactive states. As a result, many of the intended interactions were unpredictable, and thus required mock-ups to be fully explored and refined.

TWO FAMILIES OF MOCK-UPS

It is difficult to quantify the exact number of mock-ups executed during the design and construction of 7 World Trade Center. There are many physical samples, models, and photos that document the various media, but when viewed as a group the boundaries between each seem to blur into a malleable set of definitions.

GLASS CURTAIN WALL

One set of material explorations examined the glass curtain wall system and its various interactions with light, beginning with early conventional model making, but with early suggestions of the materiality at full scale. The sequence of investigation later zoomed-in, examining the particularities of different samples of textured spandrel panels being physically staged and mocked up next to one another and observed for their impact at full scale. While these specular lighting tests are full scale, they were not yet integrated into the assembly of the remainder of the building.

That occurred later in the form of two full-scale integrated mock-ups, and each varied in their motivations. While both are full-scale inhabitable building fragments, with all the suggested layers constructed, the first is a visual mock-up concerned with only the optical effects of the materials being considered. The second, a performative mock-up constructed at full scale and a full three stories high. While optically accurate, through various standardized tests, this mock-up was tested for its ability to withstand environmental stresses.

STEEL PODIUM WALL

A parallel set of physical mock-ups used a series of metal screens to test versions of the building's podium wall. Beginning with a scale model suggesting material and patterning, many physical samples of the screen were constructed at full scale. These samples were followed by a wall section mock-up testing the integration of lighting into the wall cavity; this mock-up labored over the task of concealing the lighting source.

Lastly, the architects constructed a large, full scale, multistory mock-up rehearsing a variety of construction details and serving as proof of concept. In this mock-up, the lighting was finally calibrated to the profile and placement of the fixture within the double layer.

The architects began with a design intended to convey a sense of lightness, beginning with pieces of acrylic then combining them with lighting fixtures to establish from the beginning that the building was a combination of materials interacting with light. From here, they moved through four stages of physical study: scale models, 1:1 scale models, mock-ups of full scale but with fake materials and real materials, followed by fabrication samples. When we look at this progressive family of studies, we see how each of these mock-ups builds upon the previous version, with each new study refining the design.

CURTAIN WALL MOCK-UPS: LINEAR LAP SPANDREL DETAILS

Mock-Up 01: Model and Mock-Up

Early in the design process, a number of options were considered for how to actively integrate light into the otherwise thin surface of the glass curtain wall. A variety of rain-screen systems and other options were initially considered before focusing on a ship-lap detail within the glass itself. To present this option, the drawings were produced and shared with the team from which a mock-up of the detail was constructed to present to the client.

This first mock-up of the linear lap spandrel cove was first represented in physical form as a full-scale model. Using foam-core and acrylic sheets, the model was assembled with glue and tape instead of the actual materials of its intended construction. Because of its full scale, this model occupies the transition point between a representational model and a material mock-up, something that both the design team and the client could see and feel to better understand the design.

The significant concern illustrated in this design detail was how to have the insulated glass unit (IGU) transition from inside to outside. That transition is visible in this first model as the horizontal black line where the upper panel of glass first meets the floor, but then extends past the spandrel cap creating a shallow overlap. In the model, the black line represents a thermal break, where the air temperature above is controlled internally and the air below is outside air, which can vary significantly. This detail was not typical and caused some concern that one side would heat up much more than the other resulting in thermal stress. The thermal stress could cause the IGU to expand in different amounts at different locations, leading to stress at the joints and ultimately to compromised weather tightness. In addition to thermal stress, the greater concern made apparent by this mock-up was the potential for condensation to occur where the IGU overlaps the sill. This potential was further studied and discounted through the use of computer modeling from which subsequent mock-ups physically tested these results.

Details

Ordinarily, the glass spandrel panel would be a separate piece of material from the adjacent floor to ceiling IGU, which allows a control joint between the two pieces. However, if they were to break the glass into two pieces at that line it would significantly alter the design of the curtain wall. One of the main motivations of the design was to reduce the height of the spandrel by eliminating that joint between the two typical parts, thus fusing them into the same uniform piece. This allows a much more uniform surface when viewed overall, with voids between floors filled with the volumetric presence of light.

Breaking the glass into two pieces at the edge of the floor plate would have reinforced the perception of the thickness of the floor on the exterior, marking a hard boundary instead of the desired light-filled gradients indicated. This model is a cropped sample of reality centered horizontally on the framing member, which serves as a joint between glass panels. Vertically, the model is centered on the spandrel panel represented by the warping silver panel which conceals the thickness of the floor plate behind (Figure 7.4).

Here in this first large-scale model, the shape and form of the spandrel panel is inserted with a reflective silver finish, a property that would later be changed. In front of the silver spandrel panel, the bottom edge of the glass lights hangs down, slipping past the horizontal framing member on the floor. The tops of the insulated glazing units are also visible and an initial attempt at suggesting blue spandrel reflectors are added with the intention of reflecting blue tinted light, washing the spandrel in blue reflections allowing it to fuse with the blue hues of the sky.

The model is ultimately a very large representation, not incorporating the actual materiality, but serving as a first visual rehearsal of the integration of parts and the overlaps they produce. This model acts as a scaffold, intended to suggest the scale of effects at 1:1, and particularly to begin to suggest without defining some of the material qualities which could emerge. These qualities were fine-tuned in a series of subsequent mock-ups, which utilized real materials, not the foam-core, plastic, and glue of this representational model. This model suggests the concept, picturing the forms more fully, but with the interactions still loosely observed like a sketch.

Figure 7.4 This mock-up of the linear lap spandrel was built at full scale by James Carpenter Design Associates as a presentation of the concept at full scale with representational materials such as foam-core, specular aluminum sheeting, clear acrylic, and a blue mirror glass sample. Photo taken June 18, 2002. Skidmore, Owings & Merrill and James Carpenter Design Associates, 7 World Trade Center (New York City, USA) 2007.
Image courtesy of JCDA, ©JCDA.

Mock-Up 02: Mock Reflections (Diffuse and Specular Metal Reflector Tests)

The next set of mock-ups engaged actual materials. With the design understood formally, various primitive pieces of metal were now tested for their reflective interactions with light. Unique combinations of textural finishes and colors were specified and designed to help visualize the reflections most desired when the building is constructed of actual materials. These experiments utilized materials that were laying around JCDA's studio. These mock-ups visualized the actual reflections between the blue stainless steel spandrel reflector, something that is difficult to predict without actually physically assembling the various components and observing their interactions.

One observation from the previous full-scale model was that a smooth panel would not transmit the blue light reflected onto it. As a result, several sheet samples with pressed specular textures were selected for their potential to absorb the reflected blue light and thus display it. These interactions were absorbed by simply holding the material intended for the blue reflector sill cap against a variety of textured panels and adjusting the angle of orientation to find the ideal positions for each. Two different specular textures were used in these tests, one corrugated with perforations and the other folded in a zig-zag saw tooth pattern.

Initially, a corrugated sheet of metal was fabricated in house by JCDA, scoring and folding a sheet of metal to provide more texture. This corrugated sheet was combined with two types of blue reflective metal sheets, demonstrating two specimens of projected light on its surface.

Figure 7.5
Realizing that a smooth spandrel panel would not transmit the reflected blue light from the spandrel reflector, several textures were tested for their ability to receive and display the light reflected onto their surfaces. Here a darker blue curved metal reflector on the left and a flat blue metal reflector on the right are held below a crudely scored and folded piece of sheet metal. Skidmore, Owings & Merrill and James Carpenter Design Associates, 7 World Trade Center (New York City, USA) 2007.
Image courtesy of JCDA, ©JCDA.

The two samples of blue metal were different in color and finish. One was smooth like a blue mirror providing specular reflections, while the other is more diffuse and deeper blue, providing softer ambient refraction. Both reflections were observed cast on the textured back panel, with one crisp and the other soft (Figure 7.5). With both samples held side by side and photographed together, the length of one reflection remains intact traveling higher up the panel, while the softer glow gradually dissipates as a result of its rougher texture.

Figure 7.6 A piece of blue mirrored glass is held below a rolled and perforated sheet of metal creating softer more diffuse reflections. Skidmore, Owings and Merrill & James Carpenter Design Associates, 7 World Trade Center (New York City, USA) 2007.
Image courtesy of JCDA, ©JCDA.

Figure 7.7 The same piece of blue mirrored glass held at a shallower angle to the rolled and perforated sheet of metal creating softer more diffuse reflections. Skidmore, Owings & Merrill and James Carpenter Design Associates, 7 World Trade Center (New York City, USA) 2007.
Image courtesy of JCDA, ©JCDA.

In a second set of reflection mock-ups, the spandrel panel surface is altered with a new texture that was rolled and also perforated. The reflections were softer and more subtle, both as a result of some reflections passing through the perforations of the sheet, and the tighter grain of the texture in general (Figures 7.6 and 7.7).

While materials can be specified and anticipated for their physical and structural properties, their interactions when combined are more difficult to estimate. Only as a result of this step could the reflections be understood by physically mocking them up and observing their behaviors. Ultimately, the sawtooth pattern was selected for the vibrancy of color it transmitted and is seen in the final outcome of the construction.

Mock-Up 03: Hoisted Reflections

With a better understanding of the material behavior rooted in the reflections and refractions of light, a more thorough full-scale visual mock-up was constructed to visualize the interactions of the final form. This third mock-up was constructed with a range of the actual materials of construction merging the previous two sets of mock-ups into one (Figure 7.8).

At Permasteelisa in Connecticut, major components of the tower's curtain wall and podium wall were constructed as full-scale volumetric chunks of the building. The key thematic conditions of the curtain wall are captured in the design of this mock-up, featuring the floating glass linear lap detail with the blue window sill reflector.

On the interior of the mock-up, set back from the glass, they constructed a faux-column in the accurate location relative to the glass. Because of the subtleties of

Figure 7.8
A full-scale visual mock-up constructed to test various glazing options and interior paint colors, able to be hoisted above the ground. Skidmore, Owings & Merrill and James Carpenter Design Associates, 7 World Trade Center (New York City, USA) 2007.
Image ©Richard Kress, JCDA.

light effects upon and within the curtain wall, the need to suppress the visibility of the column was of paramount importance.

This column was a placeholder for the true structural element to be constructed on-site, but because this column was visible through the glass, the design team wanted to observe its impact. They observed the visibility of the column through the various types of glass and as a result of these observations specified a uniform neutral gray color to be used building-wide on the outside face of the column, regardless of tenant color for the rest of the interior. This uniform treatment diminished the visibility of the column and assured that certain columns would not be more visible than others toward the exterior, maintaining a consistency of reflection.

The mock-up was designed as a kit of parts that allowed various spandrel reflectors to be swapped in and out for comparison, while also testing side by side two different types of glass. The glass types were standard clear glass and low-iron glass, each further varied in combination with and without the presence of ceramic frit patterns along their top edge.

At the time of this project in 2002, low-iron glass was a newer product on the market, and not many low-iron glass towers existed. Low-iron glass is ultra-clear, and provides higher transparency than more traditional float glass. This optimum clarity is achieved by removing most of the iron oxide found in the silica used to produce glass. As a result, the typical green tint of the glass is also removed, resulting in crystal clear high transparency panels.

With this additional clarity comes greater light transmission into the interior of the building, resulting in unwanted heat gain. The design team decided if low-iron glass was used, then a performance coating and a ceramic frit pattern would need to be printed on the outside face of the glass. This fritting would reduce the amount of daylight that passes through the glass into the building and thus would limit the amount of solar radiation, in order to prevent unwanted heat gain on the interior.

The design team grew concerned about the visual presence of this band of fritting and utilized this mock-up to observe the differences between glass with and without this treatment. Because the goal of the lapped spandrel panel was to reduce the thickness of the spandrel zone, if the band of fritting became visible in the surface of the panel, then the thickness of that zone would seem exaggerated instead of reduced.

When viewed side by side, the layers of fritting were noticeable at the top of the panel immediately below the floor edge. One significant concern was that this band of fritting would produce thick horizontal bands like racing stripes when viewed across the entire façade of the final building. The frit pattern was plainly visible in

Figure 7.9 The final curtain wall mock-up hoisted above the ground to test the visibility of glass frit patterns when viewed from below. Skidmore, Owings & Merrill and James Carpenter Design Associates, 7 World Trade Center (New York City, USA) 2007.
Image ©Richard Kress, JCDA.

the mock-up when viewed head-on, but because the office building sits on top of the podium, the curtain wall begins 125 feet above the street and is only visible by viewing when looking up (Figure 7.9).

Because of the high elevation of the curtain wall, the mock-up was designed to be hoisted off the ground to simulate the angle of incidence from which it would be observed. Only from this position were the effects of the fritting accurately observed and as a result it was decided that the fritting pattern would not significantly impact the thin profile of the spandrel zone.

Once brought back down to earth to be viewed close up, the new textured spandrel panels can be seen (Figure 7.10). In this mock-up, the effects of the panels JCDA developed with the manufacturer (a pressed texture stainless steel sheet with a sandstone finish) can be seen as scattered reflections from above and below, which are collapsed onto the rolled corrugations of the panel. The texture here can be observed to transmit the reflections into alternating micro bands, much more than the initial smooth panel.

The curtain wall contractor Permasteelisa also tested in this mock-up whether the glass would produce condensation. This involves cooling the interior of the chamber to see if the condensation occurs on the outside of the building or between layers of glass. So in this single mock-up, SOM and JCDA are able to verify

Mocked-Illuminations

Figure 7.10 The pressed textured spandrel panels visible in the visual mock-up breaking reflections into discrete bands. Skidmore, Owings & Merrill and James Carpenter Design Associates, 7 World Trade Center (New York City, USA) 2007.
Image courtesy of JCDA, ©JCDA.

the orchestration of all the layers, accompanied by a fine-tuned optical calibration in addition to the engineer and fabricator, all collaborating on a single mock-up. This mock-up serves as a malleable scaffolding for the design, on top of which the optical precision and engineering can be calibrated.

Mock-Up 04: Construction Research Labs: Performative Mock-Ups

At Construction Research Labs, and other testing facilities, there is a categorical distinction between the concepts of "stress" and "performance." Some of the routines which are run on the full-scale mock-ups are intended to evaluate the ability to withstand certain stresses placed upon them. Some of the other routines are intended to evaluate performance once stresses have already been placed on the building.

A building owner or design team is interested in not only knowing how the building will perform when newly completed, but also after it has endured stresses placed upon it over time. To illustrate this concept, the standard routine for testing the performance against water and air infiltration first involves pre-requisite stresses such as interstory movement, thermal cycling, wind-loading or preloading, seismic, and lateral drift, and in some cases large missile impact tests. As a result of stresses, the performance is usually reduced; however, if it remains within an allowable range, it is considered to pass (Figure 7.11).

Figure 7.11
A full-scale performance mock-up constructed at Construction Research Labs in Miami, Florida, to measure stress and performance. Skidmore, Owings & Merrill and James Carpenter Design Associates, 7 World Trade Center (New York City, USA) 2007.
Image courtesy of JCDA, ©JCDA.

PRISMATIC WIRE STAINLESS STEEL PODIUM DETAILS

Podium Mock-Up 01: Assembling Refractions

For the design of the podium wall, which defined the base of the building at street level, JCDA developed several initial conceptual studies. Each of the initial studies was intended to remain conceptually consistent with the curtain wall by embedding light into the depth of the podium wall system. After a sequence of initial design concepts, JCDA realized that a fabricator whom they had previously worked with would be the ideal supplier for one of the options. It was through consultation and significant modification to their fabrication process that they finalized the design of the podium wall, a detail they finally referred to as the "prismatic wire stainless steel podium wall system." To arrive at the final design for the prismatic steel podium wall, a progression from study models to mock-ups show the unique evolution of the design details.

To first begin to study the design of the podium wall, several small scale representational models were built. The first model was built by JCDA, constructed

Mocked-Illuminations

Figure 7.12
A first concept model demonstrating the effect of subdividing the surrounding reflections. Skidmore, Owings & Merrill and James Carpenter Design Associates, 7 World Trade Center (New York City, USA) 2007.
Image courtesy of JCDA, ©JCDA.

only to be shared with SOM and the design team for internal consideration, not to be presented to the client.

In this first model, the design is represented as a stack of two wall fragments. Each of these fragments crops a repetitive zone of the podium wall and illustrates the shifting of one atop the other to produce breaks in what would otherwise become vertical banding. This model is conventional in the sense that within the boundary of the model, all of the typical details are captured in this physical representation, suggesting a repetition of typical modules. The model shows a clear alternating stepped pattern, with one panel recessed while the other projects forward.

Evident in the observations of this model are not only the suggestions of material type and tone, but also the clear intentions of breaking up the image of the reflections. Through the shifting of depths, the legibility of the reflected image is refracted, as alternating flush and recessed surfaces transform the reflected light of its surroundings (Figure 7.12).

In this small model, a system of vertically oriented metal grills are stacked side by side, resembling shutters with horizontal slats etched within each individual grill. This system of slats reflects portions of light back, while the voids between allow the light to continue through and deconstruct the reflected image into linear bands of color and tone.

These bands effectively atomize the image of the reflections abstracting it into long pixels of light, transforming it as a result instead of simply redirecting it back. The potentials in this small scale model represent complex interactions of refractions, not simple reflections. The resulting subdivided portions of reflections, disassociate smaller-scale regions of light and color, inviting us to zoom in and inspect cropped details of a larger image of light.

This model was constructed before JCDA realized they could rotate the individual stainless steel prisms in relation to each other in order to create the field of changing reflective targets. The alternating pattern was important as the design team did not want to have a single large-scale grill covering the entire podium wall. The initial design idea seen here was to mount horizontal rods onto thinner vertical rectangular panels, which would be made legible by alternately stepping back and forth. The alternating A–B–A pattern of the vertical panels of the podium, established a behavior of reflections which remained intact throughout the development of subsequent studies. As a result of the final fabrication process later selected, JCDA realized they could rotate the rods individually, transforming the design of these alternating recesses and protrusions into a continuous layer with individual rods rotated in groups to articulate the alternating pattern.

Podium Mock-Up 02: Double Layer Podium Model

A second small scale model was constructed by JCDA, approximately 20 inches tall, but this time as a presentation model to communicate the design to the client. This model represents the effects of the revised podium wall design, which now places the linear metal wires vertically instead of horizontally. This decision was made based on the realization that the manufacturer, Johnson Screens, could individually rotate the vertical wires of the screens while welding without adding additional cost.

This more informed model calibrates the thickness of the stainless steel grill and the porosity of the screen based on the spacing of the vertical wires. Uniquely fabricated, this model was constructed using a chemical etching process, which allowed the model to represent the porosity and thickness of the wires at a very small scale. The process involved printing a resist layer onto thin gauge metal sheets and then acid etching the metal, a process ordinarily used for etching circuit boards.

In the original model, the stacked joint where the top layer shifts in relation to the lower one are still present; however, that original sample is now elevated intact, above an additional layer with a new type of horizontal joint between. This new joint is a reveal constructed from a structural element, which appears with the same material finish (Figure 7.13).

In this model, the alternating vertical panels are achieved by using different line-weights of the metal wires etched out of the sheet. This material patterning indicates that the light will be transformed into staggered sets of panels through configuration of the wires themselves instead of the stepping previously seen. The detail to produce that shift will be explored further in subsequent mock-ups, and it is surprising how accurate this very early model ends up being when compared to a subsequent full-scale mock-up which occurs much later in the process.

Figure 7.13
A second model with wires oriented vertically constructed of chemically etched metal screens. Skidmore, Owings & Merrill and James Carpenter Design Associates, 7 World Trade Center (New York City, USA) 2007.
Image courtesy of JCDA, ©JCDA.

Podium Mock-Up 03: Illuminated Model

The idea of transforming daytime reflections is present in the two initial study models. A third model was later constructed in an attempt to engage the internal illuminations of the cavity wall, in which embedded light sources cause the wall to glow at night.

This model is small scale, approximately 36 inches tall, built of chemically etched metal screens. To gain an initial impression of this light, the model illuminates a translucent piece of acrylic that glows behind the metal screen. As a result, a soft light is emitted through the screen filtered through the pattern of the vertical wires. What is notable is that the light source is not visible, only the soft illumination of the scrim of the interior.

This light is intended to illuminate the atmosphere around the building where it meets the street, transforming the hard boundary between public and private with a subtle atmospheric distinction. This double layer wall functions to both locate the source of this atmospheric light and to also transform it within the cavity of the wall by bouncing it around, creating a unique soft glow. This glowing light is more like an ambient zone articulating an interaction between the materials of the building and the spaces surrounding it (Figure 7.14).

Podium Mock-Up 04: Johnson Screens Prismatic Wire Samples

Figure 7.14 A presentation model prepared by JCDA to illustrate the thickened zone of refracted light in the podium wall. Light bounces between two layers of vertical metal wires, and the results of this initial model, would undergo substantial development through full-scale mock-ups, testing the lights' particular behaviors through its interactions with various materials and textures. Skidmore, Owings and Merrill & James Carpenter Design Associates, 7 World Trade Center (New York City, USA) 2007.
Image courtesy of JCDA, ©JCDA.

The first three physical representations of the unique light intended in the design of the podium existed at the traditional scale of representational models. A fourth model zooms in to the full-scale materiality of the screen itself. Early on, the design team found a product that already existed but for a categorically different use. These screens were a product by Johnson Screens, and were originally used as a sieve or screen in the mining industry for filtering out various size particulates and in hydroelectric dams for removing debris from the water before reaching the interior workings of the generators (Figure 7.15).

Because the screens were used in different industrial applications with different filtering requirements, the process already existed to customize the product. This allowed the product to be reconsidered.

The design team evaluated a variety of profiles, ultimately specifying wires with triangular

Figure 7.15
A series of podium screen samples fabricated by Johnson Screens to evaluate the customizable components such as wire diameter, profile, spacing, and rotation. Skidmore, Owings and Merrill & James Carpenter Design Associates, 7 World Trade Center (New York City, USA) 2007.
Photo by the author.

cross-sections which they custom designed. The advantage of this product was that the system was already set up for the design team to input and substitute components of the system. Some of the parameters which could seamlessly be specified were: spacing, the size of the wire, the shape of the profile, and orientation in which it was welded (Figure 7.16).

Beginning with a single surface, the design team ordered samples of different size wires and orientations, and eventually built up samples with double

Figure 7.16
A photograph of the fabrication process of the podium wall by Johnson Screens as triangular profile wires are individually rotated and welded. Skidmore, Owings & Merrill and James Carpenter Design Associates, 7 World Trade Center (New York City, USA) 2007.
Image courtesy of JCDA, copyright JCDA.

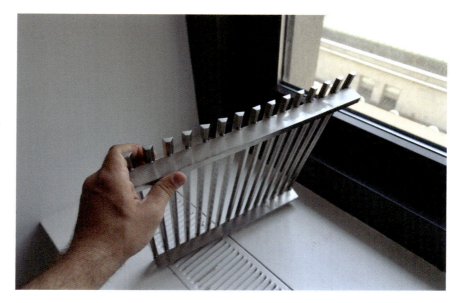

Figure 7.17
A single layer podium screen sample fabricated by Johnson Screens showing individual sets of wires rotated within the same panel. Skidmore, Owings & Merrill and James Carpenter Design Associates, 7 World Trade Center (New York City, USA) 2007.
Photo by the author.

layers. The design of the double layers further differentiated the characteristics of the wires for each surface. The double-layer mock-ups positioned thicker wire profiles on the exterior layer and thinner gauge triangular wires on the interior layer (Figures 7.17 and 7.18).

The design team inspected these samples for the quality of welds as well as surface finish, reflective properties, and ultimately ordered a range of fabricated samples to observe the possible configuration of details and their interactions with light. These samples allowed the design team to further develop the design as a result of understanding at full scale how these moves would appear and how they would impact both cost and refractions of light.

Figure 7.18
A double layer podium screen sample fabricated by Johnson Screens showing different sizes of triangular wires between exterior and interior layers, rotated and welded at varying angles. Skidmore, Owings & Merrill and James Carpenter Design Associates, 7 World Trade Center (New York City, USA) 2007.
Photo by the author.

Figure 7.19
A double layer podium wall sample fabricated by Johnson Screens, showing the difference between the exterior specular polished finish, and the interior bead-blasted diffuse finish. Skidmore, Owings & Merrill and James Carpenter Design Associates, 7 World Trade Center (New York City, USA) 2007.
Photo by the author.

The impact on cost resulted from how the podium wall would be fabricated. Specific areas of concern which each impacted cost were the side panels, which were waterjet cut called ladders, the finish of the individual triangular rods, and the tilt of the rods.

The exterior layer of the podium wires are larger in profile: one half of an inch wide with high reflectivity so that during the day you do not see the rods in the back. This outer layer is made of wires, which are cold-formed stainless steel with a brushed finish. The back layer is made of smaller profile wires, one-eighth of an inch wide, and bead-blasted, so at night the internal light hits the bead-blasted wires and they diffuse the light, absorbing it onto its surfaces and becoming more present. Through this shift in finish and light source over the course of the day, there is an anticipated inversion from day to night.

The difference in reflectivity between interior and exterior layers becomes visible as the exterior wires bounces specular reflectivity, while the interior reflections from the bead-blasted wires are more diffuse. The triangular profiles become advantageous for two reasons: the fabrication process needs a point of contact between two metals to do a resist weld and the reflections of light become more refractive based on this triangular shape (Figure 7.19).

Podium Mock-Up 05: Light Performance Mock-Up

After observing a range of material samples, the architects next designed a larger podium wall mock-up that would be constructed of the approved samples.

In a sense, these podium wall mock-ups are all visual mock-ups, as they are not subjected to the strict performance criteria of the curtain wall. However, they are also more complex in that the desired outcome is not simply that they fit together and support themselves. These mock-ups also do need to perform. Their performance is not based in terms of structure, but contingent on their own interactions with light. In this regard, they are performative because it is not enough for them just to be made and to look good; instead, once fabricated, they must be observed to interact with light in specific ways.

While the first small scale lighting model was built as a presentation tool to communicate the desired effects of the glowing light, the effects of that small scale model needed to be maintained while scaling up and constructing the actual details. This process of scaling up often changes performance in unpredictable ways.

In the presentation model, the parts were glued together and the illumination was achieved by backlighting the interior layer, which was constructed of a translucent piece of acrylic. This construction suggests glass or a scrim; however, there is no such glass in this wall and as a result the placement of the lighting system needed to be absorbed into the construction of the podium wall, hiding it from sight.

Because the podium screen was masking a Con-Edison transformer vault, there were specific airflow requirements that prevented a monolithic surface such as an interior scrim or shade. As a result, the construction at full scale was proposed as a double layer of the stainless steel. However, the effects of the lighting needed to be understood in combination with this particular materiality. So the architects had the fabricators at Johnson Screens construct a lighting mock-up at their shop in Minnesota, approximately 8 feet long, 6 feet tall, and 4 feet deep. A custom light fixture was designed to fit within the cavity, and it was placed in several locations before deciding on a final solution. Because the back layer screen was intended to be as refractive as possible, the stainless steel was specified with a bead blasted finish to allow it to diffuse the light and becoming more present when illuminated at night.

The outer screen of the double layer podium wall was specified with a brushed finish, providing a more smoothly textured surface, which increased its specular reflectivity. The light which strikes this double layer is fragmented into vertical linear bands, half of which are reflected back out to the street, and half of which pass through the exterior layer onto the back surface of the cavity wall. These light rays which pass through strike the interior bead-blasted screen and are muted and refracted within the cavity, illuminating the shallow depth of this surface. The corner condition is also constructed in the mock-up.

Working with a lighting designer this mock-up was constructed with a strip of LED lighting, consisting of alternating white and blue diodes, which enabled the mock-up to be observed within relation to a range of tones.

Upon inspection of the light, a few things were noticeable. The light did produce a sense of layering and depth, as the outer surface reflected the ambient orange-colored light of the surrounding workshop, while the interior glowed blue. The orange reflections from the shop lights where the mock-up was constructed are often present in the final building as a result of passing car headlights when it's dark.

This exterior light provides overlapping layers of different color lights, creating a dynamic shifting of the podium walls double layers.

When viewing the mock-up axially in elevation, the source of the light is not visible. When viewed obliquely the reflection of the individual diodes from the led fixtures are visible as points of light. This condition was something the architects intended to avoid, and was particularly noticeable in the corners, which allowed views parallel to the light cavity.

In order to avoid this observed phenomenon, the interior detailing of the podium wall was developed to conceal the original source emanating from the fixture. The final detail drawings show the location of the LED fixture sandwiched in the vertical joint between two panels, a detail only determined after this light performance mock-up was constructed.

Podium Mock-Up 06: Final Visual Mock-Up

A final podium wall mock-up was constructed to test the customized fabrication process in addition to many of the other issues that would be observed in the final building. In this full-scale visual mock-up, the fabricators at Johnson Screens attempted to individually rotate the triangular wires with their fabrication techniques, which is something they had not previously attempted with such variability. This represents one of the first demonstrations of a 5 foot by 10-foot unit, the actual size to be used in the construction of the building (Figure 7.20).

Figure 7.20 One of the first 5 foot by 10-foot double-layer podium screen units fabricated by Johnson Screen for the full-scale visual mock-up. Skidmore, Owings & Merrill and James Carpenter Design Associates, 7 World Trade Center (New York City, USA) 2007.
Image courtesy of JCDA, ©JCDA.

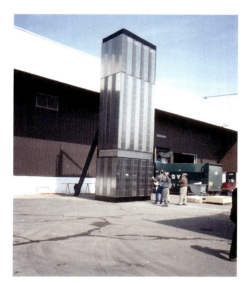

Figure 7.21 The podium wall being constructed in front of a black-painted plywood surface, which represents the surface of the waterproofed concrete transformer vault. Skidmore, Owings & Merrill and James Carpenter Design Associates, 7 World Trade Center (New York City, USA) 2007.
Image ©Richard Kress, JCDA.

Figure 7.22 The two final visual mock-ups, one of the curtain wall and its linear lap spandrel detail between floors, and the other the prismatic wire stainless steel podium wall. Skidmore, Owings & Merrill and James Carpenter Design Associates, 7 World Trade Center (New York City, USA) 2007.
Image courtesy of JCDA, ©JCDA.

Because much of the stainless steel podium wall was intended to cover the concrete surfaces with large voids, a goal of this mock-up was to determine if the screen would disguise the reading of the solid and voids in the structure behind it. The design team did not want to see a difference between the solid concrete and the aperture in the wall, and as a result mocked up that condition by painting plywood black to simulate the concrete, which would eventually be coated with a layer of black waterproofing (Figure 7.21).

A final performative mock-up procedure improvised by the architect was to beat up on the stainless steel screens by simulating graffiti on it and hitting it with projectiles to demonstrate that it was durable and easily maintained.

The final mock-up procedure of the preconstruction process involved illuminating this same podium wall and observing the final lighting specifications, checking for visible signatures of the internal LEDs. This new lighting system had the ability to shift from white to blue, and was built with an acute corner condition. The purpose of this final lighting mock-up was for quality check, with the final actual lighting fixtures and the actual welded stainless steel screen fabricated with the final specifications (Figure 7.22).

In a way, this final mock-up exists categorically in between a performative and visual integrating concerns of both. This integrative mock-up brings together the actual specified components into a final dry run. The mock-up also functions to train the contractors on how to best handle and install the final panels and LEDs. The only true performance of the screen is to reveal light in desired ways, but also to allow the required airflow requirements of the equipment housed within the podium (Figures 7.23, 7.24, and 7.25).

Over the course of the day, an inversion occurs from day to night. As the sun strikes the smooth outer layer of the podium screens, the triangular profile wires juxtapose the light from the surrounding environment with the interior illuminations by filtering it into bands and redirecting it. At night, the outer layer of screens is no longer visible, acting only as a scrim through which to view the internal and illuminated back layer (Figure 7.26). The inner layer is illuminated by LEDs attached to the backside of the outer layer, which illuminates the cavity, giving a volumetric reading to the light. Because the interior screen is bead blasted, it glows within the depth of the cavity and emits a soft volumetric ambient light back out to the street. The carefully orchestrated and dynamic performance of these interactions was successfully verified in this final mock-up.[9]

At 7 World Trade Center, the light is built-in and integrated into the surfaces of the building. This built-in model echoes the concept of transforming the light from reflections to refractions by producing deeper and more transformative interactions between the surfaces of the building and the light which it interacts with. Built-in furniture has similar capacities where the furniture is absorbed into the construction of the wall, transforming both the wall and the furniture in the process of integration. By exerting reciprocal pressures across scales, built-in conditions define an in-between scale; the scale of the architectural surface and the detail of furniture. This in-between scale is present in the podium wall where the wall is designed not simply to exist passively in relation to its environment, but specifically to receive and produce more certain interactions with light. As in a light cove, the podium wall must reveal the light while masking the source through a calibration of both elements. Through the construction of the mock-up, the location of the

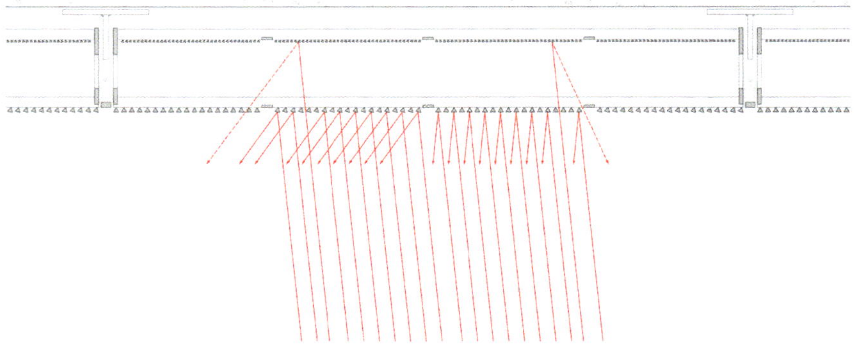

Figure 7.23 The visual mock-up of the podium wall with integrated LEDs illuminating its cavities at night. Skidmore, Owings & Merrill and James Carpenter Design Associates, 7 World Trade Center (New York City, USA) 2007.
Image courtesy of David Sundberg, © David Sundberg/Esto.

Figure 7.24 A detail drawing demonstrating the sun's light refractions, as some light rays are reflected, and some pass through to the interior cavity of the podium wall refracted from the interior layer. Skidmore, Owings & Merrill and James Carpenter Design Associates, 7 World Trade Center (New York City, USA) 2007.
Image courtesy of JCDA, ©JCDA.

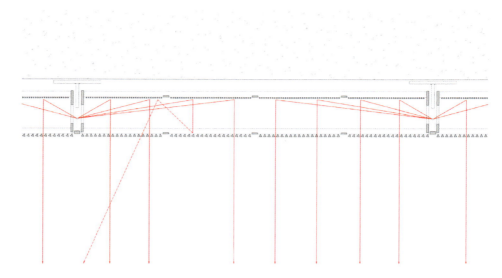

Figure 7.25 A detail drawing demonstrating the podium's LED ray tracing, as the light rays are emitted from a concealed source and bounced off the interior back layer, out through to the exterior layer onto the street. Skidmore, Owings & Merrill and James Carpenter Design Associates, 7 World Trade Center (New York City, USA) 2007.
Image courtesy of JCDA, ©JCDA.

fixture was able to be calibrated to cancel out the visibility of the light source. As a result of its integration into the prismatic screens, end baffles were added to the interior of the mock-up structure. Finally, attachment details were developed to be deeper in section, simultaneously structuring the podium wall screens, while concealing the internal light source from view.

UNIQUE TRANSFORMATIONS OF REFLECTIONS AND PRACTICE

The vast range of mock-ups constructed in service of the design of 7 World Trade Center are illustrative but unusual in many ways. We could consider them unusual for the simple fact that they are so abundant, and with this abundance comes a depth of design research that is not typical of a large corporate office building. In addition to their quantity, the mock-ups in this particular case occurred very early on in the design process, often acting as a scaffolding for collaboration to occur which advanced design concepts.

What we see in the design and execution of these mock-ups is a conceptual increase in depth; both the depth of research as well as a more basic deepening of the typically shallow curtain wall and its effects. Through the transformation of the curtain wall from a thin surface into a thickened space, an increased depth of reflections are enabled through new unique transformations of light.

 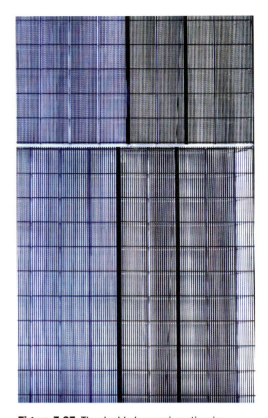

Figure 7.26 The double-layer prismatic wire screens of the podium wall visual mock-up illuminated at night, emitting a transformed set of reflections and refractions. Skidmore, Owings & Merrill and James Carpenter Design Associates, 7 World Trade Center (New York City, USA) 2007.
Image courtesy of JCDA, ©JCDA.

Figure 7.27 The double-layer prismatic wire screens of the podium wall visual mock-up illuminated at night, emitting unique transformations of light within each panel. Skidmore, Owings & Merrill and James Carpenter Design Associates, 7 World Trade Center (New York City, USA) 2007.
Image courtesy of David Sundberg, © David Sundberg/Esto.

These unique transformations result from a detailed engagement with the behavioral particularities of light, subdividing it into something less generic. Through constructed mock-ups we see an unraveling of light into its fundamental characteristics only observed through its interactions with materials. The designs of these mock-ups reveal an expanded range of behaviors, through transformations between an incident and reflected rays, reflections and refractions, and from specular to diffuse (Figure 7.27).

Mock-ups reveal the unpredictable interactions that are often difficult to represent, allowing the opportunity to balance these elusive formations in the process of construction. At 7 World Trade Center, the unusual depth of material investigations is invested in taming or domesticating the properties of light by structuring deeper, more detailed interactions between the tangible and intangible. What results are unusual transformations not only of light, but also of practice, demonstrating a depth of design collaboration most likely only achievable through the potentials of full-scale mock-ups.

Notes

1. James Carpenter, "Beyond Transparency," in *Engineered Transparency – The Technical, Visual, and Spatial Effects of Glass*, eds. Michael Bell and Jeannie Kim (New York: Princeton Architectural Press, 2009), 230.
2. Sandro Marpillero, *James Carpenter: Environmental Refractions* (Basel: Birkhauser, 2006), 72.
3. James Carpenter, "Beyond Transparency," in *Engineered Transparency – The Technical, Visual, and Spatial Effects of Glass*, eds. Michael Bell and Jeannie Kim (New York: Princeton Architectural Press, 2009), 230.
4. Richard Kress (Design Director, JCDA) in discussion with the author, October, 2018.
5. Kenneth Frampton, "Between Membrane and Microclimate: The Work of James Carpenter Design and Associates," in *James Carpenter: Environmental Refraction*, Sandro Marpillero (Basel: Birkhauser, 2006), 155.
6. James Carpenter, "Beyond Transparency," in *Engineered Transparency – The Technical, Visual, and Spatial Effects of Glass*, eds. Michael Bell and Jeannie Kim (New York: Princeton Architectural Press, 2009), 224.
7. James Carpenter, "Beyond Transparency," in *Engineered Transparency – The Technical, Visual, and Spatial Effects of Glass*, eds. Michael Bell and Jeannie Kim (New York: Princeton Architectural Press, 2009), 226.
8. Sandro Marpillero, *James Carpenter: Environmental Refractions* (Basel: Birkhauser, 2006), 85.
9. Sandro Marpillero, *James Carpenter: Environmental Refractions* (Basel: Birkhauser, 2006), 85.

Index

7 World Trade Center: beyond reflectivity 200–201; built-in-light 203; collaboration through mock-ups 199–200; curtain wall mock-ups 205–212; forms and details 201–203; illustrative power of mock-ups 223–224; linear lapped glass and spandrel daylight reflector panel 197; prismatic wire stainless steel podium mock-ups 212–223; range of mock-ups 203–205; volumetric refractions 198–199

acclimation, of wood 185–187, 189–193
actual/virtual 10
Alaskan Yellow Cedar wood 191–193
alchemical reconsiderations 32
Anthony, Ron 186, 195
architect's role 8
the Arthur M. Sackler (Harvard Art Museum) 171–173

Benitez, Solano 30, 31–32, 33, 34, 55–57, 57–58
Biarritz, France 141; *see also* Cité de L'Océan et du Surf Museum, Biarritz, France
bio-deterioration of wood 178–179, 191–193
boundaries, and uncertainty 169–170
boundary-free configuration 181
brick beam project 51–55
brick canopy slab 47–51
brick canopy vault project 42–43
brick shell project 38–42
bricks: alchemical reconsiderations 32; constraints of 30, 56–57; experimental approaches 31–32, 36; Harvard Art Museums 172; labor requirements 36; painting with 29–30; project examples 36; Quincho Tía Coral, Asunción, Paraguay 36, 47–57; strength through thinness 34–35; strength through voids 33–34, 43–47; Teletón Children's Rehabilitation Center, Lambare, Paraguay 36, 37–47; use in construction 31
Bridge of Houses project 144–145
builder's role 8

buildings: and drawings 7–8, 61–63; extensive/intensive 9–10; meaning of 5–7; use in mock-ups 162–163; *see also* construction issues
the Busch-Reisinger (Harvard Art Museum) 171–173

Cache, Bernard 91, 92
Cadwell, Mike 6
Cage, John 8
Carpenter, James 200; *see also* James Carpenter Design Associates (JCDA)
Carpenter Center for the Visual Arts 172
cast glazing 122–124, 133
CDLT House 7–8
cement, ferro-cement 176
Childs, David 199
Cité de L'Océan et du Surf Museum, Biarritz, France 141–142; building uncertainty 169–170; design through construction 147–155; final mock-up 162–163; first mock-up 146–147; glass 163–164; material tendencies 144–145; orchestrating randomness 167–169; pool form and formwork 157–161; structure 165–167
cladding, wooden 183, 194–195
Clifford, Brandon 89; *see also* Matter Design
computers: from computer model to reality 90–91, 92, 101–104; design process 96, 98–100, 112; full-scale mock-ups 21–22; hyper-precision 90; unraveling form from efficiency 96–97
"concept-mock-ups" 120
concrete: Carpenter Center for the Visual Arts 172; Cité de L'Océan et du Surf Museum, Biarritz, France 151–153; finishes 122, 124–125, 126–128, 153; Pérez Art Museum Miami 115–134; "unnatural" status and use in building 116–118; unpredictable transformations 134–135
concrete tombstones 121–122
construction issues 4–5; Quincho Tía Coral, Asunción, Paraguay, brick project 36, 47–57; strength through thinness 34–35; strength

227

Index

through voids 33–34; Teletón Children's Rehabilitation Center, Lambare, Paraguay, brick project 36, 37–47; zero tolerance 101–105; *see also* materials tests
Construction Research Labs 211
copper cladding 83–84
Copper House II, Chondi, Maharashtra, India 70–74, 85, 86, 87
copper mock-ups 79–82
corners: copper skin 83–84; mitered wooden corners 180–181
creativity 24
crumpled finishes 153–155
curtain wall, 7 World Trade Center 198, 204, 205–212

de Arquitectura, Gabinete 36, 55–56
Delanda, Manuel 9, 10–11
Deleuze, Giles 10, 11
design process: 7 World Trade Center 199, 201–203; Harvard Art Museums 173, 195; Matter Design 96, 98–100, 112; Pérez Art Museum Miami 129, 137–138; Steven Holl Architects 143; technological context 96, 98–100, 112
Dieste, Eladio 57
drawings: artists and architects 6–7; and buildings 7–8, 61–63; copper drawings 79; extensive/intensive 9–10; insufficiency of 4; Matter Design 95–96, 97–98; meaning of 5–7; representations without drawing 93–95; Studio Mumbai 63–64, 79; tape drawings 85–88; thicker forms 95–96; and watercolor 143
ductile iron truss system 174–175, 177

engineering: alchemical reconsiderations 32; boundary-free configuration 181; physical motivations 23–24
Eno, Brian 58
equilibrium 10
Equilibrium Moisture Content 189–190
Esmeraldina House 34–35
Evans, Robin 6–7
extensive/intensive 9–10

falsifiability 11–12
feasibility tests, full-scale mock-ups as 14–17
ferro-cement 176
Fiat VSS project 174–175
finishes: concrete 122, 124–125, 126–128, 153; plaster 146; Steven Holl Architects 153–155
flat canopy slab of bricks 47–51
the Fogg (Harvard Art Museum) 171–173
formwork: bricks 35, 38–40, 44, 52; concrete 118, 124, 135–136, 152–161, 165
Forty, Adrian 116, 117, 139
fritting finishes 133–134
full-scale mock-ups: 7 World Trade Center 205, 208–209, 214, 220; as feasibility tests 14–17; hard and soft materials 164; historical examples 3, 4–5; materials tests 17–20; mock-ups and models 13–14; Pérez Art Museum Miami 2; purpose of 2; simulation and prediction 20–21; Studio Mumbai 79; wood species test 187–188
funicular project 92–93

geologic impressions 155
geometry 36
glass: 7 World Trade Center 197, 205–211; Cité de L'Océan et du Surf Museum, Biarritz, France 163–164; curtain wall at 7 World Trade Center 204, 205–212; Harvard Art Museums 172; linear lapped glass and spandrel daylight reflector panel 197, 201–202, 205–211
glass fritting 133–134
glazing system, concrete 122–124, 133
glazing system, glass panel 197, 201–202, 205–211
Gropius, Walter 24

Haldane, J. B. S. 14
Handel Architects LLP 119
Harvard Art Museums 171–173; acclimation of wood 189–193; appearance of the wood 194–195; mock-ups 179–189
Herning Museum of Contemporary Art 153–154
Herzog & de Meuron, Basel, Switzerland 115–134
Holl, Steven 143; *see also* Steven Holl Architects
hot air balloon example 20–21
House with White Net, Maharashtra, India 64–70, 85
hylomorphism 9–10
hyper-precision 90

illuminated interactions 145
Incan wedge-stone construction 105–111
insulated glass units (IGUs) 205
intensive/extensive 9–10

Jain, Bijoy 62–63, 87; *see also* Studio Mumbai
James Carpenter Design Associates (JCDA): collaboration through mock-ups 199–200; design process for 7 World Trade Center 201–203; mock-ups of 7 World Trade Center 204–224; prismatic wire stainless steel podium, 7 World Trade Center 212–223
Johnson Screens 215

Kittinger, Joe 20, 21
Kröller-Müller Villa 4, 5, 13–14, 17–20
Kwinter, Sanford 117, 135, 138, 143

La Voûte de LeFevre, Columbus, OH 97–104
labor productivity 36
languages, translation between different languages 89–90
LEDs, 7 World Trade Center 202, 221–223
light: 7 World Trade Center 203, 215, 217–220, 221–223; Steven Holl Architects 145; UV weathering 136, 191–193; zero-thickness edges 107
linear lapped glass and spandrel daylight reflector panel 197, 201–202, 205–211
Lutz, Jim 7–8

Magritte, Rene 29–30
massiveness, representations 142
materials: acclimation of wood 185–187, 189–193; alchemical reconsiderations 32; appearance of the wood 194–195; bricks' constraints 30, 56–57; building uncertainty 169–170; concrete finishes 122, 124–125,

Index

126–128; concrete's "unnatural" status and use in building 116–118; concrete's unpredictable transformations 134–135; ductile iron truss system 174–175, 177; ferro-cement's flexibility 176; hard and soft 164; illuminated interactions 145; plaster finishes 146; of representation 142–143; sketching with 142–144; Steven Holl Architects 144–145, 169–170; stress and performance 211–212; wood and bio-deterioration 178–179, 191–193; wood as a local material 116; *for case study examples see under individually named materials e.g. bricks, concrete*
materials tests: full-scale mock-ups 17–20; purpose of mock-ups 23
Matter Design: from computer model to reality 90–91, 92; design process 96; funicular project 92–93; La Voûte de LeFevre, Columbus, OH 97–104; representations without drawing 93–95; Round Room, Cambridge, MA 105–111; thicker forms 95–96; translation between different languages 89–90; unraveling form from efficiency 96–97
Mayne, Thom 7–8
McGee, Wes 89; *see also* Matter Design
the Menil Collection building, Houston, Texas 173–178, 194
metal cladding 81–84
Miami Art Museum 115; *see also* Pérez Art Museum Miami
Mills, Russell 58
mitered corners, wood 180–181
mock-ups: 7 World Trade Center 203–224; broader application 25–26; building translations 111–112; Cité de L'Océan et du Surf Museum, Biarritz, France 146–147, 146–151, 162–163; from computer model to reality 90–91, 92, 101–104; as the construction of falsifiability 11–13; definitions 22–23; drawings and buildings 5–8, 61; Harvard Art Museums 179–189; image of structure 3–4; legibility through practice 22–23; materials tests 23; Matter Design 90, 99–101, 107–110; and models 13–14; novelty and creativity of falsework 24; organizational concepts 21–22; Pérez Art Museum Miami 119–122, 125–131; physical forms of representation 3; physical motivations 23–24; "prototype," "mock-up," "performative mock-up," and "visual mock-up" 111; purpose of 2, 23, 25–26; as the structure of a space of possibility 10–11; Studio Mumbai 74, 79–84; wood and bio-deterioration 178–179, 191–193; *see also* full-scale mock-ups
mode of production 92
models, comparison to mock-ups 13–14
Moe, Kiel 9–10
motivations: organizational concepts 21–22; physical motivations 23–24

natural weathering tests 191–193
Nelson Atkins Museum, Kansas City 163
Nervi, Pier Luigi 176
novelty 24

organizational concepts 21–22
oriented-strand board (OSB) 152–153

paving stones 148–150, 167–169
Pérez Art Museum Miami 1–2, 115–134
performance, and stress 211–212
performance mock-ups (PMUs) 20
perspectives in space 74–78
physical motivations, mock-ups 23–24
Piano, Renzo 174; *see also* Renzo Piano Building Workshop (RPBW)
plaster finishes 146
pool form 157–161
Popper, Karl 12
Portuguese paving 148–150, 167–169
precast board forms, Pérez Art Museum Miami 131–132
prediction, use of full-scale mock-ups 20–21
prismatic wire stainless steel podium, 7 World Trade Center 204–205, 212–223

Quincho Tía Coral, Asunción, Paraguay 36, 47–57

rebar shadowing, Pérez Art Museum Miami 136–137
reflections, 7 World Trade Center 200–201, 203, 208–211, 213–214, 215, 217–218, 219–220
refractions, 7 World Trade Center 203, 217, 219
Renzo Piano Building Workshop (RPBW) 185; appearance of the wood 194–195; materials in design process 173, 195; mock-ups 178, 180–184
representations: massiveness 142; materials and form 29–30; sketching with materials 142–144; without drawing 93–95
reveals (edges) 105
roofing, Studio Mumbai 79, 82–83
Rotondi, Michael 7–8
Round Room, Cambridge, MA 105–111
RPBW *see* Renzo Piano Building Workshop
running bond (bricks) 30

sacrificial buildings 1–2
sacrificial coatings 190
S.C. Johnson Wax Administration Building 1, 3, 13–17, 20
scale, mock-ups and models 13–14
Schaulager, Laurenz Foundation 121
simulation, full-scale mock-ups 20–21
sketching: artists and architects 6–7; Harvard Art Museums 179–180; with materials 142–144; relationship to mock-ups 156, 179–180; representations without drawing 93–95; site impressions 65–66; *see also* drawings
Skidmore, Owings & Merrill (SOM) 199–200
slag staining, Pérez Art Museum Miami 135–136
spandrel daylight reflector panel 197, 201–202, 205–211
steel frame project 144–145
steel podium wall, 7 World Trade Center 204–205, 212–223
Steven Holl Architects: building uncertainty 169–170; geologic impressions 155–157; glass 163–164; illuminated interactions 145; job of Cité de L'Océan et du Surf Museum, Biarritz, France 141; material tendencies

229

Index

144–145, 169–170; sketching with materials 142–144; wall finishes 153
stone: Incan wedge-stone construction 105–111; paving for Cité de L'Océan et du Surf Museum, Biarritz, France 148–150, 167–169
stress, and performance 211–212
stretcher bond (bricks) 30
structural vault project 89
Studio Mumbai: conventional mutations 85; Copper House II, Chondi, Maharashtra, India 70–74, 79–82, 85; corners 83–84; design at 62–63; drawings 63–64, 79, 85–88; fabricating perspectives 74–78; full-scale mock-ups 79; House with White Net, Maharashtra, India 64–70, 85; mock-ups 74, 79–84; roofing 82–83; structure 62; tape drawings 85–88; training 79–82; unconventional process of arrival 63

tape drawings 85–88
technology: from computer model to reality 90–91, 92, 101–104; design process 96, 98–100, 112; full-scale mock-ups 21–22; hyper-precision 90; unraveling form from efficiency 96–97
Tehrani, Nader 8
Teletón Children's Rehabilitation Center, Lambare, Paraguay 36, 37–47
thicker forms 95–96, 97
training, Studio Mumbai 79–82
translation: building mock-ups 111–112; between computer model and reality 90–91, 101–104; between different languages 89–90; mock-up types 111
triangulated brick beam project 51–55
triangulated brick canopy vault project 42–43

UV weathering 136, 191–193

van der Rohe, Mies 4–5, 13–14, 17–20
virtual/actual 10
visual mock-ups (VMUs) 20
voids, strength from 33–34, 43–47
volumetric refractions, 7 World Trade Center 198–199
voussoirs 99–104, 109, 110

watercolor, and drawings 143
weathering responses, wood 191–193
weatherometers 191
wedge-stone construction project 105–111
wood: acclimation of 185–187, 189–193; appearance on Harvard Art Museums 194–195; bio-deterioration 178–179, 191–193; Cité de L'Océan et du Surf Museum, Biarritz, France 152–153, 160–161; Harvard Art Museums 172–173; as a local material 116; mitered corners 180–181; Pérez Art Museum Miami 116; species test 187–188
Wright, Frank Lloyd 3–4, 9, 13–17, 20
wrinkled finishes 153–155

zero tolerance 101–105, 110
zero-thickness edges 107